WASHINGTON
D. C.
VIRGINIA
MARYLAND
DELAWARE

100
Easy Hikes

Washington, D.C. • Northern Virginia
Maryland • Delaware

by Barbara A. Noe

NATIONAL
GEOGRAPHIC

WASHINGTON, D.C.

Contents

A Landscape Mosaic

Across the sleeping landscape sometime in March, precocious rue anemones confetti the forest floor, heralding the coming of spring. From this moment onward, the woods, marshes, and stream valleys of the mid-Atlantic, along with their accompanying fauna, put on an ever changing show. It's for this reason alone that hiking in the region is so rewarding. No trail is ever the same. Following the rue anemone come the dainty pinks and whites of flowering dogwoods, contrasted by brilliant magenta redbuds. Bird songs and frog sonatas ride the wind, baby cottontails nibble spring-green grass, speckled fawns nuzzle moss-covered logs. And before you know it, summer is here, with its lush green canopies, rushing creeks, and fragrant honeysuckle and blackberry vines. Cool north winds signal another change in mid- to late September, as ridge after ridge of oaks, hickories, and maples ignites in spectacular color, marshlands shimmer gold, and clouds of migrating warblers and raptors fill the sky. Then comes winter, with its frozen waterfalls, snow-sprinkled firs, and bald cypresses locked in hoar frost, and all is silent—and magical.

This guide shows anyone—busy families, harried professionals, active grandparents—how to discover all this splendor. You don't need a backpack or special shoes, or to drive too far. Each hike measures 5 miles or less. Most are within an hour or two of Washington, D.C., or Baltimore, with a couple farther afield—perfect for an autumn weekend getaway. Hikes have been rated from easy to difficult, so you know what you're in for.

Each hike features something spectacular. Maybe it's something special about the landscape—Maryland's largest waterfall or a panorama of the Shenandoah River's seven horseshoe bends. Perhaps it's something with a historical bent—a walk through the Manassas battlefield or a visit to Harpers Ferry's industrial ruins. Or maybe it's the bird- or wildlife you're sure to spot—the great blue herons and rails of Huntley Meadows, the blizzards of snow geese at Bombay Hook. For a change of pace, some urban walks have been included, such as Maryland's colonial New Castle and Annapolis, which remain picturesque glimpses of the past.

The guide is divided into 13 chapters. Beginning in the heart of Washington, D.C., they spiral outward, visiting the green spaces of the Virginia suburbs and the Virginia Tidewater, then the history-rich Fredericksburg area, the misty Blue Ridge, and the mountain-ringed Shenandoah Valley. Then it's on to Maryland's suburbs to enjoy a boulder-scramble at Great Falls, and farther north to central Maryland's Civil War battlefields and mountain-top vistas. In Maryland's western panhandle, you are deep in the Alleghenies, domain of the black bear. Several hikes cluster around Baltimore, including one through a birdy marsh, and the Annapolis area, on the edge of the Maryland Tidewater. Finally, you explore the fertile marshlands of the Eastern Shore and the peaceful rivers and historic hamlets around Wilmington, Delaware.

All information has been verified and, to the best of my knowledge, is accurate as of press date. However, it's advisable to phone ahead when possible, as visitor information changes frequently. The suggested hiking times allow 20 minutes or more per mile, depending on the difficulty of the terrain.

Now, no matter what the season, it's time to hit the trail.

Regional Map of 100 Easy Hikes

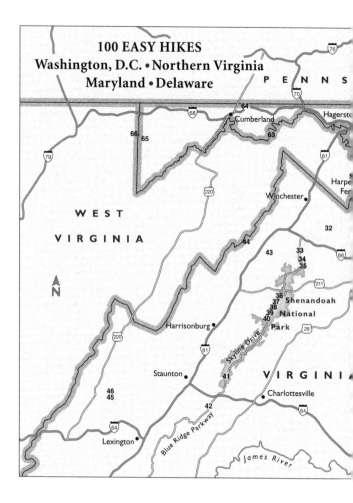

100 EASY HIKES
Washington, D.C. • Northern Virginia
Maryland • Delaware

P E N N S

WEST

VIRGINIA

Cumberland

Hagerst

Harpe
Fer

Winchester

Harrisonburg

Shenandoah
National
Park

Staunton

VIRGINIA

Charlottesville

Lexington

James River

Blue Ridge Parkway

Skyline Drive

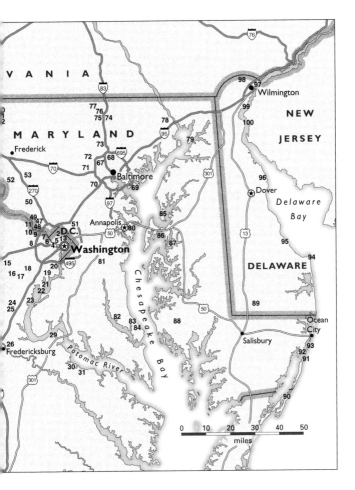

VANIA

MARYLAND

Frederick

Baltimore

D.C.

Washington

Annapolis

77 76
75 74
78
73
72 67
71
70
68
69
51
49 47
48
11 46
10 9
8
7 6
5 1 3
4 2
20
19
21
22
81
15
16 17
18
24
25
23
29
26
Fredericksburg
30
31

52
53
50

Chesapeake Bay

Potomac River

80
85
86
87
82
83 84
88
301
79
301

Wilmington
98 97
99
100

NEW

JERSEY

Dover
96

Delaware
Bay

DELAWARE

95
94
89
90
91
92
93
13
Ocean
City
Salisbury

76
83
97
695
95
270
495
50
50

0   10   20   30   40   50
miles

MAP KEY

■	Point of Interest		
P	Parking		Foot Trail
R	Rest Rooms	Featured Hiking Route (surface varies)	Sidewalk / Paved Trail
☺	Playground		Fire, Gravel Rd. / State, Local Rd.
⌂	Picnic Area		Optional Foot Trail Hike
C	Shelter		
⊛	National Capital		Other Foot Trail
✳	State Capital		Paved Trail
•	City or Town		Sidewalk
◇	Milepost		Canal
)(	Tunnel		Intermittent Stream
⊬	Waterfall		State Border
I	Dam	81	Interstate Highway
		29	U.S. Federal or Principal Hwy.
	Park or Historic District	42 47	State or Local Road
			Fire or Gravel Road
	Swamp	┼┼┼┼┼┼┼┼┼	Railroad

The symbols used in this guide are as follows:

 Leashed dogs allowed.

 Biking possible on all or part of the trail.

 The hike is easy and flat.

 The hike is moderate, with rolling hills.

 The hike is more difficult, promising a good hill or two—but nothing too strenuous.

Trail Notes

The beauty of the wilderness is tantalizing—but its wilder side should not be ignored. Storms can whip up out of nowhere, temperatures can drop quickly, dangerous animals and plants are rare, but a reality. It's smart to always be prepared. Here are some of the basics.

WHAT TO BRING ON THE TRAIL

FOOD

Even on short hikes, a snack helps maintain energy. Extra calories are especially important to keep you warm on cold days. Bring along items that are easy to transport and nonperishable. Some favorites: tuna fish on crackers; peanut-butter-and-jelly sandwiches; pita and hummus; trail mix; granola bars; cheese and crackers; carrot and celery sticks. Fruit—oranges or apples (avoid the bananas)—is another excellent energy source.

WATER

Perhaps even more important than food is water, especially on hot days. It's smart to carry more than you think you will drink. Figure about a quart per person for a day of moderate hiking, more for hot days. Don't drink from streams, which may be tainted with giardra or other trouble-causing microorganisms, as well as viruses (rotavirus, hepatitis A, and polio), bacteria (e. coli, salmonella, cholera), and man-made pollutants.

GEAR CHECKLIST

Rain or shine, layering is the best way to dress on the trail. Each layer traps warmth and provides additional insulation, and as the temperature fluctuates, you can adjust your outfit.

Hiking boots Choosing the right footwear is perhaps the most important decision a beginning hiker can make. Hiking boots help provide ankle stability and reduce wear and tear on the feet; they are traditionally classified in three categories: heavyweight, for serious mountaineering; medium weight, with substantial support and limited flexibility intended for walking over easy to moderate terrain; and lightweight, which are especially flexible. However, many of the lightweight shoes really are inadequately supportive and less durable than the other weights. The best bet is probably something in the medium weight range.

Boot material is another consideration. Nylon mesh and split grain leather boots are lightweight and breathable—ideal for short or moderate hikes in good weather. They also cost less, but tend to be less water resistant than full-grain leather boots, which are very water resistant and durable, offering plenty of support. The leather boots are heavier than the nylon/split grain combinations, but last longer.

Another choice is to find a boot that has a built-in, lightweight, waterproof barrier (such as Gore-Tex) to help enhance its water resistance.

Hiking socks The all-around favorite, in both hot and cold weather, are heavy wool ragg socks. Cotton is fine in warm or hot temperatures, but may prove uncomfortable should your feet get wet in colder weather. Some people wear a liner, available in silk, wool, and synthetics, to help lessen the chance of blisters.

Shorts or pants Keep in mind that if you're hiking through an area full of biting insects or unfriendly plants, long pants may be the better option, even on hot summer days.

T-shirt On hot days, bring along an extra long-sleeved T-shirt to protect from the sun and insects.

Shell parka or windbreaker

Rainwear Rainstorms can literally appear out of the blue, especially on summer mid-afternoons in the mountains. Bring along a nylon poncho, Gore-Tex jacket, or other waterproof covering.

Fleece pullover or sweater

Down vest or jacket Only needed on the coldest of days.

Mittens or gloves

Cap or hat

Oᴛʜᴇʀ ᴛʜɪɴɢs ᴛᴏ ʙʀɪɴɢ ᴏɴ ᴛʜᴇ ᴛʀᴀɪʟ
Day pack or small backpack
Map and compass
First-aid kit Band-aids, antiseptic cream, elastic-type bandage in case of sprained ankle, moleskin for blisters, adhesive tape.
Duct tape
Small Knife
Lightweight binoculars for wildlife spotting
Insect repellent
Sunscreen and/or sunglasses
Lip balm with sun protection

DANGEROUS CRITTERS

Snakes There are only two poisonous snakes in the area. The most prevalent is the copperhead, a pinkish to grayish brown serpent with brown or reddish-brown crossbands that are narrow on the back and widest on the sides. The head is broad and triangular. Copperheads are found in rocky, forested hillsides and wetlands. The bite is rarely fatal but should be treated immediately.

The timber rattlesnake is identified by its broad head, keeled scales, and rattle at the end of the tail. The main body color varies between yellow/brown and gray, with black or dark brown crossbands and a black tail. They are found in heavily forested areas, rocky hillsides, and fields bordered by forests. When encountered, most timber rattlesnakes will lie quietly or slip away; only in self-defense, when disturbed or stepped upon, does a timber rattlesnake shake its tail and bite. Although the bite is venomous, bites to humans are rare and fatalities from bites are extremely rare.

To avoid snakes in general, be sure to stay on the trails, and step on logs instead of stepping over them.

Bears It's truly a thrill to see a "black ghost" lumbering through the forest. Indigenous to the mountain areas, bear sightings are becoming more common, especially in spring and early summer when they are more active. Regardless, bears are generally timid animals and have a natural fear of humans; they will most likely run away from an encounter. Be extremely cautious of mother bears with cubs.

Ticks Lyme disease is transmitted only through the bite of a deer tick. The first sign is a large circular red rash. After a few months or years, aches and pains and paralysis set in. The disease is treatable with doxycycline or amoxicillin, but prevention is best: Use an insect repellent such as Deet and check yourself for invading ticks—some the size of a pinhead.

HUNTING

Hunters are a real danger to hikers, who may take the flash of moving legs for a white-tailed deer. The general hunting season runs October to January, during which time it's always wise to phone ahead your destination site to check for trail closures. If hiking is allowed, be sure to walk in groups and wear orange or another bright color.

DANGEROUS PLANTS

Poison ivy "Leaves of three, let it be." This woodsy shrub—most dangerous in spring and summer—grows 2 to 3 feet high and also climbs up tree trunks. Many people develop a rash after contact with its sap oil, either through touching the sap directly or touching something to which the oil has spread. Wash all exposed areas with cold running water as soon as you can. Relieve the itching of mild rashes by taking cold showers and applying over-the-counter preparations such as calamine lotion. Consult your doctor for severe cases.

Poison sumac The effect is very similar to that of poison ivy. It grows in swampy areas and features leaves with 7 to 13 leaflets.

Stinging nettles This wide-ranging plant is found in orchards, farmyards, old pastures, ditches, and waste places. The tiny, stinging, hollow hairs readily break, allowing the secretions to enter the skin. First you feel a painful sting, then a small, whitish swelling develops with prolonged itching and numbness. Initial reactions last only a few minutes, though some people have the sensation for as long as 24 hours. A paste of baking soda and water soothes the sting if applied immediately.

WILDERNESS ETHICS

More and more people are taking to the trails, seeking solitude and beauty. We have a responsibility to maintain the health of these areas, so future generations can enjoy them as well. Leave No Trace, an international program dedicated to outdoor ethics, provides these guidelines.

Plan ahead and prepare Know the regulations and special concerns for the area you'll visit. Obtain a good map to eliminate the use of rock cairns or ribbons. Know what weather conditions to expect and prepare for the worst. Visit in small groups. Always carry survival gear, including food and water.

Travel on durable surfaces Don't venture off existing trails, which are designed to drain water with a minimum amount of soil erosion. Shortcut switchbacks cause erosion and create unsightly scars.

Pack it in, pack it out Pack out all trash and leftover food, including peanut shells, orange peels, cigarette butts, and toilet paper. Never bury trash because animals often dig it up.

Leave what you find Preserve the past: Do not disturb historical and archaeological sites or remove any objects from them. Leave wildflowers, trees, and rock formations so everyone can enjoy their beauty. If you pick berries or edible plants, pick only those that are abundant, leaving plenty for wildlife and next year's supply.

Respect wildlife Observe wildlife from a distance so they are not scared or forced to flee. Never feed animals; it damages their health and alters their behavior. Control pets at all times or leave them at home.

Best of the Hikes

Best Wildlife Viewing
33-41 Any in Shenandoah National Park
  84 Calvert Cliffs State Park
  90 Chincoteague National Wildlife Refuge
  91 Life of the Dunes Trail
  92 Life of the Marsh Trail

Best Bird-watching
  19 Huntley Meadows Park
  20 Dyke Marsh Wildlife Preserve
  79 Elk Neck State Park
  81 Patuxent River Park
  91 Life of the Dunes Trail
  92 Life of the Marsh Trail
  96 Bombay Hook National Wildlife Refuge

Best Waterfalls
  37 Whiteoak Canyon Trail
  40 Dark Hollow Falls trail
  61 Cunningham Falls State Park
  65 Swallow Falls State Park

Best Dog Walking
   6 Potomac Overlook Regional Park
   9 Scotts Run Nature Preserve
  68 Robert E. Lee Park

Best Fall Foliage
   3 U.S. National Arboretum
  39 Hawksbill Summit trail
  41 Turk Mountain Trail
  42 Blue Ridge Parkway
  60 Hog Rock Nature Trail

Best Spring Wildflowers
   1 National Mall
   8 Meadowlark Gardens Regional Park
  11 Riverbend Park
  15 Bull Run Regional Park
  78 Shure's Landing Wildflower and Natural Area

Most Unusual

Most Remote

Great in Winter

Best Vistas

Best River Views

Best for Running

Best Beaches

Inside the Beltway

Tucked among the monuments and government buildings of the nation's capital are pocket wildernesses teeming with wildlife.

1. National Mall

In central Washington, D.C.
4-mile loop/3 hours

I t's paradoxical that the capital of the world's most suc-
cessful democracy takes its design from a monarchy.
When creating the new Federal City in the late 1700s,
young French architect Pierre L'Enfant borrowed extrava-
gantly from the layouts of Paris and Versailles. Long broad
avenues, statue-dotted squares, and flower gardens lend a
regal charm to America's capital city. In the heart of it all is
the National Mall—L'Enfant's vision of a grand central area
bordered by the city's most important buildings.

   Though it took almost a century and a half to become a
reality, the Mall now celebrates the spirit of democracy with
radiant white monuments and national museums that provide an idyllic, patriotic stroll through history. With all the
attractions along the way, it's easy to get sidetracked—this
could be a week-long adventure. There's something special

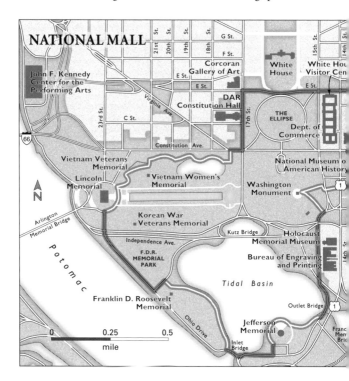

about walking along the Mall, with such iconic structures as the Capitol, the Washington Monument, and the Lincoln Memorial towering above you. Shimmery green pools lined by an ever changing display of flowers reflect the imposing monuments, and little paths wander here and there to lesser known statues, memorials, and gardens. If you're lucky, the President's helicopter may zoom right over your head as he flies to or from the White House. The museums are open year-round, but the best time to take this stroll is in the spring, when the fabled Japanese cherry trees bloom in clouds of pink and white. In the early morning you can beat the crowds.

In designing the city, L'Enfant chose the highest hill in town—then called Jenkins Hill—to showcase the **U.S. Capitol** *(Capitol Hill, E end of Mall. 202-225-6827)*. The majestic building now topping Capitol Hill is where this walk begins. Before starting, take a self-guided tour of the Capitol's interior, with its cavernous rotunda, statues honoring state individuals, and empty crypt planned for George Washington's remains. Then head up busy Pennsylvania Avenue to the **National Archives** *(7th St. and Pennsylvania Ave. 202-501-5000)*, where the original Declaration of Independence and U.S. Constitution are enshrined. Passing the **FBI Building** in

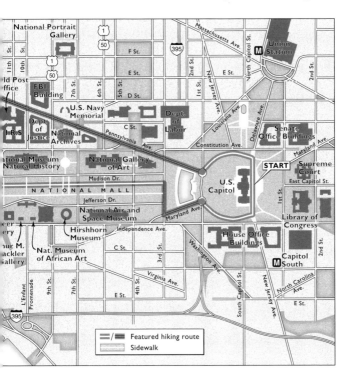

the next block, continue on Pennsylvania Avenue south, which becomes E Street. The imposing wrought-iron fence that soon looms on the right rings the **White House,** the residence of American Presidents since 1800. Sitting amid 18 lush acres of gardens and lawn, the white sandstone mansion was designed by Irishman James Hoban in the 1790s. The colonnaded wings were added by master-tinkerer Thomas Jefferson. If you want a guided tour, you'll have to contact your congressional representative several months in advance. Otherwise, line up for tickets at the **White House Visitor Center** *(1450 Pennsylvania Ave. 202-208-1631 or 800-717-1450)* to obtain same-day tickets for a self-guided tour. Tours take in a limited selection of rooms, including the elegant State Rooms and the gold-and-silver State Dining Room. The visitor center, by the way, has an excellent introductory video to the White House.

Moving along E Street, you'll come to 17th Street; turn left and proceed past the DAR Constitution Hall to Constitution Avenue and the edge of the Mall. A shaded path through Constitution Gardens leads past a lake to the **Vietnam Veterans Memorial.** Probably the most chilling of Washington's memorials, the two black wedges of granite are inscribed with some 58,000 names of soldiers either dead or missing in action in the nation's longest war. The Yale architectural student Maya Ying Lin, who designed it in 1982, said of it: "Take a knife and cut open the earth, and with time the grass would heal it." There are always crowds of people milling past, scanning grimly for the names of friends or loved ones.

Nearby looms the **Lincoln Memorial.** Built in 1922, the neoclassic structure contains the famed statue of a seated Abraham Lincoln by Daniel Chester French. Thirty-six Doric columns, signifying the number of states in the Union when Lincoln was assassinated, embellish the monument. From the memorial's west side, there's a view of Memorial Bridge spanning the Potomac and, up on the distant hillside, **Arlington House**—the former home of Confederate general Robert E. Lee (see pp. 30-31). This linking of Lincoln and Lee is not coincidental. It's meant to symbolically reunite the war-torn North and South.

Walk south past the memorial to Ohio Drive (carefully cross well-trafficked Independence Avenue). Proceed on Ohio Drive with the glimmering Potomac River on the right, aflutter with mallards and seagulls. Soon on your left you'll see the **Franklin D. Roosevelt Memorial,** where pathways lead through four outdoor marble "rooms," with waterfalls, shade trees, and quiet alcoves that convey the spirit of the 32nd

President. From here, make your way down to the **Tidal Basin** and follow the paved path to the right, beneath the bowing branches of the Japanese cherry trees. Overseeing the Tidal Basin is the **Jefferson Memorial,** a gleaming granite monument that houses a standing bronze statue of third President Thomas Jefferson. He holds the Declaration of Independence, which he wrote in just a couple of days.

From here, continue looping around the basin on the paved path, cross Independence Avenue, and head to the **Washington Monument.** During tourist season, the base of this cool white shaft is wrapped by long lines of people, waiting to be whisked to the top by elevator for spectacular, 360-degree views. Many grandiose designs were submitted in the early 1800s for a monument honoring the nation's first President, but in the end the simple marble obelisk won out. Construction began in 1848 but was stopped during the Civil War. After the war, a different contractor was used, and the marble brought from a different source. Look closely at the shaft's midriff, and you will see the difference in color.

Now cross 14th Street (east of the Washington Monument, in the direction of the Capitol) and enter the heart of the National Mall, lined by the National Gallery of Art and the museums of the Smithsonian Institution. In warm weather, the grassy fields of the Mall's interior are filled with Washingtonians playing volleyball, soccer, and softball; and perhaps you'll pass a politician out on a daily jog. You could spend years exploring America's "attic," so it's best to pinpoint what interests you—art, science, anthropology—and go from there. As you walk along, be sure to peek into alleys and back lots for pocket-size gardens, especially breathtaking in spring; don't miss the one behind the Smithsonian Castle in particular.

On the Mall's south side, you'll first come to the **Freer Gallery** *(12th St. and Jefferson Dr. 202-357-2700),* an elegant marble structure housing a world-renowned collection of art from China, Japan, Korea, South and Southeast Asia, and the Near East. Among the masterpieces is the Peacock Room, a whimsical town-house dining room that American artist James McNeill Whistler adorned with a blue-and-gold peacock design. Next door, the **Arthur M. Sackler Gallery** *(1050 Independence Ave. 202-357-2700)* contains a wonderful collection of Asian art including Chinese jades, Japanese prints, ancient Near Eastern ceramics, and Islamic manuscripts. The nearby, underground **National Museum of African Art** *(950 Independence Ave. 202-357-2700)* focuses on traditional African arts from south of the Sahara, while the **Hirshhorn Museum and Sculpture Garden** *(Jefferson Dr. at 7th St. 202-*

357-2700) boasts one of the world's best collections of modern art—featuring the likes of Georgia O'Keeffe, Edward Hopper, and Jackson Pollock. The new Sculpture Garden, showcasing Auguste Rodin's "Monument to the Burghers of Calais, 1884-89," traces sculpture's evolution to the present.

Closer to the Capitol is the **National Air and Space Museum** *(Between 4th and 7th Sts. 202-357-2700),* whose 23 galleries detail the story of man's love affair with flight. Highlights include the Wright brothers' 1903 *Flyer,* Lindbergh's *Spirit of St. Louis,* the Apollo 2 command module, and the world's only touchable moon rock.

On the other side of the Mall, a favorite stop is the **National Museum of American History** *(N side of Mall between 12th and 14th Sts. 202-357-2700),* containing items from America's past. The frayed Star-Spangled Banner that inspired Francis Scott Key to author the national anthem is here, along with actress Judy Garland's ruby red slippers from the *Wizard of Oz.* Next door, the **National Museum of Natural History** *(Madison Dr. between 9th and 12th Sts. 202-357-2700)* has recently undergone extensive restoration. Children always love the 13-foot-high mounted African bush elephant that overpowers the rotunda; the mounted remains of giant panda Hsing-Hsing, the beloved National Zoo resident who died in November 1999, are scheduled to be displayed here as well.

Lastly along the Mall you'll come to the **National Gallery of Art** *(4th St. at Madison Dr. 202- 737-4215. www.nga.gov),* first the West Wing and its classical masterpieces, then the East Wing. Renowned architect I.M. Pei designed the East Wing in the late 1970s, a light-filled interior that houses a significant collection of 20th-century art, including a bronze work by Henry Moore. An underground cafeteria sells sandwiches, snacks, and drinks.

Trip notes: There is no entrance fee to the National Mall (unless you count your federal taxes, which pay for it). For more information contact the Washington, D.C., Convention and Visitors Association, 1212 New York Ave., NW, Washington, D.C. 20005, 202-789-7000; or the Smithsonian Information Center, 51 Building, Room 153, Washington, D.C. 20560, 202-357-2700 or 202-357-2020. The web site for all Smithsonian Institution museums is www.si.edu.

Directions: The walk begins at the U.S. Capitol, on Capitol Hill, at the east end of the Mall. If you're taking the subway, get off at the Capitol South stop (blue or orange line) or the Union Station stop (red line). Park your car on surrounding streets.

2. Rock Creek Park

In northwest Washington, D.C.

Western Ridge, Pinehurst Branch, and Valley Trails
3.5-mile loop/1.75 hours

Why travel out of town in search of a wilderness escape when Rock Creek Park runs through the heart of northwest Washington? Tree-carpeted hills roll down to the boulder-scattered creek, which meanders for 9 miles through the city. As long ago as the 1820s, President John Quincy Adams used to stroll in this "romantic glen, listening to the singing of a thousand birds."

Rock Creek became the nation's first urban natural area in 1890, to preserve what Congress described as its "pleasant

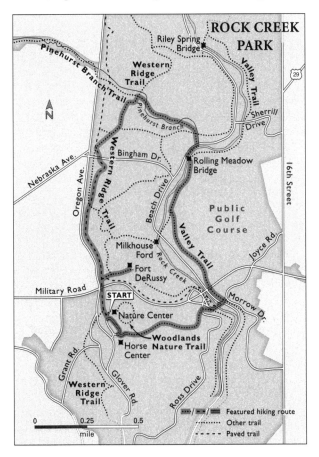

ROCK CREEK PARK

Riley Spring Bridge

Western Ridge Trail

Pinehurst Branch Trail

Valley Trail

Sherrill Drive

29

Pinehurst Branch

N

Bingham Dr.

Rolling Meadow Bridge

Nebraska Ave.

Oregon Ave.

Western Ridge Trail

Beach Drive

Valley Trail

Public Golf Course

16th Street

Milkhouse Ford

Rock Creek

Joyce Rd.

Fort DeRussy

Military Road

START

Morrow Dr.

Nature Center

Woodlands Nature Trail

Horse Center

Grant Rd.

Glover Rd.

Ross Drive

Western Ridge Trail

0 0.25 0.5	▬▬/▬▬/▬▬ Featured hiking route
mile	·········· Other trail
	- - - - Paved trail

valleys and deep ravines, primeval forests and open fields, its running waters, its rocks clothed with rich ferns and mosses." Much of the park remains the same inviting place: Thick stands of trees—tulip poplars, red and white oaks, dogwoods, black cherries—line the steep riverbanks, and the placid creek dances and riffles over rocks and logs on its leisurely descent to the Potomac.

Although Rock Creek is surrounded by heavily populated D.C. neighborhoods, wildlife thrives in this wooded sanctuary. Granted, the eastern bison, black bears, and American elk are long gone, but watch for gray and flying squirrels, foxes, beavers, opossum, and white-tailed deer. Birders will be happy with the wide variety of birdlife, including pileated woodpeckers, Carolina chickadees, wood ducks, and northern cardinals. Even the somewhat polluted creek supports life: some 35 species of fish, crayfish, turtles, and frogs. The park also contains Washington's only endangered species—a quarter-inch-long invertebrate called the Hay's Spring amphipod.

Nearly 30 miles of hiking and bridle trails lace the park. The blue-blazed Valley Trail snakes 5.6 miles along the creek's eastern ridge, while the green-blazed Western Ridge Trail meanders 4.6 miles along the creek's western ridge. A number of yellow-blazed trails connect the two, providing all kinds of possibilities for short and long loop hikes. Covering a nice cross section of the stream valley, this hike begins at the Rock Creek Nature Center and Planetarium, heads north along the Western Ridge Trail, cuts across the park at Pinehurst Branch to the Valley Trail, and heads south to the connector trail at Joyce Road.

The nature center has a wealth of exhibits concerning park geology, botany, flora, and fauna, and you can also pick up trail maps and other literature here. In front of the nature center you'll see a sign for the paved Edge of the Woods Trail. Walk past the sign and take the paved bike trail north—you're on the **Western Ridge Trail**. Cross Military Road. Just up the hill at the sign for Fort DeRussy, turn right on the now dirt, green-blazed Western Ridge Trail. It soon bears left, but continue straight ahead to the fort. In the summer of 1854 during the Civil War, Fort DeRussy supported Fort Stevens to the east of the park, providing supplies and reinforcements when Confederates attacked during Jubal Early's raid on Washington. Among the remains are the parapet surrounded by the deep dry ditch, evidence of the powder magazines inside the fort, and well-defined rifle trenches extending from the fort in each direction.

Backtrack a bit from the fort to the fork with the Western Ridge Trail. You can follow this trail north, ever following the green blazes, or go back out to the paved bike trail and continue north on it. The dirt trail gets a little confusing in this section, so the paved trail is recommended.

Assuming you return to the paved trail, you'll amble north past a flourishing community garden. Beyond Bingham Drive pass a paved road leading off to the right, then come to a dirt/gravel trail. Take this—you're back on the woodsy Western Ridge Trail. Continuing straight ahead, you pass by a trail on the left, then come to a trail junction; go left. Soon you'll see what looks like two different trails within 10 feet of each other, both leading off to the right. You can take either one, because they merge a little farther on. You are now on the yellow-blazed **Pinehurst Branch Trail,** cutting east across the park toward Rock Creek. Twice you cross Pinehurst Branch, a scenic streamlet running through the woods.

The trail brings you to Beach Drive, where you turn right and walk along the road. Rock Creek glimmers off to the left, coursing through the woods and over ancient rocks. Cross the first bridge you come to, about 100 yards down the road, turn right (south), and enter the woods. Now you're on the blue-blazed **Valley Trail.** Continue downstream in a very pretty setting, with the creek to the right. In autumn a mass of leaves casts gilded reflections on the creek, making this corner especially enchanting.

In a little over a quarter mile, you'll come to a trail junction, where you go left and uphill. (If you immediately come to Beach Drive, you've taken the wrong turn.) This brings you to a quiet wooded upland, away from the creek. Eventually, the trail comes down to Beach Drive; pay attention as you hook up to the confusing last leg of this hike. Walk beneath the Military Road overpass, continuing on the Valley Trail to Joyce Road. Turn right and walk along Joyce Road, crossing over Rock Creek. On the other side, stay on the left-hand side of the road, where a narrow trail parallels the road. Follow this until it crosses Ross Drive. Just on the other side of Ross Drive, turn left on the dirt trail, climbing uphill and back into the woods. Enjoy the supreme quiet of the woodlands and the singing of the birds, because the trail soon comes upon a horse center, which signals the end of the hike. Just follow the road back to the nature center.

More hiking: For a shorter hike, take the self-guided **Woodlands Nature Trail,** which leaves from the nature center.

Advisory: It's not wise to walk alone or at night in the park.

Trip notes: The park is open daily. There is no entrance fee. For information contact the Superintendent, Rock Creek Park, 3545 Williamsburg Ln., NW, Washington, D.C. 20008; 202-282-1063 or 202-426-6829 (nature center).

Directions: The Rock Creek Nature Center and Planetarium are located just south of Military Rd. in Rock Creek Park. From downtown Washington, take Connecticut Ave. north to Nebraska Ave. Turn right and proceed to Military Rd. Here, make another right, and, when you reach the park, take the first park road south (it's well marked). Follow the signs to the nature center.

3. U.S. National Arboretum

Off New York Ave. in northeast Washington, D.C.

Fern Valley Trail
0.5-mile loop/30 minutes

For a quick escape into nature, consider the National Arboretum—446 acres of verdant valleys, blooming flowers, and statuesque trees. Surprisingly, few locals seem to know about this wonderful sanctuary, established by Congress in 1927 and now on the National Register of Historic Places. You may well have the Fern Valley, a wild patch of nature in the heart of the arboretum, all to yourself.

Smelling of flowers and raw earth, the valley showcases a spring-fed stream shaded by century-old beeches, oaks, and tulip trees. Some 750 species of plants thrive here, all natives of the eastern United States. They've been planted in sections representing different bioregions (from the northeastern forest to southern swamp), with the most unusual plants labeled to aid horticulturists, gardeners, and students (the arboretum is one of the world's finest horticultural institutions, after all).

Begin by parking across the road from Fern Valley near the junction of Ellipse and Crabtree Roads. Cross over to the mulched path that leads into Fern Valley. Continue straight ahead, taking a map from the box immediately to the left of the main path, then passing beneath the arching pine tree that frames the entrance to the valley beyond. A bit farther, at the garden shed, look for seasonal notices about plants of interest to see along the way.

First comes the forested realm of spring ephemeral wildflowers, and then you approach a stream bank where the deciduous forest of the piedmont reigns: glorious American beeches, chestnut and white oaks, fiddlehead ferns, holly and tulip trees. Farther along, the trail passes a pond edged with alder, ferns, and sweet pepperbush. Straight ahead, plants of the southern mountains grow on your right. In spring the pink and white blooms of rhododendrons and azaleas brighten the understory.

Walk down a few steps and you'll pass through the southern lowlands, the moist domain of bald cypress (look for their knobby knees), star anise, and sweet bay magnolia, whose fragrant white flowers bloom in May and June. As the trail opens to the road, leave the stream behind and walk down the road a few steps to see the Franklin tree, a rarity discovered by pioneering botanist John Bartram in 1765 near the Altamaha River in Georgia and named for his friend Benjamin Franklin. Not seen in the wild since 1790, every Franklin tree cultivated in gardens today is believed to be propagated from seeds and plants collected by Bertram.

Return to the trail and follow it across the stream. The path loops back through more lowland and piedmont woods and leads to the northern forest, traversed by three bridges. In this shady realm, towering dark hemlocks and pines seem to scrape the sky, and wintergreen and other northern plants carpet the woodland floor. At one point a short path leads to a meadow area, flourishing with the kinds of plants that grow along roadsides and in empty fields. Follow this path to the meadow, or continue along the main path back to the parking area.

More hiking: In late April and early May, you'll want to include a visit to the arboretum's **Azalea Collections,** where thousands of colorful blooms blanket the hillsides. The mulched, meandering paths in the Collections lead up to the second highest spot in Washington, affording a stunning view of the Capitol. Beautiful during all seasons are the **Asian Collections,** where lavish plantings representing Chinese, Japanese, and Korean flora line the sometimes steep trails that lead to the banks of the Anacostia River.

Trip notes: The arboretum is open daily. There is no entrance fee. For more information contact the U.S.

National Arboretum, 3501 New York Ave., NE., Washington,
D.C. 20002; 202-245-2726. The web site is www.ars-grin.
gov/ars/Beltsville/na.

Directions: From downtown Washington, D.C., take New
York Ave. east to a right turn on Bladensburg Rd. A left on R
St. brings you to the arboretum entrance. The nearest metro
stop is Brookland-CUA on the red line.

4. Arlington National Cemetery

At the west end of Memorial Bridge in Arlington, Virginia

Cemetery trail

2-mile loop/1 hour

Hallowed, somber, serene, Arlington National Cemetery
occupies 612 rolling acres overlooking the capital city.
More than 250,000 people are buried here beneath
uniform white tablets—war casualties, veterans, and their
dependents. Shaded by trees and laced with walkways, this is a
stunning place to stretch your legs, plus take in a bit of history.

Begin at the visitor center, where you can pick up maps
and literature. Then head out the back door and up the
pedestrian walkway, crossing Eisenhower Drive. Set into the
hillside across a landscape of white tombstones looms
Arlington House, onetime home of Confederate general
Robert E. Lee.

At Weeks Drive, the first road you come to, turn right and
you'll arrive at the base of John F. Kennedy's gravesite. Walk
up to the marble terrace, admire the stately view of Washington and its monuments, and contemplate JFK's simple
grave, marked by an eternal flame. Beside him lie his wife,
Jacqueline Kennedy Onassis, their infant, and his brother,
Sen. Robert Kennedy.

Now exit the memorial the opposite way you entered,
following a small walkway left, up the hill to **Custis Walk.**
This winding path brings you to Arlington House, a mus-
tard-and-white Greek Revival mansion atop a bluff overlooking Washington. Lee resided here for 30 years and loved
it dearly, saying that "my affections and attachments are
more strongly placed" at Arlington House "than at any other
place in the world." In 1861, after declining Lincoln's offer to
head the Union forces during the Civil War, Lee left Arling-

ton for Richmond to join the Confederate war effort. He never returned. His house became the Union Army's head-quarters for the defense of Washington. Then in 1864, Union soldiers were interred on the mansion's grounds, the begin-nings of what would become the national cemetery. You can take a self-guided tour of the house, filled with Victorian-era furnishings; about 30 percent are family pieces, including landscapes Lee painted in his spare time.

From the east side of the house, follow Lee Drive south-ward to **Crook Walk** and turn left. Strolling into the heart of the cemetery, take time to study some of the old tombstones, simple markers etched only with the soldier's name and the date of his or her birth and death. Crook Walk leads to the Tomb of the Unknowns, a white-marble block that contains the remains of one unidentified soldier from each World War, and one from the Korean War (the soldier from the Vietnam War was identified in 1998 and exhumed). A stern-faced soldier guards the tomb day and night; changing of the guard takes place every half hour from April to September and every hour from October to March.

Now make your way down the pathway on the opposite (east) side of the tomb to Roosevelt Drive. Along the way, you'll pass the tombstone of world heavyweight champion (1937-1949) and World War II veteran Joe Louis, engraved with a medallion of a boxer.

Turning left on Roosevelt Drive soon returns you to the visitor center.

Trip notes: The cemetery is open daily. There is an hourly parking fee. For more information contact the Superinten-dent, Arlington National Cemetery, Administrative Building, Arlington, VA 22211; 703-695-3250.

Directions: The cemetery is located on the Arlington side of Memorial Bridge. From downtown Washington, D.C., cross the bridge to the parking lot next to the visitor center. The nearest Metro stop is Arlington Cemetery, on the blue line.

5. Theodore Roosevelt Island

In the Potomac River, Arlington, Virginia

Woods, Upland, and Swamp Trails
Up to 2.5 miles/1 hour

Y ou could almost toss a hiking boot from the Washington shoreline to 88-acre Roosevelt Island. Yet this spot in the middle of the Potomac is a wonderfully serene preserve full of wildlife.

Things weren't always so peaceful. In the early 1800s, the island—then called Analostan—held the country estate of John Mason (son of Gunston Hall's George Mason, see pp. 58-59). The Mason family lost their fortune in 1833, forcing them to abandon their beautiful island home. During the Civil War, a Union camp and hospital were established on the island. Then in the 1870s and '80s, the island was the site of an athletic club, complete with a running track, tennis courts, and a grandstand. The old Mason home finally burned down in 1906, and weeds turned the island into a veritable jungle.

In 1931 the Theodore Roosevelt Memorial Association bought the island and presented it to the federal government as a tribute to the 26th President—a fitting memorial to the man who so loved the wilderness. The Civilian Conservation Corps trimmed the weeds, removed nonnative plants, and planted some 30,000 indigenous trees. In the 1960s, the Roosevelt Memorial—a 23-foot statue of the President surrounded by elegant water fountains and granite tablets inscribed with his words of wisdom—was dedicated.

To reach the Roosevelt Memorial, cross the pedestrian bridge from the parking area. Once on the island, you'll see a bulletin board with brochures and maps. At this point, go right a short way to another trail, where you go left. This short path leads to the monument, a popular place to sit and read a book or have a picnic.

Several different trails, named for the specific habitat they traverse, create a loop around the island. The best thing to do is just wander and see what you find; you can't get lost. The **Woods Trail** and **Upland Trail** explore deep forests of sycamore and oak, hickory and maple, dogwood and ash. This is the domain of the gray and red fox, perhaps even a white-tailed deer or two. Probably the most interesting trail is the **Swamp Trail,** on the island's eastern edge. If you're quiet you may spot marsh wrens, red-winged blackbirds, belted kingfishers, raccoons, turtles, frogs, and other swamp denizens. At the island's southern tip lies a tidal freshwater marsh, vibrant with all kinds of wildflowers, including crimson and yellow flag. It's always surprising, in this haven of nature, to look across the water and see the Kennedy Center's imposing, white edifice and Georgetown University's spires.

Trip notes: The island is open daily. There is no entrance fee. For more information, contact the National Park Service, George Washington Memorial Pkwy., Turkey Run Park, McLean, VA 22101; 703-289-2530.

Directions: The island is accessible only from the north-bound lanes of the George Washington Memorial Pkwy. From Washington, D.C., cross the river on any of the bridges and take the parkway north. Just north of Theodore Roosevelt Memorial Bridge, you'll come to the island's parking area. A footbridge leads to the island. (There is a two-hour parking limit.)

If you are headed south after the hike, you'll have to first head north on George Washington Memorial Pkwy. and take the Spout Run Pkwy. exit to a U-turn point that will allow you to access the parkway south bound.

6. Potomac Overlook Regional Park

Off George Washington Memorial Pkwy. in Arlington, Virginia

Overlook, Red Maple, and Heritage Loop Trails and White Oak Way

1.2-mile loop/30 minutes

The focal point of Potomac Overlook Regional Park is not especially inspiring—a small overhang that looks out on the cars zipping along the George Washington Memorial Parkway. In winter, when the trees are bare, you can see Georgetown, 3 miles down the Potomac. Fortunately, the park has greater attributes than its namesake. It's a lovely sanctuary of oaks, hickories, and tulip poplars, laced with hiking trails and alive with bird song. To explore these fine woodlands, this hike makes a loop along several of the park's trails.

Begin on the black-blazed **Overlook Trail,** which you'll find just after entering the park gates from the parking area. In a couple of hundred yards, go left on the red-blazed **Red Maple Trail.** (If you continue straight on the Overlook Trail, you'll quickly come to the nondescript overlook.) This pleasant ramble will bring you into the heart of the forest. Watch for deer, squirrels, woodpeckers, and butterflies. In summer, the place is a riot of colorful wildflowers: tiger lilies, jewelweed (whose flowers lure hummingbirds), pokeweed (colonists used its blood-colored berries for dye), and common milkweed.

Stay on the Red Maple Trail, bearing right at two forks. Beyond the Donaldson Cemetery, where crumbling tombstones mark the graves of Donaldson family members buried here between 1877 and 1962, the trail comes to a meadow (somewhere along the way the trail has become the **Heritage Loop**—a fact that's neither obvious nor important). Continue on the trail to the right, following a little creek called Indian Springs.

The trail crosses the creek on a wooden bridge and heads uphill. At the top awaits an open meadow with several lovely gardens, including an old apple orchard dating from the early 20th century and a Native American Circle of Life garden representing nature's cycles. A nearby sign indicates that Native Americans used this land as a camp from 500 B.C. to A.D. 500, but there are no remaining signs that anyone ever lived here. Indian artifacts found here are on display at the nature center.

Now look carefully for the next leg of the hike. Off to the right, opposite the orchard, you'll see an unmarked clearing in the woods. Enter the woods, walking straight ahead until you see a sign that points to Donaldson Run. You don't want that (although a trail along the run offers good hiking as well). You do want the trail that wanders to the left, marked by the white blaze. This is (unsigned) **White Oak Way,** which rolls through pretty woodlands. Ignore two spurs that shoot left from the trail, and you'll end up at a grassy field in about a half mile or so. Walk up the steep hill to the left, which will place you back at the parking area.

Make it easier: You can cut the hike short by taking any of the intersecting trails that lead back to the nature center/ Marcey Rd.

Insider's tip: The park's nature center, located on Marcey Rd., has information and free maps, as well exhibits on local wildlife and natural history.

Trip notes: The park is open daily. There is no entrance fee. For more information contact the Northern Virginia Regional Park Authority, 5400 Ox Rd., Fairfax Station, VA 22039-1022; 703-528-5406 or 703-352-5900.

Directions: From Arlington, Virginia, follow the George Washington Memorial Pkwy. north, exiting at Spout Run Pkwy. Turn right on Lorcum Ln., then in 5 blocks turn right on Military Rd. Three blocks down, turn right on Marcey Ln., into the park. Enter the park through the gates at the head of the parking area.

7. Turkey Run Park

Off George Washington Memorial Pkwy. north of Arlington, Virginia

Big Switchback, Potomac Heritage, and Turkey Run Trails
0.75-mile loop/30 minutes

In the category of quick getaways, the **Turkey Run Loop** Trail wins hands down for its combination of natural beauty and proximity to Washington, D.C. Just 10 minutes north of the Rosslyn high-rises and right off the George Washington Memorial Parkway, the trail is tucked away in Turkey Run Park, a parcel of wild bluffs towering above the Potomac. The easy-to-follow loop actually comprises parts of three different trails—the Big Switchback Trail, the Potomac Heritage Trail, and the Turkey Run Trail.

From the parking lot at picnic area C, delve deep into a forest of tall oaks and American beeches. You'll come to a junction after about 50 yards. Go right, on the **Big Switchback Trail,** which plummets down a steep bluff to the Potomac's floodplain. Turn left at the T-intersection, onto the **Potomac Heritage Trail.** You're never directly beside the river, but you can see it sparkling a few yards away, through the trees. In spring the floodplain is resplendent with wildflowers, including Virginia bluebells, twinleaf, and trout lilies.

After crossing over narrow Turkey Run, the hike goes left, along the **Turkey Run Trail.** But before proceeding, fork right on the Potomac Heritage Trail for a close-up river view from a niche in the shade of great sycamores.

Back on the Turkey Run Trail, proceed straight ahead, with the brook on the left, through a verdant woodland setting. Just ahead, in the shadow of the parkway, the hike crosses over the run (you have to jump from rock to rock). Take the trail that wanders up the bluff to the left. (If you find yourself beneath the parkway, you've gone too far.) Climbing up, you're jolted back to reality by the whooshing of cars along the parkway and the occasional droning of an airplane headed into or out of Reagan National Airport. Before you know it, you're back at the parking lot.

Trip notes: The park is open daily. There is no entrance fee. For more information contact the Superintendent, George Washington Memorial Pkwy., Turkey Run Park, McLean, VA 22101; 703-289-2500.

Directions: From downtown Washington, D.C., take the George Washington Memorial Pkwy. north to the Turkey Run Park exit, just south of the Capital Beltway (I-95/I-495). Proceed to the parking lot at picnic area C. The trailhead is located to the left of the bulletin board, where a trail map is posted.

Virginia
Suburbs

Manicured gardens, wild stream valleys, Civil War battlefields, and forested parks speckle the neighborhoods west of Washington, D.C.

8. Meadowlark Gardens Regional Park
Off Va. 7 in Vienna, Virginia

Park loop trail
3.7-mile loop/2 to 3 hours

At this lovely 95-acre park, designed to preserve the bounty of rural Virginia, smooth paved trails wind around green lakes and grassy hills, exploring mature woods, open fields, and flower gardens. Each season brings a new look, though spring outdoes itself with daffodils, tulips, hyacinths, irises, azaleas. Three gazebos and plenty of benches entice you to relax, take your time, and listen to the birds sing.

The park loop trail is the main paved trail that lazily circles the park, making detours to different specialty gardens. To make things easier, the visitor center has a tour map that details a lake tour, a spring blossom tour, and a Virginia gardens tour. But to really experience classic Virginia countryside, continue on to the back of the park, where a short nature trail wanders through woodlands alive with scarlet-bright cardinals darting among dogwood and redbud.

Trip notes: The park is open daily. There is a $3 admission fee April through Oct. Contact the park at 9750 Meadowlark Gardens Ct., Vienna, VA 22182; 703-255-3631, ext. 301.

Directions: From the Capital Beltway (I-95/495) take the Va. 7 exit toward Tysons Corner. Drive 5 miles, turn left on Beulah Rd., and drive 2 miles to the park entrance, on the right.

9. Scotts Run Nature Preserve
Off the Capital Beltway (I-495) near Great Falls, Virginia

Scotts Run Trail
1.25-mile round-trip/1 hour

Literally yards from the busy Capital Beltway, this serene oak-and-hickory upland on the Potomac River almost became another housing development. Indeed, the plans were all drawn up: cul-de-sacs and ridge-top lots, even a small pathway along the river for strolling. Fortunately, a group of local residents fought hard to keep the place wild. Thanks to their efforts, Washingtonians and Northern Virginia suburbanites don't have to travel far to find a quiet, forested refuge.

The **Scotts Run Trail** is a wide, all-purpose path along Scott Run, a rock-strewn tributary of the Potomac River. Songbirds dart through river birch, sumac, flowering dogwood, and locust, and, at one season or another throughout the year, some 175 different species of wildflowers grace the forest floor. A quarter mile from the trailhead, where the path fords the run, you can take a narrow dirt footpath

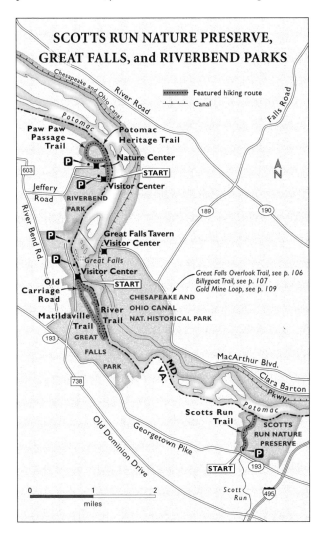

SCOTTS RUN NATURE PRESERVE, GREAT FALLS, and RIVERBEND PARKS

Featured hiking route
Canal

River Road

Chesapeake and Ohio Canal

Potomac

Falls Road

Paw Paw
Passage
Trail

Potomac
Heritage Trail

Nature Center

603

START

Jeffery
Road

Visitor Center

River Bend Rd.

RIVERBEND
PARK

189 190

Great Falls Tavern
Visitor Center

Great Falls
Visitor Center

Old
Carriage
Road

START

Great Falls Overlook Trail, see p. 106
Billygoat Trail, see p. 107
Gold Mine Loop, see p. 109

CHESAPEAKE AND
OHIO CANAL
NAT. HISTORICAL PARK

Matildaville
Trail

River
Trail

193

GREAT
FALLS
PARK

738

MacArthur Blvd.

M.D.
VA.

Clara Barton Pkwy.

Potomac

Scotts Run
Trail

SCOTTS
RUN NATURE
PRESERVE

Old Dominion Drive

Georgetown Pike

START

193

Scott
Run

495

0   1   2
miles

along the stream's right bank—you may have to scramble over some rocks and logs, but you'll be impressed by the quiet beauty here.

This little side trail soon rejoins the main path, which proceeds up and over a hill (don't take the steps off to the right). Just beyond the hill's crest, you'll glimpse the Potomac through the trees ahead and hear its roar. The trail approaches the river's edge, where you'll have a top-notch view: Wide and shallow here, the river boils with rapids. Many forested, rocky islands provide homes for waterfowl and songbirds. All around you, century-old giant sycamores shade the shoreline.

Follow the narrow dirt path upstream a little way to a secluded glen, where Scott Run tumbles 15 feet into the Potomac. Surrounded by hemlock, mountain laurel, and witch hazel, this pretty spot seems more like a Blue Ridge hideaway than a forest in the heart of suburban Washington's clamor.

After you've sat awhile and watched for deer, retrace the trail back to your car.

More hiking: The preserve is honeycombed with trails that weave through its woodlands and offer vistas of the river.

Trip notes: See map on p. 39. The park is open daily. There is no entrance fee. For more information, contact the Fairfax County Park Authority, 12055 Government Center Pkwy., Suite 927, Fairfax, VA 22203; 703-324-8700. The web site is www.co.fairfax.va.us/parks.

Directions: From the Capital Beltway (I-495), take the Va. 193 (Georgetown Pike) exit and drive west about 1 mile to the main parking area, the second lot on the right.

10. Great Falls Park
Off the Capital Beltway (I-495) near Great Falls, Virginia

River Trail, Old Carriage Road, and Matildaville Trail
2-mile loop/1.5 hours

Rugged, angry, dramatic, the Potomac River upstream from Washington rages down steep jagged rocks, then plunges through a narrow gorge. Equal to the great parks of the West, this dramatic spectacle is a sight to behold.

With splendor, of course, come the crowds. People have

flocked to Great Falls ever since the first Native Americans traded along its riverbanks. Even George Washington was lured to the spot, though his interest was more pragmatic. In spite of the obstacle created by the treacherous falls, he set out to make the Potomac River into an important trade route between Georgetown and the Ohio Valley. He headed a company that built the Patowmack Canal between 1785 and 1802. With three locks stairstepping the falls upstream and one downstream, boats were able to travel along the river all the way to Cumberland, Maryland—carrying hardware, cloth, and firearms upstream, and flour, whiskey, tobacco, and iron back down. A town called Matildaville grew up right beside Great Falls to support the canal industry. The remains of both town and canal are still apparent here. (In the end, the canal suffered financially and from extensive flooding; in 1828 it was taken over by the Chesapeake & Ohio Canal Company, which built a waterway stretching from Georgetown to Cumberland on the Maryland side of the river.)

Today, the crowds are still around Great Falls. If you're seeking peace and quiet, plan to come early in the morning or in the off-season. Crowds or no, the falls will take your breath away. The River Trail provides frontrow seats to the watery spectacle.

From the visitor center, head downstream, joining the crowds in their pilgrimage over the ruins of the Patowmack Canal to a series of scenic overlooks built for an early 20th-century amusement park. At this particular point, the Potomac River unleashes uncharacteristic energy in a series of rapids that drop a total of 76 feet. During the spring flood, 134,000 cubic feet of water crash through every second. Then all that water is squeezed into the narrow Mather Gorge, measuring just 200 feet across.

The hike continues along the main path with Washington's canal (today a grassy ditch) and picnic area on your right. In a hundred yards or so, you'll see on the left the blue-blazed **River Trail,** which plunges into a forest of sycamore, walnut, and oak. (A good part of the crowd, satisfied with the overlook views, has turned back by now.) Soon you'll hear the river's clamor, and then—all of a sudden—you're above the pounding river as it pours through Mather Gorge.

The trail darts into the woods, then to the cliff's edge, and back into the woods again. Wildflowers, meanwhile, put on their own show: Trilliums, Dutchman's-breeches, Virginia bluebells, and wild ginger brighten the understory in spring and summer. After about half a mile, you cross a bridge. Farther ahead, at Sandy Landing, turn right. Now you start heading away from the water on the wide, tree-embraced **Old Carriage Road,** which leads straight back to the visitor center.

But you want to turn off onto the **Matildaville Trail,** which wanders off the Old Carriage Road about 0.1 mile beyond Sandy Landing. The shady path ambles past the ruins of Old Matildaville, the once thriving trade village. When you come to the Old Carriage Road again, go right and soon you'll be back at the visitor center.

Advisory: Swimming and wading are not allowed; an average of seven people per year drown in the furious waters. Beware of slippery rocks along the river's edge and sheer cliffs.

More hiking: If you just haven't seen enough of the breathtaking river, continue south beyond Sandy Landing to the **Ridge Trail.** Ask for a map at the visitor center for more details.

The interpretive **Patowmack Canal Trail,** which follows the remains of the canal, tells all about the history of Washington's endeavor; obtain details at the visitor center.

Trip notes: See map on p. 39. The park is open daily. There's a park entrance fee of $4. Since Great Falls is administered by the National Park Service, be sure to take advantage of the visitor center, which has rangers to answer questions and films and information on the river and native wildlife. Ranger-led history and nature walks are offered year-round. For more information, contact the Site Manager, Great Falls Park, 9200 Old Dominion Rd., Great Falls, VA 22101; 703-285-2966. Also the George Washington Memorial Pkwy., Turkey Run Park, Mclean, VA 22101; 703-289-2500. The web site is www.nps.gov/gwmp/greatfal.

Directions: From the Capital Beltway (I-495), take the Va. 193 (Georgetown Pike) exit and go west about 4 miles to Old Dominion Dr. Turn right, into the park entrance.

11. Riverbend Park
Off the Capital Beltway (I-495) near Great Falls, Virginia

Potomac Heritage and Paw Paw Passage Trails
2-mile loop/1 hour

Riverbend Park, located on 409 acres along the Potomac River just north of Great Falls, is one of the best spots in the region to catch the April bloom of Virginia bluebells—harbingers of spring that flourish in marshy wetlands. But it's also a great place for other spring wildflowers: jack-in-the-pulpit, trillium, trout lily, cut-leaved toothwort, to name a few. The visitor center has interpretive material and naturalists on hand to teach you about the park's wildflowers, and its birds.

This hike is a combination of two trails, encompassing a stretch of the Potomac River floodplain and some fine woodlands. Begin at the river near the visitor center and follow the **Potomac Heritage Trail** to the left, upstream. Age-old sycamores drape over the water's edge, providing nesting holes for wood ducks and warblers, and spring wildflowers grow profusely along the Potomac's floodplain. About half a mile from the visitor center, take the path marked by a sign for the nature center off to the left. This interpretive trail, called the **Paw Paw Passage Trail,** makes a loop through a forest of beech, oak, sycamore, sassafras, and papaw. Be sure to look for the papaw—its mauve-red flowers bloom in May, and in autumn it produces a sweet, bananalike fruit that's relished by foxes, humans, and the zebra swallowtail caterpillar (in fact, it's the only food this black-and-white creature will eat).

When you come to the nature center, follow the asphalt path (and the Paw Paw Passage Trail sign) behind the building. Just beyond the center, at the T-intersection, turn right. The trail continues through the woodlands, home to white-tailed deer, pileated woodpeckers, and foraging squirrels. After making nearly the entire loop, you come to a dark, glassy pond where wild turkey congregate. Beyond, the path comes to the river, rejoining the Potomac Heritage Trail. Turn right, back to the visitor center.

Make it easier: Begin at the park's second entrance and take the 1.5-mile Paw Paw Passage Trail. Or stroll along the flat Potomac Heritage Trail from the visitor center and turn around when you reach the sign for the nature center.

Trip notes: See map on p. 39. The park is open daily. From Memorial Day to Labor Day, there is a $4 vehicle-admission fee for non-Fairfax County Residents on Saturday, Sunday, and major holidays. The visitor center has free trail maps and information on park flora and fauna. Contact the River-bend Visitor Center, 8700 Potomac Hills St., Great Falls, VA 22066; 703-759-9018.

Directions: From the Capital Beltway (I-495), take the Va. 193 (Georgetown Pike) exit west for 6 miles. At River Bend Rd., turn right. In about 2.5 miles, turn right again on Jeffery Rd. From here it's about 1 mile to the visitor center entrance, and about 1.5 miles to the second entrance.

12. Red Rock Wilderness Overlook Regional Park

Off US 15 Bypass near Leesburg, Virginia

White Pine Trail

1.5-mile loop/1 hour

This park's name conjures up images of a Southwest fantasyland slashed with sandstone canyons and flood-washed gullies. Of course, you'll find nothing of the sort when you pull into the parking lot of this small regional park. Maples and oaks—not cactuses—cover a rumpled landscape crossed with deep ravines, boulder-strewn streams, and trails that lead to dramatic blufftop views.

The park's not so big—67 acres—and you could stroll in any direction without getting lost. A good suggestion is to head clockwise on the **White Pine Trail,** which traces the perimeter of the park. To do so, take the trail to the left of the parking lot, and every time you come to a fork, stay to the left. Pretty soon, you'll come to the Potomac; a spur ambles down to the river's edge, alive and peaceful with songbirds, ducks, and the smooth-running river lapping gently on the muddy bank.

Veering inland, the trail rambles up and down tree-carpeted ravines, crossing over brooks. In April, flowering dogwoods and redbuds put on a showy display of pink and white blooms, and wildflowers flourish during spring and summer. In autumn, the canopy of white ash, black birch, black cherry, and red maple explodes in rich hues.

Soon you'll find yourself atop a cliff high above the river. Overlooks (guarded by ugly black chain-link fences) treat you to sweeping views of the Potomac, with the shadowy blue hills of Maryland beyond. Watch for birdlife: perhaps a regal green heron reflected in the glassy water or even a bald eagle perched regally on a snag. As you scan the scene, don't forget to look beneath your feet—the bluff you're standing on is made of red sandstone…Virginia's version of a Southwest fantasyland and the park's namesake.

The trail loops back to the parking lot through young woods of Virginia pine and eastern red cedar.

Make it easier: To avoid the hilly ravines, head counterclockwise on the trail from the right side of the parking lot. The trail through the pine and cedar forest is flat, and the overlook is just half a mile away.

Insider's tip: The park itself is easy enough to find, but because the park surrounds a private home the trail entrance can be confusing. Look for a trail map to the left of the parking lot.

Trip notes: The park is open daily. There's no fee. There's also no rest room around for miles. Contact the Northern Virginia Regional Park Authority, 5400 Ox Rd., Fairfax Station, VA 22039-1022; 703-352-5900.

Directions: From the Capital Beltway (I-495) take Va. 267 (Dulles Access Rd.) and the Dulles Greenway to Leesburg. Here, follow the US 15 Bypass north. At Edwards Ferry Rd. go right. The park is 1.5 miles down the gravel road, on your left.

13. Manassas National Battlefield Park

Off I-66 near Manassas, Virginia

Bull Run loop
1.4-mile loop/1 hour

The velvet-soft hills surrounding Manassas appear serene and calm—the safe, storybook kind of place far removed from world problems. Yet during the Civil War, these very hills saw two intense battles that left thousands of soldiers dead. The first began on July 21, 1861, when Yankees fired a 30-pounder Parrott rifle about a mile east of Bull Run, along the Warrenton Turnpike (now Lee Highway). This action initiated the Civil War's first major battle; the Battle of Second Manassas ignited a year later (see p. 45).

This hike takes in the knoll above a stone bridge where Southern troops had gathered, as well as languid Bull Run (the North called it the Battle of Bull Run). While the **Bull Run loop** has an official name and is blazed with very faded white clovers, this region is crisscrossed with trails—some marked, some not. To make things easier, this hike negotiates the least complicated route—not always the official loop.

Beginning from the parking area, follow the boardwalk off to the left, through an oak-filled bottomland. Soon the trail switchbacks up a knoll, *the* knoll. First enjoy the scenery: the picture-perfect countryside of rolling, grassy meadows and patchy woods. Then, to see the view with a soldier's eyes, read the plaques that detail the opening salvos of the battle.

The trail meanders across an undulating field to the Van Pelt home site, where the Confederates not only had a good view of the stone bridge, but also of the signal station on the Wilcoxen farm 7 miles to the southeast (known as Signal Hill today). Shortly before 9 a.m. on that fateful day, Colonel Evans, headquartered at the Van Pelt House, received a signal message warning him of the Union movement at Sudley. Evans realized that the action in his front, at the stone bridge, was merely a diversion and quickly moved most of his brigade to intercept the Union flanking column. His actions delayed the Union advance and perhaps saved the day for the Confederacy.

At the trail fork here, go right. You ramble along the edge of the woods, with fields off to the left. The trail soon plunges into the forest, passes a trail on the right, and comes to a T-intersection. A sign here indicates that the stone bridge is half a mile to the right. Take it. You go downhill and come alongside meandering, shallow Bull Run. It's hard to imagine what an important role this unassuming ribbon of water played in the battle. A little ways ahead, an interpretive sign at Farm Ford describes how Col. William T. Sherman led four regiments across the run here to join the Union drive at Henry House Hill (where the most intense fighting took place). Later that day, the ford was used again, this time by retreating Yankees. (The Confederates ended up winning the battle, destroying any hope for a quick end to the war.)

Amble along the stream bank, a flat, easy stroll through pretty woods. Rounding a bend, you soon catch sight of the legendary stone bridge, its two arches spanning the green stream. Behind it, cars zip past on a larger, modern span, bringing you back to the world of this century.

Make it easier: From the parking area, head in the opposite direction of the hike, toward the stone bridge, to stroll along Bull Run to Farm Ford. This way, you'll avoid the big hill at the beginning of the hike but still get a flavor of the history and scenery.

More hiking: To learn more about the battle, take the 1-mile walking tour around **Henry House Hill,** where most of the critical fighting took place. The trail begins behind the visitor center at the rebuilt Henry House (you'll have to hop in your car to get there).

Trip notes: The park is open daily. There's a $2 fee. The visitor center has a hiking map for 50 cents. For information and a free park brochure, contact Manassas National Battlefield Park, 12521 Lee Hwy., Manassas VA 20109; 703-361-1339 or 703-754-1861. The web site is www.nps.gov/mana.

Directions: From the Capital Beltway (I-495), follow I-66 west to Manassas. Then take the Va. 234 (Sudley Rd.) exit and go north. The visitor center entrance is half a mile ahead. For the stone bridge parking lot, drive past the visitor center entrance and turn right on US 29 (Lee Hwy.) for about a mile and park in the parking area on the west side of Bull Run.

14. Manassas National Battlefield Park

Off I-66 near Manassas, Virginia

Unfinished Railroad Loop Trail
2.5-mile loop/2 hours

On a sultry summer day in 1862, two lines of enemy troops—Union and Confederate—faced each other across an old unfinished railroad bed. All of a sudden, shells screamed and cannon roared and young men collided face to face. The Battle of Second Manassas had begun. After two days, 3,300 men would be dead, and the Confederacy would rise to new heights of power.

The **Unfinished Railroad Loop Trail** covers the scene of the heavy fighting. These days, birds chirp and breeze-tousled oaks and maples bear no trace of war, though the railroad bed that parallels the trail offers some element for imagination; here, waves upon waves of Union soldiers advanced their attack upon entrenched Confederates. What makes this trail especially poignant are the plaques scattered throughout the forest, which share some of the thoughts, observations, and fears of the soldiers—Yankee and Rebel both.

From the Sudley United Methodist Church, strike off through the woods, following the railroad bed. About a quarter mile in, you come to a fork. You can go either way— left leads through a field while right goes through cool woods. Both trails merge not far ahead.

About a third of a mile beyond, you come to another fork. Go left, down the stairs and across the bridge. Murmuring streams crisscross this lush, woodsy area, just as they did more than a century ago. You have entered the ground where Union troops pressed their attack.

After about a mile, the trail comes to the parking lot for the Deep Cut Trail and wraps back on the other side of the railroad bed, through the woods. Now you're in Confederate territory. Here, Southern troops secretly waited for the enemy with bayonets and clubbed muskets poised to kill. After awhile, climb down some wooden stairs, cross a wooden bridge, and come back to the point where the two trails split the second time. Return to the parking lot straight ahead, the way you came.

More hiking: Two spur trails off the main route reveal more events of those days of battle. The 0.6-mile trail at Sudley, near Sudley Church, offers a glimpse of Bull Run. And the 1-mile **Deep Cut Trail,** at the far end of the loop (across the street from the parking lot; look for the big sign), winds through woods where some of the most vicious combat— including a rock fight—took place.

Trip notes: The park is open daily. The entrance fee is $2 (pay at the visitor center). The visitor center has a somewhat helpful hiking map for 50 cents. For a free park brochure and other information, contact the Superintendent, Manassas National Battlefield Park, 12521 Lee Hwy., Manassas VA 20109; 703-361-1339 or 703-754-1861. The web site is www.nps.gov/mana.

Directions: From the Capital Beltway (I-495), follow I-66 west to Manassas. Take the Va. 234 (Sudley Rd.) exit and go north about 2 miles, past the visitor center entrance, to the small parking area adjacent to the Unfinished Railroad and the Sudley United Methodist Church.

15. Bull Run Regional Park
Off I-66 near Centreville, Virginia

Blue Trail (Bull Run-Occoquan Trail)
1-mile round-trip/45 minutes

This trail has a lot to live up to—"the most beautiful wildflower trail in Virginia," it's often called. You'll be skeptical as you enter the regional park, a busy place that caters mostly to picnickers and campers. But if it's mid-April, when the Virginia bluebells bloom, you're in for a treat.

The trail begins near the visitor center/camp store, at the arched wooden bridge. It's officially part of the Bull Run–Occoquan Trail, an 18-mile path along the Occoquan River to Fountainhead Park; the park singles out this particularly beautiful section as the **Blue Trail.** You walk through a swampy floodplain—sometimes through mud, sometimes on wooden boardwalks. Spring beauty and other delicate blossoms decorate the forest floor in springtime.

Ignoring all side trails, continue straight ahead until you come to Cub Run, where in mid-April millions of nodding blue blooms carpet the stream banks and creep into the forest beyond. Turn right, along the riverbank, and you can't help but be entranced by the scene: a narrow footpath winding beside a trickling stream; the luminous light diffusing through towering birch and ash trees; the raw, pure, Technicolor hues of the blue flowers and purplish green leaves. If you're wondering how a regional park obtained such a prize—75 acres of bluebells, the largest stand on the East Coast—it's because the area's vast, marshy floodplain (the same that makes hiking here sometimes difficult) nurtures the delicate blossoms.

Proceed to the point where the trail reaches Bull Run, turn around, and experience it all anew.

Trip notes: The park is open mid-March through November; the bluebells bloom occurs around mid-April (call ahead to make sure you get the timing right). There's no fee if you're a resident of Fairfax, Loudoun, or Arlington Counties or a citizen of Alexandria, Fairfax, or Falls Church. All others are charged a $4 vehicle-admission fee. For more information, contact Bull Run Park, 7700 Bull Run Dr., Centreville, VA 22020; 703-631-0550.

Directions: From the Capital Beltway (I-495), take I-66 west to the US 29 exit at Centreville. Drive south about 2 miles and turn left on Bull Run Post Office Rd. Follow the sign to the park entrance, and park at the lot near the visitor center/camp store.

16. Bull Run-Occoquan Trail

Off Va. 28 near Centreville, Virginia
4-mile round-trip/1.5 hours

One of the most unsung trails in the Washington area, the 18-mile **Bull Run-Occoquan Trail** wanders through wooded hillsides and deep ravines cloaked with tall beech and birch, poplar and pine, traversing marshes and tributary streams alongside sparkling Bull Run and the Occoquan Reservoir. Several parks dot the trail, so hearty backpackers can enjoy an entire weekend escape into the wilderness. Extremely well marked, the trail is accessible at several places, including Bull Run Regional Park, Hemlock Overlook Regional Park, Bull Run Marina, and Fountainhead Regional Park.

For those not as ambitious, a good, easy hike begins at the small parking area on Va. 28. Walk down the hill toward the river and you'll see the blue-blazed trail. Go north (right), with Bull Run on your left, gently flowing south on its way to join the Occoquan River and, finally, the Potomac. You enter a silent woodland belonging to white-tailed deer and bald eagles, mourning doves and bull frogs.

Midway along, you cross a stream on a rustic plank footbridge, pass beneath Ordway Road, and continue through creek-crossed woods. When you cross the next footbridge, over Cub Run, you'll know you've reached the boundaries of Bull Run Regional Park. Just ahead, the trail—this segment of which is a'.o called the Blue Trail (see p. 49)—shoots off to the right; watch carefully for the turnoff. Now you wander beside lovely Cub Run, whose banks are dotted with millions of bluebells in mid-April.

The trail continues across the cleared path of a natural gasline, then bears left through marshland to another little bridge, dropping you into the heart of Bull Run Regional Park. You'll find a small visitor center and camp store just off to the right, where cold drinks are sold. Then turn around and enjoy the hike anew.

Trip notes: The trail is open daily. There is no entrance fee. For more information, contact the Northern Virginia Regional Park Authority, 5400 Ox Rd., Fairfax Station, VA 22039-1022; 703-352-5900.

Directions: From the Capital Beltway (I-495), follow I-66 west to the Va. 28 exit. Follow Va. 28 south through the Compton Rd. intersection and, just before crossing the bridge over Bull Run, turn into the driveway on the right.

17. Fountainhead Regional Park

Off I-95 near Lorton, Virginia

Nature Trail
1.5-mile loop/1 hour

Verdant, pristine, wonderfully remote, Fountainhead Regional Park is a little known parcel of heavily wooded land overlooking the scenic Occoquan Reservoir. The trails are well maintained and well blazed—all you have to do is remember to follow the yellow blazes. The park is probably best known for being the terminus of the 18-mile Bull Run-Occoquan Trail. Fortunately, for those who prefer a nice afternoon hike, there's also the Nature Trail.

You can't miss the trailhead. It's marked by an archway with **Nature Trail** splashed across it in large letters. You pass through it onto a dirt trail and enter a wilderness sanctuary of hickory, oak, and pine. As you stroll up and down the wooded ravines, watch for white-tailed deer, scurrying squirrels, or even a bald eagle soaring above the treetops.

At one point you come upon a serene little inlet along Lake Occoquan, then you reenter the forest again. Climbing up, you're suddenly atop a bluff overlooking the placid water, with boats gliding across its smooth surface. Along this stretch, small trails wander off here and there to informal lake lookouts, where you can sit and enjoy a picnic lunch.

After awhile, the trail darts back into the woods and soon emerges just below the parking lot where you started. Take a right, and head about 100 yards back up the road.

Trip Notes: The park is open between mid-March and mid-November. There is no entrance fee. For more information, contact the Northern Virginia Regional Park Authority, 5400 Ox Rd., Fairfax Station, VA 22039-1022; 703-352-5900. Or call the park (during opening months) at 703-250-9124.

Directions: From the Capital Beltway (I-495), take I-66 west to Fairfax. Exit south on Ox Rd. (Va. 123) and drive about 10 miles to Hampton Rd. Turn right and in 3 miles turn into the park entrance on the left.

Or take I-95 south to the Lorton exit. Turn right on Lorton Rd., then right on Furnace Rd., and right again on Ox Rd. (Va. 123). At Hampton Rd. turn left for the park entrance.

18. Burke Lake Park
Off the Capital Beltway (I-495) in Burke, Virginia

Burke Lake Trail
5-mile loop/3.5 hours

As beautiful as it can be, Burke Lake—a 218-acre wooded oasis in the heart of suburbia—is a madhouse in summer. That's why the gravel and dirt trail around the lakeshore is best taken early in the morning or evening, or even in late fall or winter. After all, the tree-fringed lake is noted for its birds, such as the migrating Canada geese and ducks that stop by in November and December. Forested Vesper Island, in the center of the lake, is a state waterfowl refuge.

The **Burke Lake Trail** starts at the marina parking lot near the park's main entrance. Look for the sign. Indicated by green markers on redwood-stained posts, the trail proceeds in a clockwise manner along the lake's edge. In a bit you come to a paved park road. Turn right on this for 100 yards or so, then follow the dirt trail as its darts back into the woods.

For most of the way, you'll be eye-level to the large, glassy lake, weaving in and out of thickly wooded coves. Every turn offers another choice spot for bird-watching, both in the woods (red-headed woodpeckers, northern cardinals, warblers, chickadees, bluebirds) and out on the water (black ducks, mallards, pintails, and the occasional bald eagle that has flown in from nearby Mason Neck).

In about 2 miles you'll reach the dam over South Run; cross over it and follow the trail to the right, as it wends along the water's edge. Before you know it, you'll be back to the marina bustle.

Trip notes: Park facilities close in winter, but park grounds are open daily year-round. The park is free to Fairfax County residents. A vehicle-entrance fee of $4 is charged to noncounty residents on weekends between April and November. For more information, contact the Park Manager, Burke Lake Park, 7315 Ox Rd., Fairfax Station, VA 22039; 703-323-6600.

Directions: From the Capital Beltway (I-495), follow Braddock Rd. west. At Burke Lake Rd., turn left and drive 5 miles. At Ox Rd. (Va. 123) turn left again to the park entrance.

19. Huntley Meadows Park
Off US 1 in Alexandria, Virginia

Cedar, Heron, and Deer Trails
2-mile loop/2 hours

Of all of Washington's wilderness areas, this one takes the prize for its amazing array of wildlife—especially birds. Walking its shady trails through low-lying woods, then traversing the boardwalk above rich wetlands, you will feel like you've entered the Everglades or some other animal-rich kingdom. But this seemingly remote place lies in the heart of suburban Alexandria, where the occasional muffled roar of a distant airplane doesn't seem to disturb the regal egrets, singing toads, browsing does, beavers, northern cardinals, or bluebirds.

The 1,424-acre park occupies the site of an ancient

channel of the Potomac. In colonial times, the land was part of the vast holdings of prominent statesman George Mason, who lived at Gunston Hall Plantation, 5 miles to the south (see pp. 58-59). For centuries the land was farmed, and only in past decades has it been allowed to revert to its natural state. Because of the diversity of habitats, the park provides interesting wildlife watching year-round.

A single trail with three different names—depending on the type of terrain it's traversing—begins just outside the nature center's doors and loops through the park. Along the way, informative plaques point out such natural features as looping grapevines and beaver lodges; plenty of benches provide perches to take in a songbird chorus.

Begin on the **Cedar Trail,** which snakes through a young forest of sweet gum, red maple, and Virginia pine. The dark canopy is cool on a hot summer's day, and tree frogs, thrushes, flycatchers, and katydids thrive. Six species of woodpeckers are permanent residents, including the uncommon red-headed woodpecker. When you come to a fork, go straight on the **Heron Trail,** and soon you enter the open wetlands. Here the trail becomes a lengthy boardwalk that hovers just above the cattail-rich expanse of marsh. Stroll along, pause frequently, and watch and listen for wildlife. You may spy egrets, bullfrogs, great blue herons, king rails, red-shouldered hawks, northern water snakes, American toads, wood ducks, and painted turtles. One of the most intriguing events occurs in early spring—the famed amphibian symphony. For six weeks beginning in March, male frogs sing at sunset to woo their mates; green frogs and bullfrogs belt out their love songs a little later in the season.

The trail wanders about half a mile over the wetlands, quickly ducks into the woods, then comes back out over the wetlands. Pass a trail on the left (this is the Deer Trail; you'll pick it up farther ahead), continuing straight. An observation tower just beyond rises 19 feet above the wetland, providing a bird's-eye view of a 400-foot-long beaver dam. Farther along, the water on the right is prime territory for king rails and other rails that visit the park in migration. The scent of honeysuckle is overwhelming in summer as you enter the woods. The main path is now called the **Deer Trail,** because deer are often spotted foraging here or bounding through the woods. At the Y-intersection, go right on the **Cedar Trail.** At the next Y-intersection, go right again, still following the Cedar Trail, and return to the nature center.

Trip notes: The park is open daily. There is no entrance fee. The nature center has lots of free information on the wildlife and land formations to watch for. Trail maps are available. The park offers highly recommended guided tours. For more information, contact Huntley Meadows Park, 3701 Lockheed Blvd., Alexandria, VA 22306; 703-768-2525.

Directions: From the Capital Beltway (I-95/I-495) in Alexandria, take the US 1 south exit. Drive 3.5 miles south to Lockheed Blvd. and turn right. You'll come to the park entrance in half a mile. The hike leaves from the nature center.

20. Dyke Marsh Wildlife Preserve

Off George Washington Memorial Pkwy.
in Alexandria, Virginia

Dyke Marsh Trail
1.5-mile round-trip/45 minutes

D uring the past two centuries, development in the Washington metropolitan area has virtually eliminated the freshwater tidal wetlands that once edged the Potomac River. But, wedged between the Potomac and the George Washington Memorial Parkway, one small swatch remains. This hike takes you into this pristine world of bygone days, where more than 300 species of birds have been spotted.

You might not think you're heading toward yesteryear as you park at the busy Belle Haven Picnic Area and walk past all the bikers, joggers, anglers, and picnickers. But on the road leading down to the Belle Haven Marina, a big sign announces the **Dyke Marsh trailhead,** and soon you're entering a bottomland of willows, river birches, gums, and oaks, whose quiet, cool canopy provides welcome shade on hot summer days. Within minutes, the trail brings you to the sailboat-dotted Potomac River, its green waters lapping upon driftwood-strewn beaches. Then, curving left, you enter a marshy realm where beds of wild rice compete with cattails—resplendent in July and August as a sea of fuzzy brown "tails."

Here and there, spur trails wander off to the river and the marsh, accessing perfect wildlife-viewing spots where you can blend into the surroundings and quietly observe. Near the water you should see leopard frogs, snapping and painted turtles (in summer), and northern water snakes. On higher ground watch for cottontails, gray squirrels, shrews, field mice, even red foxes. And signs of beavers at work are everywhere: wood-cutting marks on trees, piles of sticks and mud. But Washingtonians mainly come here to bird-watch, scanning the area for wood ducks, long-billed marsh wrens, egrets, herons, and red-winged blackbirds (pick up a bird list at the trailhead).

Just three-quarters of a mile from the start, the trail dead-ends in the heart of the marsh. When you're ready to return, go back the way you came.

Insider's tip: Bird walks led by the Friends of Dyke Marsh start year-round at 8 a.m. on Sundays in the Belle Haven Marina south parking lot.

More hiking: If you'd like to further explore the banks of the Potomac River, continue north or south on the **Mount Vernon Trail,** a 17-mile paved hiker-biker path that links Washington, D.C., with Mount Vernon.

Trip notes: The preserve is open daily. There is no entrance fee. Contact the National Park Service, George Washington Memorial Pkwy., c/o Turkey Run Park, McLean, VA 22101; 703-289-2500.

Directions: Take the George Washington Memorial Pkwy. 1 mile south of Old Town Alexandria to the Belle Haven Picnic Area.

Tidewater Virginia

The Potomac landscape south of Washington, D.C., harbors reclaimed forests, eagle-rich marshlands, and historic houses.

21. Gunston Hall Plantation

Off I-95 near Lorton, Virginia

Barns Wharf Trail
3-mile loop/1.5 hours

Winding through the backyard wilderness of an 18th-century plantation, this quiet hike provides plenty of time to ponder one of history's most elusive figures. George Mason—gentleman planter and the "father of the Bill of Rights"—lived on these splendid grounds, and his house, Gunston Hall, is the beginning of the hike. Mason consistently demurred from holding public office, but the ideas in his Virginia Declaration of Rights, published in final form in 1776, resound in Thomas Jefferson's Declaration of Independence, France's Declaration of the Rights of Man, many state constitutions, and the United Nations Charter of the Rights of Man. To gain historical perspective, you may wish to take a tour of the Georgian-style country manor. Its Palladian Room, whose ornate woodwork was created by indentured servant William Buckland, has been called the most beautiful room in America.

More beauty—of the natural sort—waits outdoors. To the right of the front facade, look for the Nature Trail sign. This will bring you to the head of the **Barns Wharf Trail,** about 20 feet away. Take the trail to the right; the one on the left will be your return route.

You immediately plunge into a lush forest of towering cedars, oaks, maples, and walnuts. (Ignore the numbered posts—they're left over from a former nature trail.) Walking through these woodlands, crossing clear-running streams on rustic bridges, you can easily imagine Mason himself strolling this way. About half a mile in, you come to a crossroads. Go right, following the sign to the Potomac. You soon come to a swampy stream and then a cove shaded by trees. At one point, a split-log bench provides the perfect vantage to watch birds flitting by and deer grazing.

Emerging from the trees, the trail reaches the Potomac River, wide and calm. In Mason's day, transatlantic sailing ships and river vessels came to call, picking up tobacco and grain and carting them off to England.

Retrace your steps back to the crossroads and turn right to continue the loop. The rest of the trail rambles through woodlands and over more streams, skirting a fine meadow

Mason used as a deer park. At one point, you can detour down to the Canal Overlook, where small boats were once moored.

Climbing back up the bluff to Gunston Hall, you come to the trail's finale: an English boxwood allée, planted by Mason himself.

Trip notes: The site is open daily. Admission to Gunston Hall is $5, even if you only want to hike the grounds. For more information, contact Gunston Hall Plantation, Mason Neck, VA 22079; 703-550-9220 or 800-811-6966. The web site is www.gunstonhall.org.

Directions: From Washington, D.C., take I-95 south about 20 miles to the Lorton exit and turn left onto Lorton Rd. Turn right onto Armistead Rd, then at the light turn right onto US 1 south. At the third light, turn left onto Gunston Rd. (Va. 242). After about 3.5 miles look for the Gunston Hall entrance on the left.

22. Mason Neck National Wildlife Refuge
Off I-95 near Lorton, Virginia

Great Marsh Trail
1.5-mile round-trip/45 minutes

Here's a hike that's best taken in the winter, when you can easily scan the spindly tops of leaf-free trees for bald eagles. Just 26 miles from the nation's capital, the 2,276-acre Mason Neck NWR, established in 1969, was the first refuge specifically created for America's endangered national bird. Thirty years ago, just a few eagles could be spotted in the Mason Neck area, their numbers decimated by logging and the pesticide DDT. But now they are making a comeback, and at least two nesting pairs inhabit this refuge.

The **Great Marsh Trail** cuts through woodlands on an old road along a peninsula. At first glance, it's just a lot of trees—and in winter, it's just a lot of really stark-looking trees. But if you stop for a moment, you might spy some forest residents: bluebirds, screech-owls, tree frogs, white-tailed deer, mink, foxes, and bobcats. Also be alert for pileated and red-bellied woodpeckers.

The trail ends with a sweeping panorama of the Great Marsh—the largest freshwater marsh in Northern Virginia. An observation platform overlooks placid waters dotted with snags and an island where tall trees cluster—ideal bald eagle country. Bring binoculars or a spotting scope for a better view.

The best months to visit are November through February, when eagles commonly feed in the marsh; nesting season is April and May. Look closely: Those vulturelike birds soaring overhead may well be eaglets. (Bald eagles don't develop their trademark white head until they are three to five years old.)

If you don't want to brave the icy air of wintertime, there are plenty of goings-on the rest of the year. In April, great blue herons court (Mason Neck manages one of the largest rookeries in Virginia—more than 1,500 nests) and spring wildflowers carpet the woodland floor. Songbirds fill the forest with their melodies in May. By July the heron young are learning to fish and spotted, newborn fawns huddle against mossy logs. Egrets and herons are abundant in September. And in October, the woods ignite in a spectacular display of fall color.

You'll have to retrace your steps from the Great Marsh to return to the parking area.

Trip notes: The refuge is open daily. There is no entrance fee. For information, contact Mason Neck National Wildlife Refuge, 14344 Jefferson Davis Hwy., Woodbridge, VA 22191; 703-490-4979.

Directions: From Washington, D.C., follow I-95 south about 20 miles to the Lorton exit. Proceed east on Lorton Rd., right on US 1, then left on Gunston Rd. (Va. 242). Go 6 miles (past the entrance to Mason Neck State Park) to the parking area for the Great Marsh Trail.

23. Leesylvania State Park
Off I-95 near Dale City, Virginia

Lee's Woods Trail
2-mile loop/1 hour

Just minutes from the frenzied Potomac Mills outlet mall (a top Virginia tourist attraction) sprawls a tranquil gem of a park, resplendent with waterscapes, hardwood forests, bald eagles, and a respectable dose of history.

Here, at Leesylvania State Park, the **Lee's Woods Trail**
winds across forested bluffs above the Potomac, taking in
traces of the past: Henry Lee II—the grandfather of Robert
E. Lee—settled here in the mid-1700s with his beautiful
young wife. He called the place Leesylvania, meaning "Lee's
Woods." A century later, John Fairfax resided here in a brick-
and-stone house before becoming a colonel in the Confederate Army. During the Civil War, Freestone Point was used as
a Confederate gun battery involved in the blockade of Washington. At the trailhead you can pick up an interpretive
brochure that does a good job in bringing the history to life.

The trail—well marked with bright red signs—begins at
the end of the park road, just beyond the monument com-
memorating Henry Lee II. It makes a figure eight, the first
loop wrapping around Freestone Point, the second delving
deep into the woods. Begin by heading left at the bulletin
board, up the wide dirt path. Within 50 yards, the hike veers
right, uphill and onto a smaller trail leading into the woods.
Soon the Potomac can be glimpsed through the trees, then
suddenly you come to a clearing with a magnificent
overview of the river. This is the tip of Freestone Point, the
domain of the bald eagle and osprey. An old Civil War cannon sits among worn-down earthworks, and a placard
details how Confederate soldiers tracked enemy Union
sloops in an attempt to blockade the river—Washington's
main avenue for supplies and communication.

The trail enters a green forest full of large-leafed papaw
trees and follows a ridge above Occoquan Bay. At one point
(stop no. 4), a bench provides a place to sit and take in the
view. Coming down to a wide road, you complete the first loop.

Now go right, uphill on the road, and at the top you
come to another scenic overlook (at least a sign tells you it's
scenic; the view of the parking lot in the foreground is a bit
distracting). Just a little farther on, you'll see a crumbling
brick chimney and some sandstone block foundations—all
that remain of gentleman farmer John Fairfax's house. Once
fields of corn, rye, wheat, and oats swayed in the breezy
slopes below the house; horses and cows filled a large barn,
and at least one outbuilding housed farm tools and other
supplies. Note also the earthen pit that is probably the
remains of an icehouse (the refrigerator of the time), and the
handsome remains of the brick-lined well.

Beyond this point you come to a junction with another
road; go right, following the sign that announces Lee's
Woods Trail, Lee's Homesite Ruins, and Cemetery. The trail
snakes uphill through woods tangled with wild grapevines,

to a pretty ridge top shaded by tall hackberry trees. This is the Lee Homesite, where Henry Lee—a locally prominent colonial leader and country gentleman—and his wife entertained neighboring gentry, including George Washington. There's no sign of the house anymore, but with a little imagination you can see the colonial residence ablaze with candlelight, as guests inside passed platters of turkey and beef and debated the prospect of independence.

Follow the trail downhill, where the 250-year-old escaped gardens makes for a short detour around a little valley. These were the Lee family gardens, and many of the plants that now grow wild here are descendants of plants cultivated in the Lees' time. The park has set up plaques that identify the plants and describe their colonial uses. The nuts of the American beech, for instance, were roasted to make a kind of coffee; daylilies were eaten as greens; and the hard wood of the dogwood was perfect for making tool handles and mallet heads.

From here you climb up a gentle hill to the Lee family cemetery—an iron-fenced plot with an engraved memorial. A little bit farther ahead, at stop no. 10, a view takes in a man-made valley created so trains could get through.

The hike backtracks to the cemetery and proceeds through the woods, soon bringing you back to the Fairfax homesite and the completion of the second loop. Go left to return to the parking lot.

Make it easier: At the end of the first loop, instead of continuing the hike to the right, go left on the wide road, back to the parking lot.

Trip notes: The park is open daily. The entrance fee is $1 to $3, depending on the day and time of year. Be sure to pick up the pamphlet, "A Potomac Legacy," at the trailhead. For more information contact Leesylvania State Park, 2001 Ludwig Dr., Woodbridge, VA 22191; 703-670-0372.

Directions: From Washington, D.C., take I-95 south about 25 miles to the Ribbon Landing east exit in Dale City, by the huge Potomac Mills sign. Follow Rtes. 784 (Dale Blvd.) and 642 (Neabsco Mill Rd.) to US 1, where you turn right. At the first light, Neabsco Rd., go left for about 2 miles to the park entrance. The trailhead is off the picnic area parking lot at the end of the park road.

24. Prince William Forest Park

Off I-95 near Woodbridge, Virginia

High Meadows and South Valley Trails, Taylor Farm Road
4.1-mile loop/2.5 hours

Y ou'd never know that backups on interstate highways and fast-food eateries lie just hundreds of feet from the quiet woodlands of Prince William Forest Park. Quiet, that is, but for the murmuring of streams, the melodies of songbirds, and the rustling of leaves being tousled by the wind.

This hike is a sampler of the park's best assets: pretty forestland, meadows, pastoral valleys, and several streams. Park your car at the parking lot H, accessed by Scenic Drive. The hike begins on the **High Meadows Trail,** marked by orange blazes, in the direction of South Fork Quantico Creek. You cross several ridges, with white and red oaks towering above and beech and yellow poplars shading slow-flowing creeks. In autumn, motley scarlets, oranges, and golds set the forest ablaze.

After about 0.8 mile, you come to the gentle-moving South Fork Quantico Creek. Take a left onto the **South Valley Trail,** marked by white blazes. For 1.8 miles you follow the creek banks through a quiet valley. Watch for beaver and white-tailed deer.

After crossing over Scenic Drive, the trail leaves the creek, plunging once again into woodlands. After 0.1 mile, take a left onto **Taylor Farm Road** (marked by blue blazes), an old road that climbs up about half a mile to the High Meadows Trail and the ruins of Taylor Farm; you can still see the old family cemetery. A left on the High Meadows Trail (blazed with orange) will bring you back through the forest to your car.

Make it easier: Leave your car at parking lot I and stroll along the stream; this is the prettiest part of the trail and it's flat.

Trip notes: The park is open daily. There's a $4 vehicle-admission fee. Contact Prince William Forest Park, 18100 Park Headquarters Rd., Triangle, VA 22172; 703-221-7181. The web site is www.nps.gov/ncro/prwi/.

Directions: From Washington, D.C., take I-95 south about 35 miles to the Triangle exit and head west. The park entrance is a couple hundred yards up on the right.

25. Prince William Forest Park

Off I-95 near Woodbridge, Virginia

Farms to Forest Trail
1.1-mile loop/30 minutes

When Europeans came to Virginia in the 1600s, they uprooted beautiful old-growth trees to grow tobacco—a move that made many of them rich, but the soil poor. In 1936 the National Park Service set aside a parcel of former tobacco land as part of a reclamation program. Trees were planted and native plants allowed to grow. The result: the beautiful forest at Prince William Forest Park. The interpretive **Farms to Forest Trail,** which begins near the entrance to the Oak Ridge Campground, provides insight into the process of reforesting land.

Pick up a brochure, keyed to ten stations, at the visitor center or the trailhead. As you walk along, you'll see human traces amid the forest: an old cemetery with crumbling gravestones dating from antebellum times, a colonial road that once led from fields to farmsteads, tall pines that once bordered farm fields. But most of all, you'll see the forest returning to its natural state.

About half way along the trail, a 2.8-mile detour wanders along Quantico Creek into the splendor of a dense, dark forest. The main reason to take this side trail, though, is the large beaver population. Look for their dams and telltale gnawed trees. (Remember that the last half mile is a fairly steep descent, which you'll have to climb up coming back.)

Trip notes: The park is open daily. There is a $4 vehicle-admission fee. Contact Prince William Forest Park, 18100 Park Headquarters Rd., Triangle, VA 22172; 703-221-7181. The web site is www.nps.gov/ncro/prwi/.

Directions: From Washington, D.C., take I-95 south about 35 miles to the Triangle exit and head west. The park entrance is a couple hundred yards up on the right.

Fredericksburg
Area

Colonial Fredericksburg and the neighboring Northern Neck embrace Civil War battlefields, historic museums, ancient fossils, and bald eagles.

26. City of Fredericksburg
2.25-mile loop/1.5 hours

Founded as a tobacco port on the fall line of the Rappahannock, Fredericksburg took root in 1728 and flourished throughout the century, manufacturing munitions for the Revolutionary War. It became known nationwide in the 1860s, when four Civil War battles unfolded in nearby fields. This walk focuses on prerevolutionary Fredericksburg, whose tidy colonial buildings still form the historic heart of downtown.

Begin at the **Visitor Center,** where you can pick up maps and brochures, plus watch a short orientation video. Then walk up (north) Caroline Street, past old brick facades that now house antique shops, boutiques, and cafés. At the next block, Hanover Street, go left a block, then turn right on Princess Anne Street. Here stands the **George Washington Masonic Museum** *(803 Princess Anne St. 540-373-5885. Adm. fee)*, where young George Washington was raised as a Mason; the lodge now contains memorabilia and relics relating to his membership, including a Gilbert Stuart portrait. Washington knew colonial Fredericksburg well, often stopping by to visit friends and family (he bought his mother, Mary, a house on Charles Street). Next stop, the **Court House** *(815 Princess Anne St. 540-373-1776 or 800-678-4748)*, just up Princess Anne Street. The Gothic Revival building, designed by James Renwick, the architect of the Smithsonian Castle, was built in 1851-52. Inside you'll find such historic documents as Mary Washington's will.

Go left on George Street, then right on Charles Street to the **James Monroe Museum and Memorial Library** *(908 Charles St. 540-654-1043. Adm. fee)*. A young James Monroe practiced law in this dormered brick edifice between 1786 and 1789. The old structure now contains the oldest collection of Monroe-related materials, including much of the Louis XVI furniture the fifth President and his wife bought during his stint as minister to France from 1794 to 1797. Don't miss the directoire-style desk with secret compartments, on which in 1823 Monroe penned his annual message to Congress, parts of which became known as the Monroe Doctrine.

Continue up Charles Street to William Street, turn right, and proceed across Princess Anne Street to the **Fredericks-**

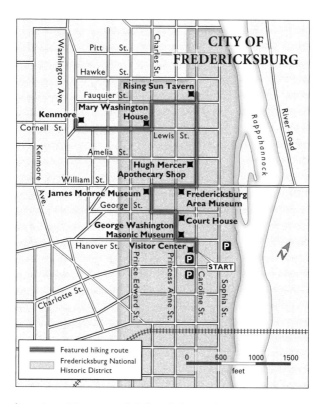

CITY OF FREDERICKSBURG

- Pitt St.
- Hawke St.
- Fauquier St.
- Rising Sun Tavern
- Mary Washington House
- Kenmore
- Cornell St.
- Lewis St.
- Amelia St.
- Hugh Mercer Apothecary Shop
- William St.
- James Monroe Museum
- George St.
- George Washington Masonic Museum
- Hanover St.
- Visitor Center
- Fredericksburg Area Museum
- Court House
- START

Washington Ave. · Charles St. · Kenmore Ave. · Prince Edward St. · Princess Anne St. · Caroline St. · Sophia St. · Charlotte St.

Rappahannock · River Road

Featured hiking route
Fredericksburg National Historic District

0   500   1000   1500
feet

burg **Area Museum and Cultural Center** *(907 Princess Anne St. 540-371-3037. Adm. fee)*. Housed in the former town hall and market house, it was once the trading place of political ideas as well as meat and produce. It now contains a host of artifacts relating to Fredericksburg history: furniture, pottery, toys, tools, and paintings.

Walk up William Street one block to Caroline, and turn left for one block to the **Hugh Mercer Apothecary Shop** *(1020 Caroline St. 540-373-3362. Adm. fee)*. Inside, curious bottles crowd the highly polished drawers and shelves, recalling the time when George Washington's pal Hugh Mercer practiced medicine here until the Revolutionary War. Washington used the sitting room and small library as an office, and some of his handwritten notes are on display. The shop features living history presentations that demonstrate such colonial-day healing practices as leaching and cupping.

Stroll up Caroline Street a couple of blocks to the **Rising Sun Tavern** *(1304 Caroline St. 540-371-1494. Adm. fee)*, built circa 1760 by Charles Washington, George's brother, as his residence and later operated as a tavern.

Now mob-capped women guide visitors on a tour of the hostelry, restored with period furnishings.

Backtrack to Fauquier Street, turn right (away from the river), and walk two blocks to Charles Street, where you turn left and go a block to the corner of Lewis Street. Before you stands the humble **Mary Washington House** *(1200 Charles St. 540-373-1569. Adm. fee)*, which Washington built in 1772 for his mother. It still contains many of her favorite possessions, including her "best dressing glass," and some of the boxwoods she planted thrive in the English garden out back.

For the last stop, turn right on Lewis Street and walk three blocks to Washington Avenue, and turn right again. Midway down the block you'll come to the gates of **Kenmore** *(1201 Washington Ave. 540-373-3381. Daily March-Dec., Sat.-Sun. rest of year; adm. fee)*, the elegant, one-time home of George's sister Betty. The Tidewater mid-Georgian manor house is noted for its intricate ceiling plasterwork. In a nearby exhibit building, the Crowinshield Museum is full of decorative arts, as well as furnishings and memorabilia from former Kenmore residents. The best part of the tour comes at the end, when visitors are offered ginger cookies.

Trip Notes: There are individual opening hours and entrance fees as noted for historical houses and museums along the route.

Directions: The walk begins at the Fredericksburg Visitor Center, 706 Caroline St.; 540-373-1776 or 800-678-4748.

27. Fredericksburg and Spotsylvania National Military Park

Off Va. 3 west of Fredericksburg, Virginia

Chancellorsville History Trail
4.6-mile loop/1.5 hours

W alking the tangled thickets of Chancellorsville, you won't see many reminders of the grisly combat that erupted here during the Civil War—just some interpretive plaques, old embankments, and the crumbling foundations of the Chancellorsville Inn. But the silence of the brooding woods fuels willing imaginations with ghostly thoughts of tattered troops fighting desperately to the end. There's also something spooky about knowing that this is where stalwart Confederate general Stonewall Jackson was shot, victim of friendly fire.

It was 1863 when the Union Army, led by Maj. Gen. Joseph Hooker, crossed the Rappahannock and entrenched itself at an inn known as Chancellorsville, 6 miles west of Fredericksburg. The Confederates, headed by Robert E. Lee, met them there and attacked the Union line's right wing. Most of the decisive fighting took place on May 3, along both sides of Orange Plank Road (now Va. 3). In four hours, the Confederates captured the elevated clearing of Fairview, south of the road, and moved on to the open ground of Chancellorsville, which they captured as well. Hooker and his Union troops fell back to their earthworks, where they stayed quietly for two days before crossing back over the Rappahannock under a nighttime veil. It was a stunning victory for the South, the one that led to Lee's invasion of Pennsylvania.

The **Chancellorsville History Trail,** marked by blue blazes, traverses this historic ground, including parts of the May 3 battlefield and the final Union line. Before you start, stop by the visitor center for a quick briefing on all that took place. Then find the trailhead on the north side of the parking lot, about 50 yards from the visitor center. You enter dense woods that, according to the visitor center slide program, caught fire on that long-ago day, wrapping wounded soldiers in its smothering blaze and burning them to death.

After 0.2 mile, you come to some earthworks belonging to the Union line. At this trail junction, go right. Nearby trenches were dug by Confederates in their preparation to face the final Federal position.

Farther along lies a grassy, open field—Chancellorsville clearing, where vicious fighting surged back and forth on the morning of May 3. From here you can see two key positions: Fairview to the right, and the Chancellorsville inn site to the left, with the Orange Plank Road (Va. 3) in between.

Follow the blue-blazed trail to the left, along the edge of the forest. Just beyond the parking lot for the inn, you cross Route 610 and proceed to the left-hand corner of the field. Take the mowed trail into the woods. After a little less than half a mile from the inn, you come to Hooker Drive. Turn left and walk along the road—paralleling Hooker's last defense. Maybe 50 yards down, the trail reenters the forest.

Just before coming to Route 610 again, you reach the apex of Hooker's last line. Cross the road, entering the one-way Bullock Road (there's a big "Do Not Enter" sign, marked with a blue blaze). Go about 50 yards down the road, until you come to an interpretive plaque that describes how Hooker found himself, about noon on May 3, falling back to a new position, the beginning of his retreat back across the Rappahannock.

Go behind the sign, back into the forest. The visitor center lies just 1.1 miles from this point. Cross Bullock Road, reenter the woods, and soon you'll recognize the junction of the first earthworks you came to. Turn right; the visitor center parking lot awaits just 0.2 mile farther.

Trip notes: The park is open daily. There is a $3 entrance fee. Ask at the visitor center for a free trail map. Contact Fredericksburg and Spotsylvania National Military Park, 120 Chatham Ln., Fredericksburg, VA 22405; 540-371-0802. The web site is www.nps.gov/frsp.

Directions: From Fredericksburg, go west on Va. 3 for 11 miles; take a right into the Chancellorsville Battlefield Unit of the national military park and park at the visitor center parking lot.

28. Fredericksburg and Spotsylvania National Military Park
Off Va. 3 west of Fredericksburg, Virginia

Bloody Angle Trail
1-mile loop/30 minutes

The waist-high meadow along the **Bloody Angle Trail** looks much as it might have in 1864, when this pastoral setting hosted some of the Battle of Spotsylvania's most decisive fighting. Now, silent monuments stand where valiant soldiers once held their ground.

It all began on May 8, when Union general Ulysses S. Grant moved his troops to seize the village of Spotsylvania Court House, in an effort to control the shortest route to Richmond. For several days following, Robert E. Lee's Confederate troops built earthworks and staved off the Union attacks. Then on May 12, the action focused around a narrow bend in the Confederate works, nicknamed "Bloody Angle." The name itself evokes the desperate fighting that unfolded here over a period of 20 hours.

This trail cuts right through the heart of the battlefield,

beginning at a mural depicting the battle movements. As you proceed along the trail through a wildflower meadow, interpretive plaques help to picture the scene those many years ago: In a torrential rainstorm, the Confederates crouched in the trenches you step across. They sighted the gray silhouettes of Union soldiers making their advance across the field. As gun shots crackled, the Union troops stormed the trenches. Perhaps the words of one northern soldier best describe the cruel experience: "The dead and wounded were torn to pieces by the canister as it swept the ground where they had fallen . . . The mud was halfway to our knees . . . Our losses were frightful."

On the other side of the meadow lies a road; about 500 yards to the right stands the site of the Landram House, which Union general Hancock used as a headquarters. The hike continues to the left, back across the meadow, offering a perfect vantage of the bitterly contested trenches.

The hike soon finishes, with much to contemplate. In the end, the outnumbered Confederates fell back to a new line, and the May 12 battle ended. But Bloody Angle will always be remembered for its terrible slaughter.

Trip notes: The park is open daily. There is a $3 entrance fee. For more information contact the Fredericksburg and Spotsylvania National Military Park, P.O. Box 679, Fredericksburg, VA 22404; 540-373-4461. The web site is www.nps.gov/frsp.

Directions: From Fredericksburg, go southeast on Va. 1 Business, which becomes Va. 208. Follow the road until it ends at Spotsylvania Court House. Turn right onto Va. 613 and proceed to the battlefield, approximately 2 miles down the road on your right.

29. Caledon Natural Area
On Va. 218 east of Fredericksburg, Virginia

Fern Hollow, Poplar Grove, Laurel Glen, Benchmark, and Cedar Ridge Trails
4.6-mile loop/1.5 hours

Up to 60 bald eagles have been spotted at this national natural landmark, perched on spindly snags protruding from the smooth Potomac, gliding regally over the gray-blue water, sometimes even cavorting over the meadow near the parking lot. You probably won't see them from this forest trail—which really is beside the point, given the beauty of the landscape. Caledon's woods were named for the fabled Scottish forest. Here, tall, graceful trees, many of them old growth, carpet rolling ridges; birds sing cheerful tunes; frogs splash in cool-running streams. A well-maintained, well-marked trail system runs through this splendid place. It consists of five connecting loop trails, each ring melding with the next. By following the outer edge of these rings, always bearing left at the trail junctions, you trace their perimeter for a super loop hike.

Begin the hike from the far end of the parking area, near the large trail map. Follow the arrow down the hill, turn right, and enter the thick forest. Another large map provides even better detail of the loop trails—each with an individual name and color code.

You set off on the red-blazed **Fern Hollow Trail,** which—like all the trails—climbs up and down ridges forested mostly with second-growth oaks and hickories. Near a wooden bridge across a tiny stream tower old-growth oaks and beeches, majestic and supreme.

Soon you come to the blue-blazed **Poplar Grove Trail.** Bear left, ever following the outer perimeter of the overall loop. The fallen remains of massive American chestnut trees, killed by blight in the mid-1900s, scatter across the woodland floor. Along the yellow-blazed **Laurel Glen Trail,** which traverses wetter soil along a creek, wildflowers create a burst of springtime color. The heralding of the orange-blazed **Benchmark Trail** brings a fairly steep climb. But you're not the first to tackle this hill; pause midway to study the old stone survey benchmark, dated 1754. The trail now flattens out, winding through more pretty woods.

Shortly you arrive at the white-blazed **Cedar Ridge Trail** and the oldest part of the park, where old-growth forest reigns. As you walk up and down the shady ridges, stop for a moment and look above at the sky-reaching trees, luminous with diffused sunlight. Most of these trees stood 400 years ago, when the European settlers first explored Virginia's wilds. The only sounds here come from the breeze purring through the treetops and the more than 122 species of birds that frequent the forest, singing and cackling, darting and gliding. The most common include red-tailed hawks, mourning doves, ruby-throated hummingbirds, pileated woodpeckers, Carolina chickadees, and tufted titmice. Chattering gray squirrels join in the melee, and white-tailed deer crackle the understory.

The Cedar Ridge Trail brings you round to the other side

of the Benchmark Trail. Keep bearing left at the trail junctions; you'll trace the Laurel Glen Trail and the Poplar Grove Trail, and finally you'll be back on the other side of the Fern Hollow Trail. Along this portion of the hike, you'll spy signs forbidding you to trespass into the forest to the left—into the Eagle Wildlife Area. The end of the trail is near.

More hiking: The 3.5-mile **Boyd's Hole Trail,** marked with blue blazes, is a new trail that leads to a Potomac River stretch that is protected for bald eagles, with good chances for sightings in fall, winter, and spring. Find the trailhead at the kiosk at the parking area's north end.

Insider's tip: Another way to see bald eagles is to sign up for a tour of the protected area from mid-June to September.

Trip notes: The park is open daily. There is no entrance fee. For more information, contact Caledon Natural Area, 11617 Caledon Rd., King George, VA 22485; 540-663-3861.

Directions: From Fredericksburg follow Va. 218 east for 22 miles. The park entrance will be on the left.

30. George Washington Birthplace National Monument

Off Va. 3 east of Fredericksburg, Virginia

History Trail
0.5-mile loop/45 minutes

Virginia's Northern Neck is quiet now, a backwater province of small towns and farms. But in colonial times, this remote, wooded peninsula bristled with plantation life. Armies of slaves worked fields while aristocratic farmers lorded over manorial estates. And it was on one of these tobacco farms, on a chilly February morning in 1732, that the father of our nation was born.

George Washington spent the first three years of his life on his father's plantation along wooded Popes Creek. After his family moved to Little Hunting Creek Plantation (later called Mount Vernon), young George returned to Popes Creek every summer. Here he hunted, rode horses, and learned the virtues of gentleman farming. Indeed, he considered himself first and foremost a farmer, taking on public duty only when needed by his country.

The Washingtons' land is now preserved as the George Washington Birthplace National Monument, providing a glimpse into the genteel Virginia that George so loved. The **History Trail** winds along Popes Creek to the heart of the restored tobacco plantation. It's just a short walk, but travels more than 250 years back to a time when young George ran across these very fields, dipped his toes in the cooling creek waters, and hunted frogs and salamanders.

You may first wish to watch the film on Washington at the visitor center, for a historical perspective. Then walk out the back door and follow the gravel path. Along the way, plaques share Washington's thoughts about this landscape. Scan the creek for birds: bald eagles perched on snags, canvasbacks, Canada geese, and in wintertime, graceful tundra swans.

When you come to an intersection, continue to the right, along Burned House Point. The name refers to the fact that the Washingtons' house was burned down sometime during the Revolutionary War. To this day, no one knows exactly what the house looked like. The manor that you'll soon visit is considered a memorial house, fashioned after typical period architecture and built in the 1930s.

The trail wanders through a copse of aging cypress trees, providing a shady canopy on hot summer days. Where the trail wraps around the point, a bench provides a place to sit and admire the view. Farther on, you'll come to a colonial garden and see the memorial house off to the left. But continue straight ahead on the trail; soon it bears left, uphill, bringing you into the heart of the old plantation. Poke your head into the memorial house, barn, kitchen, and weaving room, to get a fuller flavor of life on a colonial farm.

Trip notes: The park is open daily. There is a $2 entrance fee. For more information, contact the Superintendent, Rural Route 1, Box 717, Washington's Birthplace, VA 22443; 804-224-1732.

Directions: From Fredericksburg, take Va. 3 east 38 miles to Va. 204, where you turn left into the monument. Follow signs to the visitor center.

31. Westmoreland State Park

Off Va. 3 east of Fredericksburg, Virginia

Big Meadow Interpretive Trail and Turkey Neck Trail
2.5-mile loop/2 hours

Deep in the heart of Virginia's Northern Neck—a remote, tree-clad peninsula dipping into the blue Potomac—Westmoreland State Park embraces a remote realm of ravine-gouged woods and coastal plain wetlands. But this natural splendor is not what makes Westmoreland unique. For here you'll find multihued Horsehead Cliffs, a veritable open book of geology. Embedded in these sand-and-silt bluffs are billions of tiny fossils dating back to the Miocene Age, when porpoises, crocodiles, sharks, whales, and other creatures cavorted in the tepid waters of an inland sea. As wind and rain and other erosional forces wear away the cliffs, bit by bit, fossils are revealed. In fact, there are so many fossils that it's okay to keep whatever you find (avoid walking beneath the cliffs or digging into them; they're extremely unstable).

This hike combines the Big Meadow Interpretive Trail with the Turkey Neck Trail, providing a sampling of the park's best attributes. Park near the restaurant or nature center (which, by the way, merits a peek inside, if only to examine fossils picked up by other people, so you know what to look for). Then walk down the paved road in the direction of the park's easternmost group of cabins. The road splits; go right. You'll see a grassy parking area and the trailhead for the **Big Meadow Interpretive Trail.** Keyed to points of interest along the way, this self-guided trail helps visitors imagine what the region looked like in the days before colonization (pick up a brochure at the trailhead or nature center). You're actually walking along an old logging road, which brings you into the depths of the forest, populated by oaks, tulip poplars, American beeches, and red and silver maples. In spring the understory teems with flowering dogwoods and mountain laurel, spicebush and rhododendron. Carpets of wildflowers include three species of orchids.

At signpost no. 8, you come to a trail junction. To see the Potomac and its towering, ancient cliffs, detour left for a short way. A little beach here, fringed by cattails, provides a pretty place to sit, swim, even picnic. Sift the sand for fossils—looking for that ever-coveted shark's tooth (they're pretty small, so look carefully)—and admire the nearby cliffs.

Backtrack to the trail junction and bear left over the boardwalk. Now you're walking over Yellow Swamp—covered in spring by bright green cattail shoots and wildflowers, it resembles a "big meadow," hence the trail's name. An observation tower offers a bird's-eye view of the lively marsh; even if you don't see the springtime frogs, you'll surely hear them boinging, twanging, croaking in their annual mating ritual.

Continuing along the boardwalk, walk slowly. You never know what may appear: a copper-colored salamander, a shy frog peering from beneath the murky waters, a turtle or two. In a little way, the boardwalk ends, and you come to a T-intersection with the blue-blazed **Turkey Neck Trail.** For an extension of the hike, go left, though this portion of the trail can be overgrown. Our hike continues right from the T-intersection, leaving the marshland, reentering the woods. Cross over a wooden bridge, and huff and puff up a hillside on a series of stairs. At the top, be assured the rest of the trail is flat and simply winds through pretty woods.

Ahead you'll come to an intersection of trails. Bear right, following the sign that points in the direction of "campground C and park office." Farther along, you'll come to another trail junction; bear right again, following the sign that says "park office."

Soon the trail sweeps beside the main park road, paralleling it for a bit. Cross over the bridge, read a placard describing the Turkey Neck Trail, and presently the trail brings you to the road. Walk along the road, turning right into the parking lot where your car is parked.

More hiking: If you are impatient to see the cliffs, take the 0.4-mile **Beach Trail,** which quickly brings you in close range.

Trip notes: The park is open daily. The entrance fee varies from $1 to $3, depending on day and season. For additional information, contact the Manager, Westmoreland State Park, 1650 State Park Rd., Montross, VA 22520; 804-493-8821.

Directions: From Fredericksburg, go east on Va. 3 for 40 miles to Va. 347, and turn left into the park. Shortly after passing the contact station, watch for the restaurant and nature center on your right. Turn right; the trailhead lies near the end of the road.

Blue Ridge

**Virginia's fabled mountains are
in perfect view at Shenandoah National
Park, where 500-plus miles
of trails lead to mountain streams,
crashing waterfalls, quiet coves,
and sheer-faced canyons.**

32. Sky Meadows State Park

Off I-66 near Paris, Virginia

North Ridge and Piedmont Overlook Trails
1.2-mile loop/1 hour

S ky Meadows State Park couldn't be more aptly named:
Forested mountains surround rolling meadows dotted
with fat black cows, all beneath a bright blue sky.
There's really no need to step one foot on a trail to enjoy the
park's beauty; it's all right there as you drive up to the visitor
center. But the network of trails that lace the property showcase the genteel Virginia countryside to perfection, and you
would do well to sample at least this one splendid hike.

This part of Virginia has been farmed extensively for
hundreds of years. Landowners have included Lord Fairfax,
George Washington, and Revolutionary War captain John
Edmonds. In the 1830s, a postmaster named Isaac Settle
constructed the fieldstone Mount Bleak House (now the visitor center). He gave the house to his son as a wedding gift,
and within 20 years the land flourished with hogs, chickens,
turkeys, oxen, and horses, and luxuriant fields of wheat and
corn waved in the gentle breeze. Times haven't changed
much—cattle graze over 400 acres of the park.

There's probably no better time to take this hike than
during the peak spring bloom, when the woods are brightened with redbud and dogwood trees, and conventions of
wildflowers carpet the forest floor. Summer is also nice,
when white daisies and yellow crownbeard run riot in the
pastures. The meadows now are at their richest green, providing nice contrasts to the white barns and bright blue sky.
(The Piedmont Overlook Trail can be uncomfortable on the
hottest of days.) In autumn, the trees put on a flashy display
of reds, oranges, and yellows. And in winter, when the fields
are blanketed with snow and silence fills the air, the park is a
pleasant place to hike, sled, and cross-country ski.

The hike begins at the far end of the parking lot, away
from the park entrance and the visitor center on an old
gravel road. You can't miss the sign that says "Hiking Trails."
After walking perhaps 50 yards on the tree-shaded road,
you'll see a sign that indicates the direction of four or five
different trails. Go right, in the direction of the North Ridge,
Piedmont Overlook, and Appalachian Trails, up and over a
cattle stile, and into a pasture. Follow the trail that climbs

the grassy hill; as you're walking, be sure to look behind you at the pastoral view that's unfolding.

At the top of the hill, bear left (in the direction of the Appalachian Trail); the trail evens out a bit as it enters a wooded area. Climb up and over another stile, and through more woods. Watch for a trail junction, which indicates that the red-blazed **Piedmont Overlook Trail** takes off to the right. Turn right and follow this trail about 150 yards, through yellow summer wildflowers, to the incredible perch above the Virginia countryside. Far below, you see grazing cows, dark copses of trees, shimmering ponds, white barns dotting green and gold patches of fields. Benches provide a place to sit and enjoy. The trail, now a mowed path, heads down the face of the hill, through a meadow scented of clover and wildflower.

At the bottom of the hill awaits another trail junction. Go right, past a cluster of weathered farm buildings, over a small creek, and back to the first stile you encountered. Climb over it, turn left on the old gravel road, and in no time you'll be back at the parking lot.

Trip notes: The park is open daily. The fee ranges from $1 to $5 per car, depending on the season. For more information contact Sky Meadows State Park, 11012 Edmonds Ln., Delaplane, VA 20144; 540-592-3556.

Directions: From the Capital Beltway (I-495) take I-66 west about 45 miles to the US 17 N/Delaplane/Paris exit. Follow US 17 north about 6 miles to the park entrance on the left. Park in the main parking area.

33. Shenandoah National Park
Mile 4.6 on Skyline Drive

Fox Hollow Nature Trail
1.2-mile loop/1 hour

Exploring the glorious mountain beauty of Shenandoah National Park, you may come across the remains of an old homestead, or a small cemetery of crumbling tombstones, or a moss-covered stone wall. All these are reminders that before there was a national park, mountain people inhabited the pristine ridges and hollows of the Blue Ridge, where they cultivated corn and grain and lived in log and white frame houses. But then, in 1926, the U.S. Congress decided the East Coast needed a national park. Their choice? Virginia's lovely Blue Ridge mountains—preferably without the people. In a controversial move, some 2,000 mountain people were displaced from their land, some forcibly. Acre by acre, farmsteads were patched together and allowed to revert to their natural state. In 1935 Shenandoah National Park became a reality; the Washington area's favorite playground was born.

The **Fox Hollow Nature Trail** introduces an Appalachian family that lived in this supreme spot for nearly a century. The trail begins directly across Skyline Drive from the Dickey Ridge Visitor Center. From the trailhead, marked by a big sign, go left, past blackberry brambles (great in midsummer). You enter a forest of black locust, hickory, and oak trees, and in about 100 yards come to the Dickey Ridge Trail. Keep to the left and continue about 300 yards, to a concrete cairn engraved with the words "Fox Hollow." Turn right at this junction, down into Fox Hollow.

The first signs of human life are piles of rocks. In his memoirs, Lemuel Fox, Jr., who lived in the hollow until 1936, said these piles were then probably "over a hundred years old." Family members gathered them as they cleared the fields for farming. Farther ahead you'll come to the old family cemetery, a small walled plot shaded by black locust trees and carpeted with periwinkle. Among the gravestones stands that of Lemuel Fox, Sr., whose parents in 1856 bought 450 acres in Fox Hollow for $5,000. Lemuel Sr., along with his two brothers, served in the Confederate Army, and upon his release from a Union prisoner of war camp in 1863, he returned to the farm. He died here in 1916 at the age of 73.

Just beyond the cemetery, look for the flat area on the left. This was where the Fox family had a little garden. Down on the right you'll pass a concrete-enclosed spring, built as a park water supply after the Fox days. This was also the location of a spring the Foxes used to keep perishables cool, even in the heat of summer. Nearby, a round millstone leaning against a tree, located near the site of the Fox family barn, was used for ornamentation.

Continuing on the trail, you go downhill a bit and cross a stream somewhat hidden beneath large rocks. Beyond, the path joins an old farm road that linked the Fox family home with Front Royal. Bear right to stay on the Fox Hollow Nature Trail. Now begins the slow descent back to the trailhead.

The objects of interest become more of a natural sort: singing birds, a hardwood forest, jungle-size wild grapevines draped from trees, white-tailed deer bounding through the woods. Just imagine, though, how different it looked in the Foxes' day. "All this was clear," Lemuel Fox, Jr., recalled. "You could see all the way to the top of the mountains. All of it was cleared fields."

Follow the old farm road for a little less than half a mile, then take the trail that goes to the right, uphill. Cross the Dickey Ridge Trail and continue uphill, back to where you started.

More hiking: If you'd like to visit another old homesite, try the nearby Snead homesite, accessible via the **Dickey Ridge Trail.** At the end of the Fox Hollow Nature Trail, when you come to the Dickey Ridge Trail, go left instead of continuing uphill. Consult the map at the beginning of the Fox Hollow trail for more explicit direction.

Trip notes: The park is open daily. The park entrance fee is $10 per vehicle; $20 for an annual park pass. An interpretive trail brochure may be purchased for 50 cents at the trailhead and at bookshops throughout the park. For information on all park activities and facilities stop by the Dickey Ridge Visitor Center *(closed mid-Nov.–mid-March),* at mile 4.6 along Skyline Drive. Or contact the National Park Service, Route 4, Box 348, Luray, VA 22835; 540-999-3500. www.nps.gov/shen.

Directions: The park's northern entrance is near Front Royal, about 75 miles west of Washington, D.C. From the Capital Beltway (I-495), head west on I-66 to Front Royal. Follow US 340 to the park entrance a mile south of town. Once you get on Skyline Drive, go 4.6 miles to the Dickey Ridge Visitor Center, and park in the parking area. The trailhead is across the road.

34. Shenandoah National Park

Mile 9.2 on Skyline Drive

Lands Run Falls Trail
1.3-mile round-trip/1.5 hours

This isn't one of Shenandoah's most spectacular hikes, but if you're in the park's north end and are seeking out a small taste of the Blue Ridge—including a small mountain waterfall—this is it. The **Lands Run Falls Trail** (really a wide fire road) is at its peak in October, when the leaves of maples, oaks, and poplars paint the landscape brilliant hues of scarlet-red, orange, and gold. Spring is also lovely, when trillium, wild orchid, and other wildflowers carpet the forest floor, and Lands Run, swollen with snowmelt, falls in a magnificent torrent of water.

Begin by parking at the Lands Run parking area, on the west side of the drive. At the far end of the lot, walk around a chain-link gate, and proceed down the hill, through the woods. In 0.6 mile, you'll come to a clear-running stream. Just 15 or 20 feet off to the right lies the top of the falls, a series of cascades that drop some 80 feet total into a flora-choked gorge. You can't see the entire drop, and there's no trail cut down the steep, rugged slope. But to see the first cascade, cross the stream to the left bank and make your way (carefully) down the rocks. When you're done listening to the music of the falls and enjoying the surrounding solitude, return the way you came (uphill).

Trip notes: The park is open daily. The park entrance fee is $10 per vehicle; $20 for an annual park pass. For information on all park activities and facilities stop by the Dickey Ridge Visitor Center *(closed mid-Nov.–mid-March),* at mile 4.6 along Skyline Drive. Or contact the National Park Service, Route 4, Box 348, Luray, VA 22835; 540-999-3500. The web site is www.nps.gov/shen.

Directions: The park's northern entrance is near Front Royal, about 75 miles west of Washington, D.C. From the Capital Beltway (I-495), head west on I-66 to Front Royal. Follow US 340 to the park entrance a mile south of town. There are plenty of signs to lead the way. Once you get on Skyline Drive, park in the parking area at mile 9.2.

35. Shenandoah National Park

Mile 10.4 on Skyline Drive

Compton Peak trail (Appalachian Trail)
2-mile round-trip/2.5 hours

High atop this mountain peak, a jumble of gray boulders juts into a vast, empty space, providing a balconylike perch above a wide-open expanse of mountains—ridge after misty ridge rolling far off in the distance. Not many people take the **Compton Peak trail,**

possibly because the beginning is a little bit hard to find. You just have to know where to look, and you're in for a treat.

Park at the Compton Gap parking area, on the east side of Skyline Drive, and walk across the road. Just off to the left you'll see an unassuming cut in the bushes—the famed Appalachian Trail (A.T.) and the beginning of the hike. You'll walk through the woods, following the A.T.'s white blazes, up, up, and up. The rocks scattered along the trail are granodiorite. Then, about 0.2 mile from the start, you'll see a big basalt boulder on the left indicating a change in the geology beneath your feet. It's made of the same Catoctin lava that forms Compton Peak—your destination.

After climbing 0.8 mile, you'll spot a cement cairn that indicates two different trail spurs, both blazed in blue. To reach the best view, take the one on the right. This 0.2-mile leg is a bit rocky, and rather overgrown in midsummer. But keep going, and soon enough you'll come to the aforementioned boulders and a fabulous vantage of the Blue Ridge off to the right, outside the park, and Dickey Ridge farther left.

Return to the cement cairn, but don't go down the hill just yet. Follow the other spur, which leads shortly to a 10-foot boulder that rises before you. If you scramble atop it, you'll see a less spectacular view than the one previous, but a good one just the same. The piedmont is straight ahead, and to the right is the Blue Ridge (look for Skyline Drive), including the two summits of Marshall Mountain. If you're a geology buff, follow the blue blazes to the left side of the rock. In about 50 steep, downhill yards, you'll come to the base of a cliff. Look back up for a superior example of columnar jointing. Some 800 million years ago, lava poured from ancient volcanoes, hardened, and cracked into giant prisms. Then, as the mountains were uplifted, the columns tilted. Erosion followed, and the bottom of the cliff crumbled away, leaving what you see today. When you're done with the geology lesson, return back down the A.T. the way you came.

Trip notes: The park is open daily. The park entrance fee is $10 per vehicle; $20 for an annual park pass. For information on all park activities and facilities stop by the Dickey Ridge Visitor Center *(closed mid-Nov.–mid-March)*, at mile 4.6 along Skyline Drive. Or contact the National Park Service, Route 4, Box 348, Luray, VA 22835; 540-999-3500. The web site is www.nps.gov/shen.

Directions: The park's northern entrance is near Front Royal, about 75 miles west of Washington, D.C. From the

Capital Beltway (I-495), head west on I-66 to Front Royal. Follow US 340 to the park entrance a mile south of town. Plenty of signs lead the way. Once you get on Skyline Drive, go to mile 10.4, and park in the Compton Gap parking area on the left; the trailhead is across Skyline Drive.

36. Shenandoah National Park

Mile 41.7 on Skyline Drive

Passamaquoddy, Appalachian, and Stony Man Nature Trails

3.5-mile loop/2.5 hours

Views, views, and more views—that's what this splendid hike is all about. From two different elevations (atop Little Stony Man and Stony Man Mountains), you peer down on the fabled Shenandoah Valley, its patchwork of farms interspersed with pocket-size woods. You'll also see the quintessential Blue Ridge scenery of hazy ridges rolling off into the distance, and, if it's springtime, lush green flora draped with the puffy white and pink blooms of mountain laurel.

Begin the hike at the Stony Man Nature Trail parking lot, located at the north entrance to Skyland. From your car, walk west along the sidewalk, away from Skyline Drive. About 50 feet beyond the parking area, you'll come to a bridle trail. Go left, following it to the paved road, and turn right. Follow the road past where it forks, keeping to the right. Just ahead you'll see a concrete marker for the **Passamaquoddy Trail**. Turn right, onto the trail, which soon passes through a marvelous grove of hemlocks. Thanks to George Freeman Pollock, who founded the nearby Skyland resort in 1894, the area was never logged, so the ancient trees still stand.

In just a little bit you'll come to a dirt road. Go right, past an old road on the right, to another fork in the road. Here you'll see a concrete post indicating that the road to the right leads to a pump house. About 5 yards to the left of this post stands another concrete post, this one marking the Passamaquoddy Trail. This is the trail you want.

Go downhill through the trees. Now you're traipsing more or less along the Passamaquoddy Trail's original route, built in 1932 by Pollock to link Furnace Spring with Little

Stony Man. (Watch on the right, just a couple of feet up the slope, for traces of the old trail.) Pollock must have had a sense a humor, because he called the trail Passamaquoddy, after the Maine Indian word for "abounding in pollock." Of course the Indians were referring to a kind of fish, not the man. Cut into a steep mountain slope, this rolling, rocky stretch of trail offers superior views through the trees of the Shenandoah Valley, far below. About a half mile from the concrete marker you'll pass some overhanging rocks, on the right, decorated in winter with icicles. Directly above you tower the Stony Man Cliffs.

About 0.3 mile beyond this point begin the upper cliffs of Little Stony Man, popular among rock climbers. Soon you'll reach the first panoramic viewpoint, at Little Stony Man summit, looking out on the little valley town of Luray and, beyond, Massanutten Mountain. If you look up to the left, at the higher cliffs of Stony Man Mountain, you can with a little imagination see how the mountain got its name: It looks like the face of a bearded man gazing out on the Shenandoah Valley.

Continuing on, about 200 yards beyond this overlook, you'll come to a fork in the road. The trail to the left leads to the Stony Man parking area at Skyline Drive. You don't want that. You want to go right, following the white-blazed **Appalachian Trail** uphill. Depending on the time of year, Queen Anne's lace, mountain laurel, and purply morning glories speckle the trailside flora. The rocky trail snakes uphill, finally coming to the junction with the brown-blazed **Stony Man Nature Trail.** Go right.

From this point, it's just a third of a mile to the summit of Stony Man Mountain. Along the way you'll come to a fork in the trail; it doesn't matter which way you take, since this is a loop up to the top. Try going right, and coming back on the left. Walking along, you'll notice numbered posts. These are keyed to an interpretive nature guide that you can purchase at the trailhead and at bookshops throughout the park.

Once atop the rather inconspicuous summit (the second highest in the park, at 4,010 feet above sea level), you'll pass two trails on the left—the first is the downhill portion of the loop trail (which you'll descend a little later), the next is a yellow-blazed bridle trail. Continue walking straight ahead until you come to the end of the world, one of the park's most breathtaking spots. Scramble over the jumbled boulders as far as you can go for the full effect. Before you sprawl the gold and green farms of Page Valley, with wooded

Massanutten Mountain beyond. Just to the right, down below, you can see the cliffs of Little Stony Man, where you just were. To the left, look down on Skyland, and farther left you can make out Hawksbill, the highest peak in the park (see pp. 91-92). The beauty of this spot is overwhelming, which is why you won't be alone—it's a popular place.

After peeling your eyes away from the view, take a minute to look at the vegetation around you. On this high, rocky, exposed peak, where winds are dry and temperatures cool, trees normally found in more northern forests thrive, including red spruce, balsam fir, and white pine.

The hike returns to the parking lot via the Stony Man Nature Trail—a 0.75-mile downhill trek.

Insider's tip: Before embarking on the hike, purchase for 50 cents a Stony Man Nature Trail guide at the Stony Man trailhead. You can use this for a small portion of the hike to learn in more detail about the surroundings. It also has a map of the Passamaquoddy Trail on the back.

Make it easier: Instead of starting off at the far end of the parking area, in the direction of the Passamaquoddy Trail, simply take the **Stony Man Nature Trail,** located at the end of the parking area nearest Skyline Drive. You'll have a bit of a climb to the top of Stony Man, but will be rewarded with the most magnificent view the entire hike has to offer.

Trip notes: The park is open daily. The park entrance fee is $10 per vehicle; $20 for an annual park pass. No dogs are allowed on the Stony Man Nature Trail, but are allowed on the other trails. For information on all park activities and facilities stop by the Harry F. Byrd Sr. Visitor Center at Big Meadows, at mile 51.0 along Skyline Drive. Or contact the National Park Service, Route 4, Box 348, Luray, VA 22835; 540-999-3500. The web site is www.nps.gov/shen.

Directions: To reach the park's central entrance from the Capital Beltway (I-495), follow I-66 west for 24 miles to the US 29 exit, and head south about 10 miles to Warrenton. Here pick up US 211, following it west about 35 miles to the park entrance, just beyond the little town of Sperryville. After you get on Skyline Drive, go south to the north entrance of Skyland, at mile 41.7. Park in the nature trail parking lot, and walk west on the sidewalk, away from Skyline Drive.

37. Shenandoah National Park

Mile 42.6 on Skyline Drive

Whiteoak Canyon Trail

4.6-mile round-trip/4 hours

Of all the trails to walk and explore in Shenandoah National Park, there's one that always stands out: the **Whiteoak Canyon Trail.** The trail leads through pristine forest to a steep-walled canyon, where six different waterfalls drop over bedrock ledges. (This hike takes in just the tallest one.)

The seasons bring ever-changing variety to this beautiful niche. In winter you'll find a silent refuge, where powdery snow dusts dark green hemlocks, ice-cold streams are mere trickles, and the only signs of life are the footprints of foraging deer. In summer, puffy white mountain laurel decorate the trailside, mountain streams splash over moss-covered stones, the waterfalls fall in torrents, and the forest is filled with joyful birdsongs and the laughter of young kids dipping their toes in moss-fringed pools. Anytime, it's a magical place.

The hike begins at the north end of the Whiteoak Canyon parking area, at mile 42.6 along Skyline Drive. Walking down a gentle slope, you'll cross over a clear-running, rock-strewn stream. Take note of this gentle rush of water, because during the course of the hike it joins the forces of other streams to become a raging waterfall. About the time that you cross over the Limberlost Trail (see pp. 90-91), about a half mile ahead, you'll begin to notice the giant hemlocks towering above you. Ancient, silent, magnificent, these trees create so much shade that almost nothing can grow beneath their branches. In summer you might spot some ferns, mushrooms, Indian pipes, and other plants that thrive without much light or nutrition; otherwise, the forest floor is bare.

The trail crosses over the Old Rag Fire Road, then, about a quarter mile on, crosses the Limberlost Trail again. Continue straight, downhill. The sound of rushing water grows louder and louder, and you'll see clear, cool streams gurgling over moss-covered stones. Shafts of sunlight slant through towering trees like gold-dipped fingers, illuminating the forest's bright green flora. This fantasyland is the pure essence of Shenandoah.

Farther ahead, cross the modern metal-and-wood bridge to the other side of a stream. Soon you'll be walking on the right bank of the Robinson River, the sculptor of the sheerfaced Whiteoak Canyon, the source of the waterfalls. The trail becomes steeper from this point on, strewn with more rocks—watch your footing. Soon you reach the first noticeable cascade (not one of the main falls, but just a sampling of what's to come): the stream tumbling over rocks into a pretty green pool. The river will stay to your left, its riffles and sparkles—and occasional cascade—visible through branches of trees.

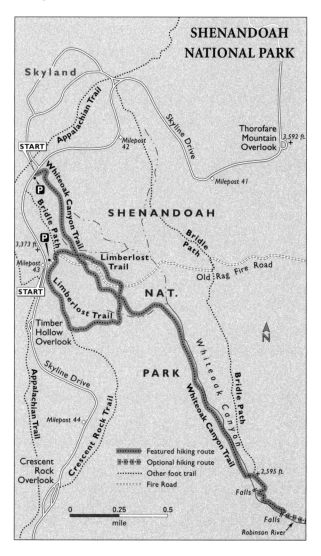

It's 1.3 miles from the last time you crossed the Limberlost Trail to the point where you cross back over the Robinson River. You can't miss the spot: Another metal-and-wood bridge spans the water here. Continue along the trail, wider now, on the river's left bank. The top of the first falls is ahead on the right, but not really worth stopping at, since you can't view the falls from atop. So walk about a third of a mile, to two rocky ledges. The farthest one provides the best perch from which to watch the amazing gymnastics of the Robinson River as it drops 86 feet into a cool, green pool.

The hike ends at this point. When you're ready to peel your eyes from nature's spectacle, turn around and return the way you came (not to spoil a perfectly good hike, but the only way out is uphill).

Make it easier: If you just want to see some classic Blue Ridge scenery, go as far as the first bridge and turn around the way you came. You won't get to see the beautiful waterfall, but you also won't have to climb back uphill.

More hiking: You can make a loop by returning from the falls via the bridle path and the Old Rag Fire Road.

To see the other waterfalls—truly a lovely sight, with fewer people—you can continue past the first one, down the narrow, steep, rough trail for 1.4 miles. Remember: The drop in elevation is 1,110 feet—something to consider, since you'll be turning right around and coming right back up the way you came. Another popular hike is to continue down Whiteoak Canyon to Cedar Run Canyon, a narrow, rocky gorge with a small waterfall; consult park literature for details.

Trip notes: The park is open daily. The park entrance fee is $10 per vehicle; $20 for an annual park pass. For information on all park activities and facilities stop by the Harry F. Byrd Sr. Visitor Center at Big Meadows, at mile 51.0 along Skyline Drive. Or contact the NPS, Route 4, Box 348, Luray, VA 22835; 540-999-3500. The web site is www.nps.gov/shen.

Directions: See map on p. 88. To reach the park's central entrance from the Capital Beltway (I-495), follow I-66 west for 24 miles to the US 29 exit, and head south about 10 miles to Warrenton. Here pick up US 211, following it west about 35 miles to the park entrance, just beyond the little town of Sperryville. After paying the park entrance fee, go south on Skyline Drive to mile 42.6. The Whiteoak Canyon parking area will be on the left.

38. Shenandoah National Park

Mile 43 on Skyline Drive

Limberlost Trail
1.3-mile loop/1.25 hours

Ir you're a bit unsure about venturing far into the
Shenandoah wilderness, here's the perfect trail. There's
absolutely no way to get lost, for the crushed greenstone
walkway measures 5 feet wide, and its gray-green color
starkly contrasts with the area's rich brown soil. All you have
to do is step to the left of the big Limberlost Trailhead sign
and follow the trail in a clockwise loop.

The **Limberlost Trail** begins in some woods, and then—
all of a sudden—you enter the dark, shady realm of giant
hemlocks, called the Limberlost. The canopy of these
conifers is so dense that light, even at high noon, can barely
penetrate. The soil is acidic and stripped of nutrients, so
there aren't a lot of plants growing on the forest floor. In
summer you might spot ferns, mushrooms, Indian pipes,
mosses, pine drops, and other plants that thrive in dark
shade and don't need much nutrition. Why are these trees
still here, you ask, when the rest of the forest was cut and
farmed? These lovely trees were saved by George Freeman
Pollock, whose dedication to the area in the late 1800s
brought about the founding of Shenandoah National Park. It's
said he paid a lumberman $10 for each tree not cut down.
Sadly, virtually all of the national park's hemlocks are infested
with the hemlock woolly adelgid—a tiny insect that sucks sap
from twigs, causing the tree to lose vigor and prematurely
drop needles to the point of defoliation, and oftentimes death.
These along the Limberlost Trail have been sprayed, but the
canopy is noticeably thinner than it once was.

Continue on the trail across the Whiteoak Canyon Trail,
the Old Rag Fire Road, and the Whiteoak Canyon Trail
again. Then you'll cross over a small stream and, after bearing west, enter a boggy area. A boardwalk keeps your hiking
boots dry. In spring, look for the bright green sprouts of
false helibore and the yellow blooms of marsh marigolds.

From here, the trail veers north (turn right at the intersection with the Crescent Rock Trail) through a thicket of
mountain laurel, whose white and soft pink blossoms appear
fairyland-like in spring. Look for the old apple trees leftover
from the days when this land was farmed. In spring, their

blossoms explode in delicate pinks, and in fall the spindly branches are laden with small, wormy apples. The trail soon loops you back to the parking area.

Trip notes: The park is open daily. The entrance fee is $10 per vehicle; $20 for an annual park pass. For further park information, stop by the visitor center at Big Meadows, at mile 51 along Skyline Drive. Or contact the NPS, Route 4, Box 348, Luray, VA 22835; 540-999-3500. The web site is www.nps.gov/shen.

Directions: See map on p. 88. To reach the park's central entrance from the Capital Beltway (I-495), follow I-66 west for 24 miles to the US 29 exit, and head south about 10 miles to Warrenton. Here pick up US 211, following it west about 35 miles to the park entrance, just beyond the little town of Sperryville. Once you get on Skyline Drive, drive south to the Limberlost parking area, on the left at mile 43.

39. Shenandoah National Park
Mile 46.7 on Skyline Drive

Hawksbill Summit trail
2.1-mile round-trip/1.25 hours

Hawksbill Summit—the park's highest peak—floats above a misty landscape of tree-carpeted mountains and green-and-gold countryside, its steep slopes plunging 2,500 feet from where you stand. On a crisp fall day, when the surrounding trees are ablaze in golds, scarlets, and oranges, you can see forever. This is the time of the hawk migration, when the majestic birds ride by on invisible thermals. In winter, glistening hoarfrost covers the summit, creating an enchanting setting as hushed as a cathedral. Haze and pollution often obscure the view in summertime.

No matter what season, there's only one way to reach this supreme vista—up. This hike from the Upper Hawksbill parking area is the easiest of several summit trails. Beginning from the parking lot, follow the **Hawksbill Summit trail** near the drinking fountain into the woods. You're going to start climbing pretty quickly, but take your time; enjoy the young oak forest around you. You might even wish to rest on the park bench part way up; listen to the various bird songs and watch for deer that graze the forest floor.

After 0.7 mile, you'll hit a dirt fire road. Go right on this, and climb 0.3 mile up to the summit. (Along the way, ignore the trail that cuts sharply across the fire road about a quarter mile up—to the left it leads to the A.T., to the right it goes down to Skyline Drive.) At the summit you'll see a shelter called Byrds Nest No. 2 (no camping) and be treated to breathtaking western views of the Shenandoah Valley and the Alleghenies. But don't stop now.

Continue on the trail about 75 yards to a stone observation area. Here, atop Shenandoah's loftiest peak, you're greeted with a nearly 360-degree view of misty blue ridges undulating ridge after ridge into the distance. Far off on the left you can make out the town of Stanley. Moving to the right you'll spot Nakedtop Mountain, then Buckraker Hollow, Bushytop Mountain, Stony Man Mountain, and, far to the right, venerable Old Rag.

Now take a moment to look closer around you. Sprinkled among the red oaks, birches, and other trees are balsam firs and red spruces. Found in few other spots in the park, these relics of the last ice age thrive at this high elevation (4,049 feet), where lower temperatures and abundant moisture provide a climate similar to that of more northern climes.

Return to the parking lot the way you came.

Trip notes: The park is open daily. The park entrance fee is $10 per vehicle; $20 for an annual park pass. For information on all park activities and facilities stop by the Harry F. Byrd Sr. Visitor Center at Big Meadows, at mile 51.0 along Skyline Drive. Or contact the National Park Service, Route 4, Box 348, Luray, VA 22835; 540-999-3500. The web site is www.nps.gov/shen.

Directions: To reach the park's central entrance from the Capital Beltway (I-495), follow I-66 west for 24 miles to the US 29 exit, and head south about 10 miles to Warrenton. Here pick up US 211, following it west about 35 miles to the park entrance, just beyond the little town of Sperryville. Once you get on Skyline Drive, drive to the Upper Hawksbill parking area at mile 46.7.

40. Shenandoah National Park

Mile 50.7 on Skyline Drive

Dark Hollow Falls trail
1.4-mile round-trip/1.5 hours

Gracefully spilling over a crumbling greenstone ledge, Dark Hollow Falls is one of the greatest spectacles of Shenandoah National Park. Even Thomas Jefferson, who knew every corner of these mountains like the back of his hand, admired their solitary beauty. Perhaps the best news, though, is that of all the falls the park has to offer, Dark Hollow is the closest to Skyline Drive.

From the north end of the Dark Hollow Falls parking area, follow the trail into pretty woods, cross a stream called Hog Camp Branch, and amble along beside the water for about half a mile. At this point, the stream tumbles 70 feet into a pool below—creating Dark Hollow Falls. You can't see the falls from atop, but a sign of a stickman tumbling head-first into the water indicates what may happen if you get too close to the slippery rocks near the edge.

Now the trail curves briefly away from the falls, crests a small hill, and delves into a steamy, almost junglelike world of moss-covered boulders and waves of ferns. Moisture drips from everywhere—from trees above, between cracks in boulders, even running across the trail. You'll pass a gigantic rock, its moist face resplendent in winter with stalactites of ice.

Finally the trail reaches the base of the falls. Here you are treated to a full-on view of the cascading water, framed by jungly green foliage—a supreme mountain setting, the epitome of Blue Ridge beauty, indeed.

Backtrack to your car the way you came.

More hiking: If you still have the energy—remember the return trip is all uphill—the trail wanders another 300 yards or so past smaller waterfalls, ending at Rose River Fire Road.

Trip notes: The park is open daily. The park entrance fee is $10 per vehicle; $20 for an annual park pass. For information on all park activities and facilities stop by the Harry F. Byrd Sr. Visitor Center at Big Meadows, at mile 51.0 along Skyline Drive. Or contact the National Park Service, Route 4,

Box 348, Luray, VA 22835; 540-999-3500. The web site is
www.nps.gov/shen.

Directions: To reach the central entrance to the park
from the Capital Beltway (I-495), follow I-66 west for
24 miles to the US 29 exit, and head south about 10 miles
to Warrenton. Here pick up US 211, following it west
about 35 miles to the park entrance, just beyond the
little town of Sperryville. Beyond the entrance station,
go south on Skyline Drive to mile 50.7, and park in
the Dark Hollow Falls parking area, on the left.

41. Shenandoah National Park
Mile 94.1 on Skyline Drive

Appalachian and Turk Mountain Trails
2-mile round-trip/1 hour

Shenandoah National Park boasts many spectacular
hikes to scenic overlooks, and each one is beautiful in
its own right. This hike to the top of Turk Mountain,
though, outshines the competition for two reasons. First, the
trail's pretty easy, considering you're climbing to the top of a
mountain. The ascent is gradual, and all along you're treated
to magnificent mountain views. And second, since it's
located at the park's southern end, you're less likely to come
across fellow nature lovers. Chances are, even at the peak of
the fall foliage season, you'll have the place all to yourself.

Taking off from the Turk Gap parking area, cross Skyline
Drive. At the cement cairn marking the **Appalachian Trail,**
bear left, into the woods. It's a fairly level walk beneath a
sunshade of maple, dogwood, sassafras, and elm. After 0.1
mile, you'll come to another cement cairn marking a trail
junction. Go right on the blue-blazed **Turk Mountain Trail.**
The trail descends into the saddle between Turk Mountain
and the main ridge; ahead looms Turk's tree-carpeted
peak—your destination.

Now the narrow dirt path gradually makes its ascent,
offering distant mountain views along the way. To the left
your eyes feast on the geologically pleasing view of rumpled
ridges, rising and swelling off into the distance—these are
rock talus slopes formed by the accumulation of rock debris.

After about three-quarters of a mile from the beginning,

the trail switches back, bringing you into the summit's barren, rocky realm. Make your way to the tiptop, where a jumble of rocks (Erwin quartzite), poised above tree line, makes a perfect spot to sit and admire the nearly 360-degree view. Way up here, the sky somehow seems bigger, the sun closer. At your feet (westward) spreads the storied Shenandoah Valley, with its plush green pastures and copses of trees. Behind you (eastward) tower the same magnificent mountain peaks you've been watching throughout your ascent. In autumn, this is a fabulous place to watch the annual hawk migration, as hundreds of raptors float by on invisible currents.

The rest of the hike entails simply retracing your steps back down the mountainside, a most enjoyable task indeed.

Trip notes: The park is open daily. The park entrance fee is $10 per vehicle; $20 for an annual pass. For further information, stop by the visitor center at Big Meadows, at mile 51.0 along Skyline Drive. Or contact the NPS, Route 4, Box 348, Luray, VA 22835; 540-999-3500. The web site is www.nps.gov/shen.

Directions: To reach the park's southern entrance from Charlottesville, travel west on I-64 about 20 miles to Rockfish Gap and the exit for Skyline Drive. Go north 11.3 miles from the south entrance station to the small parking area on the right for Turk Gap. The trail begins across Skyline Drive.

42. Blue Ridge Parkway

Mile 6 on Blue Ridge Pkwy.

Blue Trail
2-mile round-trip/1 hour

Ancient, rumpled, wonderfully remote, the southern Appalachians have been the subject of many a song and ballad. This is the remote, rocky landscape of mountain folk, who have lived hardscrabble lives for centuries, of flower-scented breezes of springtime, when thousands of rhododendron and azalea festoon the lush green understory, and of wildfire that ignites in autumn, as ridge after tree-fringed ridge bursts into vibrant oranges, scarlets, and golds.

This hike at the northern end of the Blue Ridge Parkway offers a small sampling of this singular place of beauty.

Granted, it's a little steep, but if you take your time and take advantage of the trailside benches, you'll do fine. The destination is Humpback Rocks, a greenstone outcrop that locals simply call the "Rocks." At 3,210 feet above sea level, the Rocks, jutting westward, provide a wide-sweeping, unobstructed view of the Shenandoah Valley as it rolls in green and golden swathes to the feet of the Alleghenies.

The hike begins at the southern end of the Humpback Gap parking area, following the blue-blazed trail up the rugged mountain. Up and up you go, ascending beneath a splendid canopy—chestnut oaks, white oaks, red oaks, pignuts, sweet birches, serviceberries, red maples.

After about half a mile, the trail climbs up some stairs, switchbacks farther up, and finally swings around to the north on flatter terrain. At 0.8 mile from the parking lot you come to a trail junction, where a left turn brings you to Humpback Rocks. Climb up on them, and be taken in by the heavenly view. You may just be inspired to write a ballad yourself.

The hike returns the way you came.

More hiking: Nearby at mile 5.8 along the Blue Ridge Parkway lies the Humpback Rocks Visitor Center, where you can walk a short, easy trail around some restored rock-and-timber homesites belonging to early mountaineers.

Insider's tips: The trees at higher elevations peak earlier in autumn than those on lower lands. So remember, if it's mid-October and Washington's trees are still green, you should be in the mountains. Keep in mind that the southern Blue Ridge generally peaks before the northern Blue Ridge, since the mountains are higher.

Trip notes: The parkway is open daily. There is no entrance fee. For more information contact the Blue Ridge Parkway, 200 BB & T Building, Asheville, NC 28801; 828-298-0398. Or contact the Appalachian Trail Conference, P.O. Box 807, Harpers Ferry, WV, 25425; 304-535-6331.

Directions: From Charlottesville, go west on I-64 about 20 miles to Rockfish Gap and the entrance to the Blue Ridge Parkway. Go south on the parkway to mile 6, and park in the Humpback Gap parking area, on the left.

Shenandoah and Beyond

Virginia's storied Shenandoah Valley and the bordering Allegheny Mountains offer some of the region's wildest, most breathtaking trails.

43. George Washington National Forest

Off I-81 near Woodstock, Virginia

Woodstock Lookout Tower trail
0.3-mile round-trip/15 minutes

One of the most tremendous Appalachian views lies at the end of a very short trail. If you're in the neighborhood of Woodstock, make a point of driving the windy, narrow road up Powell Mountain, ambling up a couple of stone steps, and traipsing through an oak and pine forest for 0.15 mile. You'll then see the Woodstock Lookout Tower—the most challenging part of this hike is climbing its stairs. As you climb higher and higher, above the trees, brace for this 360-degree vantage:

To the west sprawls the plush emerald green Shenandoah Valley, spotted with farms and groves of trees. In the distance rises tree-clad Great North Mountain, and, farther than that, Long Mountain in West Virginia. What's most impressive about this view, though, lies in the foreground—the seven horseshoe bends of the Shenandoah River. Between Edinburg and Strasburg, a distance of only 15 miles or so, the curling, meandering river travels 50 miles.

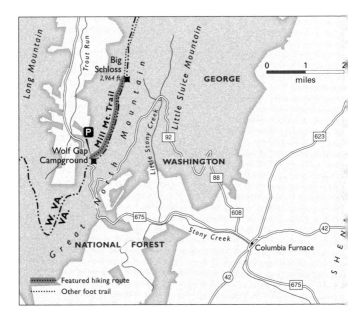

To the east take in Massanutten Mountain and, beyond that across Page Valley, the Blue Ridge within Shenandoah National Park. Note the formation created by the western flank of Massanutten Mountain and the ridgelines of Green and Powell Mountains, located north and south respectively from where you stand. The positioning of these mountain slopes creates a bowl with steep, impenetrable walls. Named "Fort Valley" by George Washington, who had planned to use the valley as a retreat in case of defeat at the Battle of Yorktown, the valley creates a natural fort.

Return to your car the way you came.

Advisory: Owing to steep, windy, precipitous curves, driving here is not recommended in winter; the road may be closed in adverse weather conditions.

Trip notes: The trail is open daily. There is no entrance fee. For more information, contact the Woodstock Chamber of Commerce, N. Main St., Woodstock VA 22664, 540-459-2542; or the U.S. Forest Service, Lee Ranger District, 109 Molineu Rd., Edinburg, VA 22824, 540-984-4101.

Directions: From the Capital Beltway (I-495) take I-66 west beyond Front Royal to I-81 and go south. Take the Woodstock exit, heading east on Va. 42. At US 11, turn left and head into town. At Cemetery Rd./Rte. 758, turn right and

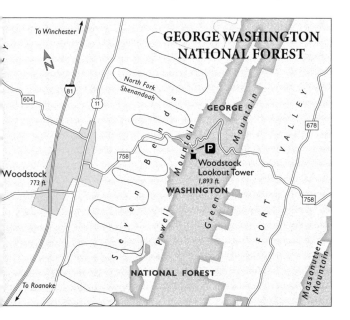

follow the road up the mountain. The road becomes gravel and switchbacks to the top of the mountain, about a 5-mile trip in all. Leave your car at the second parking area you come to, on the right, and head up the trail by the "Woodstock Tower" sign.

44. George Washington National Forest

Off I-81 near Columbia Furnace, Virginia

Mill Mountain and Big Schloss Trails
4.4-mile round-trip/2.5 hours

Suspended above misty green valleys and engulfed by steep, rugged mountains, the stony outcrop of Big Schloss lives up to its German name—castle. Indeed, the incredible 360-degree view from this vantage takes in one of the last vestiges of pure, unbroken wilderness in all of eastern America, a natural fortress in the midst of civilization.

The trailhead to the orange-blazed **Mill Mountain Trail** begins near campsite no. 9 in the Wolf Gap Campground of the George Washington National Forest. You start off climbing up rocky Great North Mountain fairly steeply beneath a cool canopy of oaks and maples, leveling off in about three-quarters of a mile as you bear left along a spiny ridge. Every now and again, beautiful views of Shenandoah Valley appear off to the east, completely surrounded by tree-cloaked mountains with names like Little Sluice and Massanutten. In wintertime, through the trees ahead, you can make out the gray outcrops of Big Schloss—your destination. Local denizens include white-tailed deer and even black bear.

About a mile farther, watch for the double orange blazes that indicate a trail junction. At this point, the Mill Mountain Trail continues its wanderings straight ahead, through other parts of the George Washington National Forest. You want to turn right, onto the white-blazed **Big Schloss Trail.** Climbing a bit, the trail becomes rockier and rockier, while fabulous views emerge from outcroppings on both sides.

A wooden bridge crosses over a deep crevice. On the other side, walk all the way to the very tip of Big Schloss, and its astounding 360-degree wilderness view. To the west are Trout Run Valley and Long Mountain (in West Virginia); north lies Mill Mountain; eastward you'll recognize the same view that you saw previously from the ridgeline trail; and to the south looms Great North Mountain.

You'll want to linger awhile and enjoy this heavenly place. If you're lucky, you may spot a peregrine falcon; the Forest Service has placed a hatching box at Big Schloss to help reintroduce these magnificent birds of prey back into the wilds.

When you're done enjoying this true return to nature, go back down the way you came.

Advisory: The trail is rocky; sturdy hiking boots will help.

Make it easier: You could just do the 0.75-mile climb to the first views and turn around.

Trip notes: The trail is open daily. There is no entrance fee. For more information contact the U.S. Forest Service, Lee Ranger District, 109 Molineu Road, Edinburg, VA 22824; 540-984-4101.

Directions: From the Capital Beltway (I-495) take I-66 west beyond Front Royal to I-81, then go south to the Woodstock (Va. 42) exit. Follow Va. 42 west about 7 miles to Columbia Furnace. When you reach town, turn right on Rte. 675. (Just after you take this turnoff you'll cross over a stream; Rte. 675 veers left, alongside the stream, not straight ahead.) From Va. 42 it's 6.5 miles to the Wolf Gap Campground. Park in the big parking lot. The trail takes off near campsite no. 9.

45. Douthat State Park

Off I-64 west of Lexington, Virginia

Buck Hollow, Mountain Top, and Mountain Side Trails
5.7-mile loop/3 hours

Unspoiled views of ancient, rumpled ridges; a lovely little mountain lake; tree-filled coves that burst into flames of color in autumn: These are some of the scenes that highlight this hike through Douthat (DOW-thit) State Park. Granted, the park is a bit of a jaunt from the Washington, D.C., area—four hours or so. But try to set aside some mid-October weekend, when autumn splashes rich hues of color on the tree-covered mountains.

With 40 miles of hiking trails—more than in any other

park in the state—it's hard to choose which hike to take. You can't really go wrong. Though this particular hike is a bit long, it brings you to the top of a mountain, far out in the wilderness, with wide-reaching views of nothing but misty ridges. You won't be disappointed.

Before beginning, make sure to admire lovely Douthat Lake at surface level, because in about an hour you're going to have quite a different perspective. Taking off from the parking lot near the Lakeview Restaurant on Douthat Lake, cross the park road to the trailhead for the red-blazed, 1-mile **Buck Hollow Trail** (this is also the trailhead for the Buck Lick Trail, a short interpretive trail through a climax forest). Follow the gurgling stream in a woodsy hollow, and soon you'll come to a T-intersection. Go left, crossing the stream on a little wooden bridge. Just beyond lies another trail intersection. Go right, in the direction of Buck Hollow and Mountain Top. You parallel the rock-riven stream, crossing over it a couple of times, making your way gradually up the hollow.

After about half a mile the hollow becomes narrower, its walls steeper. At this point, the trail crosses over to the left bank and begins switchbacking up that side of the hollow. As you climb up and up, you'll begin to notice views westward of tree-covered mountains. Farther up, the trail curves around the head of the hollow, and soon you're standing on flatter ground, atop a ridge, at a trail junction. You want to go left, on the yellow-blazed, 2.3-mile **Mountain Top Trail.** Switchbacking up to the summit of Beards Mountain, you're treated to breathtaking views off to the north and south of tree-blanketed ridges. You finally reach the mountain top, which is a little disappointing, given that trees block any potential views. No matter, the best is yet to come.

Now the narrow trail dives pretty steeply down the other side of the mountain. Farther ahead, in a clearing, you get a bird's-eye view off to the west of little Douthat Lake, a sparkling indigo jewel cradled by massive mountains. Soon after, you come to another trail junction. Go left, on the 1.4-mile **Mountain Side Trail**—the best part of the hike. On a narrow trail cutting across a steep mountain slope, you wrap around coves and hollows filled with maples, sassafras, elms, and oaks. Autumn sunlight filters through the thousands and thousands of orange and red and yellow leaves that fill these little valleys, so the whole forest looks like a sunlit stained-glass mosaic. Between the branches you get magnificent vistas of distant mountain ridges.

Eventually the trail brings you back to the first trail

junction above Buck Hollow. Duck into the hollow and return the way you came.

Insider's tip: Douthat is a bit of a drive from D.C., but in about four hours you'll be a world away. Make a weekend of it; rent one of the cabins and do nothing but hike, boat, and fish.

Trip notes: The park is open daily. There is a $2 entrance fee per vehicle. The park office has trail maps. For more information contact Douthat State Park, Rte. 1, Box 212, Millboro, VA 24460; 540-862-8100.

Directions: From Lexington, go west on I-64 about 30 miles to the Clifton Forge exit. Head north on Rte. 629 for 5.5 miles to the park entrance; park in the Lakeview Restaurant parking area inside the park.

46. Douthat State Park

Off I-64 west of Lexington, Virginia

Heron Run Trail
2.5-mile round-trip/1.3 hours

Dark and glossy, Douthat Lake reflects the high mountain peaks of the surrounding Alleghenies, the reddish orange of changing maples along its shoreline, the silhouette of a canoe cutting its smooth waters. Get to know this beautiful mountain lake along the **Heron Run Trail.**

The trail begins along the lakeside loop of campground A. Don't be put off by the "campers only" sign set up at the campground's entry gate. If you're not camping, simply park outside and walk in. As far as directions go, the trail is self-explanatory. From beginning to end, it hugs the shoreline, wandering for a spell beneath tall, shady hemlocks, wrapping around a small cove, and, after half a mile or so, coming down to a dam. You can walk across the dam for nice lake views, then backtrack the way you came.

Trip notes: The park is open daily. There is a $2 entrance fee per vehicle. The park office has trail maps. For more information contact Douthat State Park, Rte. 1, Box 212, Millboro, VA 24460; 540-862-8100.

Directions: From Lexington, go west on I-64 about 30 miles to the Clifton Forge exit. Head north on Rte. 629 for 5.5 miles to the park entrance; travel along the park road, around the lake, to the left-hand turnoff for campground A.

Maryland Suburbs

North of the nation's bustling capital, a handful of seemingly remote wilderness sanctuaries offer crashing rivers, majestic forestlands, and plenty of wildlife sightings.

47. Chesapeake & Ohio Canal National Historical Park (Great Falls Tavern section)

Off MacArthur Blvd. near Potomac, Maryland

Great Falls Overlook trail
0.5-mile round-trip/30 minutes

█▬

As the Potomac River drops 77 feet out of the pied-mont into the coastal plain, it creates Great Falls—rather a series of rapids than a true waterfall. There's a Maryland side and a Virginia side, and much debate over which side offers the prettiest views. While Virginia provides beautiful panoramas (see hike on pp. 40-42), only in Maryland can you stand on an island in the middle of the river, amid all the thunder and spray.

The hike begins in front of the Great Falls Tavern, a whitewashed structure dating from 1828, when canal boats on the Chesapeake & Ohio Canal floated by its door. Cross the footbridge to the towpath that runs along the historic canal, and turn left. Farther on, at the **Great Falls Overlook** sign, turn right. The footbridge spans a narrow shoot of the Potomac River called the Fish Ladder—beneath you a powerful gush of water swirls, circles, and spits through a narrow channel.

At the bridge's end lies Falls Island, crisscrossed by a boardwalk to protect its fragile ecosystem. Indeed, a unique habitat of plants, called a bedrock terrace forest, thrives on both this island and on the one you're about to cross. The rocks here look pretty barren, not conducive to life at all. But floods and high waters have deposited enough silt and other alluvium in cracks and crevasses to sustain some unique plant species. On the island's drier parts you'll recognize Virginia pine, red oak, and post oak. In wetter soils grow pine oak, river birch, and swamp oak. But look closer to the ground for some really unique plants: hairy wild petunias, erect water hyssops, tall tickseeds. Even in these small places, white-tailed deer graze the underbrush, and the birdlife is overwhelming: Some 150 species have been spotted throughout the year.

The trail leaves Falls Island, crosses another surging side channel, then winds across Olmstead Island. Soon you come to the Great Falls Overlook at the end—undoubtedly crowded for a good reason: The crashing waters are mesmerizing. Scan the scene for bald eagles gliding overhead, reckless kayakers fighting the current downstream, and rock climbers spidering up the cliffs across the way.

When you've had enough, return the way you came.

More hiking: Check out the **Billygoat Trail** just downstream (see below).

Trip notes: The park is open daily. There is a $4 parking fee at the Great Falls Tavern. The tavern has trail maps, as well as some interesting exhibits on historic floods in the area, a small bookstore, and rangers to answer questions. For more information, contact the National Park Service, Great Falls Tavern, 11710 MacArthur Blvd., Potomac, MD 20854; 301-299-3613.

Directions: From Washington, D.C., take the Clara Barton Pkwy. north to MacArthur Blvd. Turn left and follow it past the Old Angler's Inn to the junction with Falls Rd. A sign here indicates that you've reached the entrance road to the C&O Canal National Historical Park, on the left. Follow this past the toll gate to the large parking area. The trail begins from the Great Falls Tavern.

48. Chesapeake & Ohio Canal National Historical Park (Great Falls Tavern section)

Off MacArthur Blvd. near Potomac, Maryland

Billygoat Trail
4-mile loop/3 hours

They don't call this the Billygoat Trail for nothing. At times you're leaping from rock to rock, clambering over large boulders, climbing angled rocks, and teetering beside steep cliffs above the Potomac River. A billy goat would have an easier time of it, no doubt. But this rocky hike along the edges of Bear Island just downstream from Great Falls, by no means simple, is one of the best loved in the Washington area. The Potomac Electric Power Company bought the 96-acre island in the 1940s with the idea of building a hydroelectric station and a dam across

Mather Gorge. However, the floods that periodically sweep the island finally dissuaded the company, which donated the land to the Nature Conservancy in 1996. The National Park Service now oversees Bear Island, with the Potomac Appalachian Trail Club maintaining the trail. The Billygoat Trail itself, as designated by a group of hikers in the 1930s, ambles beside the Potomac River for more than 8 miles between Great Falls and Carderock. It's made up of three segments; this hike takes in the part referred to as section A, the closest portion to Great Falls Park.

From the Great Falls Tavern, cross the footpath across the canal and walk downstream along the towpath for about half a mile to Lock 16. Here you'll see a large sign on the right, marking the **Billygoat Trail.** Enter the grove of Virginia pine, noting the blue blazes that indicate the trail.

Soon you'll spot the Potomac's surging waters through the trees. Little by little, you'll find yourself stepping around some rocks scattered across the trail. At first it's not too bad, but these rocks seem to grow and grow. The trail turns southward, paralleling the Potomac, and all of a sudden you realize there's no more dirt beneath your feet. You're climbing over a jumble of boulders (gneiss and schist), and you're using your hands and derrière to negotiate the trail. The blue blazes mark the trail in the oddest of places—on fallen trees, on sides of boulders—because there's nowhere else to paint them.

Be sure to stop now and again, because at this point of the trail you have a completely unobstructed, panoramic view of the Potomac River as it tears voraciously through the narrow rock channel of Mather Gorge. Over eons, the river cut this vertical, smooth-walled gorge straight through the rock. Notice the huge potholes in the rock beneath you; when this rock was part of the riverbed way back when, surging eddies on the river bottom swirled cobbles that over time created these smooth, gaping holes. Across the river, rock climbers clamber up the cliff-lined Virginia side.

The trail continues along the wide Potomac's edge, crossing rocky hills and ravines. At one point you scramble diagonally up a rock face. Then the trail ducks on and off into woods crisscrossed with streams and dotted with bright spring wildflowers and small beaver ponds. Finally, when you think you've surely traveled 10 miles, not just 1.5, you come to an overview above a river channel that's dry during low water; but during high water it's a rapid-filled surge popular with kayakers. A little rock perch here provides the perfect rest spot. The land across the way is wooded Sherwin Island, and beyond that lie Virginia's wooded heights.

From here, it's just a hop and a skip beside the channel and Sherwin Island back to the towpath. Once you reach the towpath, turn left for the easy, pleasant 2-mile walk back to the tavern. Along the way you'll pass Widewater—once the riverbed of the Potomac—and, farther ahead, fabulous cliff-top vistas of the Potomac. Consider taking the easy walk out to the **Great Falls Overlook** (see pp. 106-107).

Insider's tip: You can park at the Old Angler's Inn on MacArthur Blvd. and walk down to the towpath, go right, and do the trail backwards—for no fee.

Trip notes: The park is open daily. There is a $4 parking fee at the Great Falls Tavern. The tavern has trail maps, as well as some interesting exhibits on historic floods in the area. For more information, contact the National Park Service, Great Falls Tavern, 11710 MacArthur Boulevard, Potomac, MD 20854, 301-299-3613; or the Potomac Appalachian Trail Club, 118 Park St., SE, Vienna, VA 22180, 703-242-0693.

Directions: From Washington, D.C., take the Clara Barton Pkwy. north to MacArthur Blvd. Turn left and follow it past the Old Angler's Inn to the junction with Falls Rd. A sign here will indicate you've reached the entrance road to the C&O Canal National Historical Park, on the left. Follow this past the toll gate to the large parking area. The trail begins from the Great Falls Tavern.

49. Chesapeake & Ohio Canal National Historical Park (Great Falls Tavern section)

Off MacArthur Blvd. near Potomac, Maryland

Gold Mine Loop
4.2-mile loop/2.5 hours

While the Great Falls area is known for the Potomac River's explosive drama, a more peaceful side to the park is found in the wooded uplands above the falls. Here, a network of trails ambles beneath oaks and maples and hollies, where the silence is broken only by the drumming of a pileated woodpecker on a dead tree limb, the lonesome chortling of a great blue heron, the sweet melody of a warbler.

But this corner hasn't always been so quiet. As long ago as the 1600s, when Capt. John Smith sailed up the Potomac as far as Great Falls "to search for a glistering metal," the quest for gold has tantalized many. No mother lode was ever discovered, but there were enough rumors in the general vicinity to keep people searching. In 1861 a Union private discovered traces of gold near Angler's Inn while washing dishes in a stream. Returning in 1867, he purchased the lands for what would become known as the Maryland Gold Mine, triggering an explosion of gold-mining activities over the next six decades.

On this hike you can visit the gold mine ruins. But the real treasures are the splendid canopy of oaks and maples that sparkle golden and red and orange in autumn, the deer, fox, and woodpeckers that reign throughout this rich kingdom.

The blue-blazed **Gold Mine Loop** begins uphill just behind the Great Falls Tavern. At first you amble along a dikelike ridgeline—a former rail bed. Ahead you'll come to the junction of the yellow-blazed Lock 19 Loop. Keep straight, on the Gold Mine Loop. As you traipse along, watch for the sawdustlike dirt mounds that speckle the forest floor, built by Allegheny mound-builder ants. (See pp. 118-119 for a description of these ants.) Soon you come to a T-intersection, where the Gold Mine Loop heads in both directions. Go left (you'll return the other way). Continue along, enjoying the tranquility, until you reach a branch trail that wanders off to the left. A sign posted here says "Falls Road." Just uphill on this trail you'll see the first of the ruins—rusted shacks with corrugated aluminum roofs. Farther up the hill a sign explains the local history.

Backtrack to the "Falls Road" sign; the trail continues dipping, winding, weaving through the woods. You pass the Rockwood spur (to Rockwood School), then the yellow-blazed Angler's Spur, the yellow-blazed Woodland Trail, and the yellow-blazed Lock 16 spur. And soon you come full circle around the loop. Follow the sign left down the hill, retracing your steps past the Allegheny mound-builder ants to the tavern.

Make it easier: Just walk as far as the gold mine and retrace your footsteps.

Trip notes: The park is open daily. There is a $4 parking fee at the Great Falls Tavern. The tavern has trail maps, as well as some interesting exhibits on historic floods in the area, a small bookstore, and rangers to answer questions. For more information, contact the National Park Service, Great Falls Tavern, 11710 MacArthur Blvd., Potomac, MD 20854; 301-299-3613.

Directions: From Washington, D.C., take the Clara Barton Pkwy. north to MacArthur Blvd. Turn left and follow it past the Old Angler's Inn to the junction with Falls Rd. A sign here indicates you've reached the entrance road to C&O Canal National Historical Park, on the left. Follow this past the toll gate to the large parking area. The trail begins from the Great Falls Tavern.

50. Seneca Creek State Park
Off I-270 near Gaithersburg, Maryland

Lakeshore Trail
3.7-mile loop/2.5 hours

At first glance, Clopper Lake—a glistening body of water snuggled amid Seneca Creek State Park's timbered hills—seems to teem with people…boy scouts, picnicking families, strolling couples. But if you take the trail that loops the lake, you'll find yourself in a quiet realm far away from humans, where the only signs of life are local denizens: white-tailed deer, opossums, raccoons, foxes, cottontail rabbits, wild turkeys, groundhogs. In addition, some 150 species of birds have been spotted here, including the magnificent bald eagle.

The 6,609-acre park embraces Seneca Creek as it flows from Gaithersburg to the Potomac River. As long as 10,000 years ago, Native Americans lived in this area; in fact, the site of Maryland's earliest Indian dwelling is located within park boundaries. Later, in the 17th and 18th centuries, colonists farmed the land, cultivating peaches and apples, tobacco and grains. One of their old gristmills still stands in the park's southern section. Since those times, much of the land has been allowed to revert to wilderness—what you see today. Clopper Lake itself was created in 1976, when Long Draught Branch was dammed.

The hike begins from the parking area near the boat center; stroll down to the lakeside, where you'll see the narrow, dirt **Lakeshore Trail**. Go right (counterclockwise), staying close to the water's edge, and you'll find your way around. The trail cuts through pretty woodlands and traces quiet inlets where fishermen cast for largemouth bass. In spring and summer old farm fields bloom with colorful wildflowers, while golden sagegrass flourishes in fall.

Along the way, watch for wildlife. Plump Canada geese lumber near the water's edge; scarlet-red northern cardinals dart playfully through the woods; families of turtles sun on floating logs; perhaps a black rat snake drapes itself across the trail, enjoying an afternoon snooze. And the songbird symphony—starring cedar waxwings and bluebirds—plays in spring.

The presence of people will alert you to the fact that you've looped the lake and are returning to the trailhead.

Trip notes: The park is open daily. There is a $1 entrance fee per person on weekends May through Sept., and 50 cents per car on weekends Oct. through April. A trail map and bird list are available at the visitor center. For more information contact the Park Manager, Seneca Creek State Park, 11950 Clopper Rd., Gaithersburg, MD 20878; 301-924-2127.

Directions: From the Capital Beltway (I-495), go north on I-270 to the Clopper Rd. exit. Proceed 2 miles west, through the Gaithersburg section of the park. Watch for signs to the park entrance, on the left. Park at the boat center parking lot; the hike begins down near the water's edge.

51. Greenbelt Park
Off the Capital Beltway (I-495) in Greenbelt, Maryland

Perimeter and Blueberry Trails
2.3-mile loop/2 hours

Washington's sprawling suburbs completely embrace Greenbelt Park, a 1,300-acre wilderness island administered by the National Park Service. Within this lush green kingdom hides a great deal of wildlife: white-tailed deer, red foxes, raccoons, squirrels, groundhogs, and 320 species of birds that go about their daily lives just as if millions of people weren't going about *theirs* nearby. In spring, dogwood, laurel, and azalea put on a magnificent display, and in fall, the changing leaf color is sensational.

Perhaps the most interesting thing about Greenbelt Park, though, is its success in reforestation. Denuded of trees by colonist broadaxes to grow tobacco, corn, and other crops in the rich soil, Greenbelt's land has been allowed to recover since the early 1900s. Today a mixed pine and deciduous forest—the middle step toward an eastern climax forest—thrives, and within the next few decades, a hardwood forest will take over again, just as when the colonists first arrived.

Greenbelt Park has several short hiking trails that wind through the wilderness. A favorite hike uses both the Perimeter Trail and the Blueberry Trail, making a loop in the south end of the park.

From the ranger station, turn left on the paved park road and walk about 100 yards to Park Central Road; turn right. You'll see the vehicle barrier that blocks the paved bike trail. Pass through the barrier and take a sharp right onto the dirt trail, into the woods. Almost immediately, bear left on the yellow-blazed trail, the **Perimeter Trail,** and soon you'll be snaking downhill beneath a canopy of pines—Virginia, white, pitch, and shortleaf—mixed with maple, oak, and sweet gum trees. In about a half mile, the trail flattens out, and you come to the boardwalk, which skims across a marshy area created by Deep Creek. Early in spring the marsh is at its wettest, when salamanders and newts hide beneath rotting logs and skimmers glide across its surface.

The trail then winds uphill; at the T-intersection, go right. Off to the left you'll see some houses, reminders that development is never too far away. Continue along, with the slow-moving Deep Creek on your right.

Soon you come to another T-intersection that crosses over the stream. Make a sharp right, across the stream, which will bring you to a V-intersection. The trail on the right leads to the campgrounds. Take the one on the left, still following the yellow blaze.

Farther ahead, cross over two little wooden planks and, immediately beyond, cross a fire road. About 50 yards beyond this point, you'll come to a V-intersection with the **Blueberry Trail.** Veer to the left (you'll see the trail now is blazed both blue and yellow, meaning the Blueberry Trail has merged with the Perimeter Trail).

At the next fork, follow the blue-blazed Blueberry Trail as it leaves the Perimeter Trail, to the right. This trail wanders through tall, skinny trees, ending at a sign that says "Blueberry Nature Trail." Go left on the paved road and back to the ranger station.

More hiking: The park boasts two other short nature trails that also are worthwhile: the 1.2-mile **Azalea Trail** and the 1.4-mile **Dogwood Trail.**

Trip notes: The park is open daily. There is no entrance fee. Pick up a free park map at the park headquarters, located near the entrance. For more information, contact the Park Manager, Greenbelt Park, 6565 Greenbelt Rd., Greenbelt, MD 20770-3207; 301-344-3948.

Directions: From the Capital Beltway (I-95/I-495), take Kenilworth Ave. south. At Greenbelt Rd., turn left and follow signs to the nearby entrance on the right. To find the trailhead, follow Park Central Rd. to its end, and turn right toward the campgrounds. Park at the ranger station, almost immediately on your right.

Central Maryland

Among central Maryland's lush farmland and tree-covered mountains, a mélange of trails unveils hidden waterfalls, supreme vistas, Civil War battlefields, and more.

52. Sugarloaf Mountain

Off I-270 south of Frederick, Maryland

Mountain Loop, Northern Peaks, A.M. Thomas, Monadnock, and Sunrise Trails
1.3-mile loop/1.5 hours

Jutting above the manicured farm country of central Maryland, Sugarloaf Mountain stands alone, a defiant stronghold of wilderness amid pastoral calm. This protruding anomaly in the earth's surface is called a monadnock, a lonesome mountain created when all the land around it erodes. It took some 14 million years for Sugarloaf to attain its height, as surrounding lands wore away. As mountains go, this one's not particularly high—just 1,282 feet above sea level—but it's high enough to provide sweeping views of the lovely countryside all around.

Since there's only one way to go—UP—most trails here are fairly steep. Happily there's one hike, if you can stand a few sharp ascents, that circles the mountain a couple of hundred feet below the mountain top, then climbs straight to the summit. Your reward: staggering views of the surrounding land, and of the Blue Ridge beyond. The well-blazed trails are easy to follow. Be forewarned that on weekends they can be popular.

Starting at the white-blazed **Mountain Loop Trail** near the bulletin board, pick up a trail map and plunge into the woods. For a second, you'll think you've really lucked out, because the trail goes downhill for a spell, then flattens out. Only then does it begin its climb (and climb and climb). At the blue-blazed **Northern Peaks Trail,** about half a mile ahead, turn left, up a fairly wicked hill brightened with tulip poplars, red maples, and beeches.

The Bill Lambert Overlook at the top is worth the climb. Before you spread the green and gold fields of the Monocacy River Valley, and on a clear day the misty Blue Ridge rises in the distance. Geologists say that Sugarloaf is actually an outpost of the Blue Ridge; indeed, its 570-million-year-old erosion-resistant rock is quite similar to that found in the Blue Ridge. The trail levels out now, traveling through chestnut oaks as it wraps around the mountaintop. Moss and lichen cover gray stone outcrops, and in June the white and pale-pink blossoms of mountain laurel ornament the trailside understory. Through the leaves and tree branches on the right, you get occasional glimpses of the fields far below.

When you reach the West View parking area, take the green-blazed **A.M. Thomas Trail,** a 0.25-mile "improved trail"—rather, a dirt footpath with log steps and then a series of stone steps—which is good, because this is a seriously steep trail. Up and up you go, seemingly high into the sky. Just when you think you can't go any more, you find yourself surrounded by strange, elephantine boulders, and still you climb. And then you're on the boulders. At the top of the stairs, follow the trail as it bears left, and finally—the summit. Walk over to the giant boulders scattered atop a sheer cliff face, providing an idyllic, unobstructed 180-degree vantage of the Frederick Valley. In autumn, this makes the perfect place to watch the annual migration of hawks, which catch the updrafts generated by the monadnock.

Only when you feel like heading back, meander along the red-blazed **Monadnock Trail,** which leads away from the view, into the woods. A short way ahead, turn right on the orange-blazed **Sunrise Trail** and watch your step as you make the steep 0.25-mile descent back to the East View parking area.

Make it easier: When you come to the West View parking area, forgo the steep climb up to the summit. Instead, walk along the paved park road for 1.25 miles, back to the East View parking area.

If you want to avoid absolutely any uphill climbs, park at the West View parking area and take the **Northern Peaks Trail** to the Bill Lambert Overlook (in the opposite direction from what is described above). From the overlook, follow the **Mountain Loop Trail** down to the East View parking area. Return to your car via the 1.25-mile paved park road.

Trip notes: The park is open daily. There is no entrance fee. Free maps are available at the trailhead. For more information contact the privately owned Stronghold Incorporated, 7901 Comus Rd., Dickerson, MD 20842; 301-869-7846.

Directions: From the Capital Beltway (I-495) take I-270 north to the Md. 109 exit. Go southwest, continuing 3 miles to Comus Rd. in the crossroads of Comus, and turn right through pretty countryside. At the park entrance, follow the only road up the mountain to the first parking lot, the East View parking area. The Mountain Loop Trail begins by the bulletin board.

From Baltimore, take I-70 west, then go south on Md. 75. When the road ends at Md. 355, turn left toward Hyattstown, then go right on Md. 109 (Old Hundred Rd.). Go under I-270, continue 3 miles to the crossroads of Comus, and proceed as stated above.

53. Little Bennett Regional Park

Off I-270 south of Frederick, Maryland

Bennett Ridge, Mound Builder, Beaver Valley, Stoney Brook, and Hickory Hollow Trails
3-mile loop/2 hours

A pocket wilderness amid suburbia, Little Bennett Regional Park is a wild, beautiful sanctuary seemingly far away. A birder's paradise, it showcases breeding vireos and warblers, plus resident northern bobwhites and wild turkeys. The centerpiece is cool-running Little Bennett Stream which, with the help of its tributaries, has carved the piedmont upland into a rolling land of hills and low ridges. The trails here are well maintained and well signed—making it difficult to get lost and a delight to walk. This hike links several trails that together showcase the park's prettiest and most interesting aspects. The downside is that, in order to do all this, you'll have to walk along a park road for a quarter mile.

Begin at the nature center, walking toward the camping loop (away from the park entrance). When you reach the loop, go to the right of the fork and follow the road to the **Bennett Ridge Trail.** This wide, grassy path shoots across a ridge top, whose forest floor is resplendent with ferns and mosses. Chestnut trees abound, thriving on the ridge's poor, dry soil.

You'll pass the Antler Ridge Trail, Beaver Valley Trail, and Woodstock Hollow Trail. Continue on, about half a mile total, until you come to a sign on the right that says "Mound Builder Trail to Beaver Valley." Take this, the **Mound Builder Trail,** downhill.

As the path becomes rougher and the grass thins, pay close attention to your surroundings. Soon you should be seeing soil mounds, some as high as 2 or 3 feet, dotting the forest floor. These are the works of Allegheny mound-builder ants. Look down at your feet, and you'll see zillions of ants running around (don't stop too long; they'll crawl up your legs and

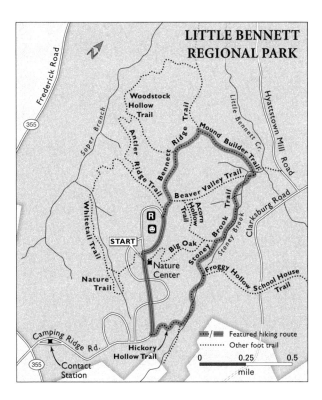

LITTLE BENNETT REGIONAL PARK

Frederick Road

Woodstock Hollow Trail

355

Soper Branch

Antler Ridge Trail

Bennett Ridge Trail

Little Bennett Cr.

Hyattstown Mill Road

Mound Builder Trail

Beaver Valley Trail

Acorn Hollow Trail

Stoney Brook Trail

Stoney Brook

Clarksburg Road

Whitetail Trail

R

START

Big Oak

Nature Center

Nature Trail

Froggy Hollow School House Trail

Camping Ridge Rd.

Hickory Hollow Trail

355

Contact Station

Featured hiking route
Other foot trail

0   0.25   0.5
mile

bite you). The half-red, half-black ants build these colossal structures to insulate themselves from searing summer heat. In winter, the mounds provide the perfect place to hibernate; the ants stay warm and dry even during the worst of blizzards.

You pass through the mound-builders' domain for about a quarter mile; continuing downhill, you'll come to the T-intersection with the **Beaver Valley Trail.** Go right, into a woodsy area. Follow the trail to the **Stoney Brook Trail,** where you bear left. This narrow trail enters a forest of tulip poplars and red maples, alongside clear-running Stoney Brook. Take time to stroll through this pretty woodland, listening to the murmuring of the stream, the joyful tunes of springtime warblers, the wind rustling through towering white oaks.

After ambling along for about a mile, passing by the Acorn Hollow Trail and Froggy Hollow School House Trail, you'll come to the junction with the **Hickory Hollow Trail.** Go right (a sign indicates the nature center and camping loops are this way, too), and start switchbacking gently uphill. In this little hollow, hickories reign over a regal forest that also includes sweet gums and maples. Shafts of sunlight slant through the tall trees. All too soon, you come to the park road. Turn right, and in a quarter mile or so you'll return to the nature center.

Insider's tip: If the park entrance gate is closed in wintertime, park next door in the maintenance area and walk up the park road to the nature center.

Make it easier: To see the mound-builder ants, wander out on the Bennett Ridge Trail to the Mound Builder Trail and stroll along until you've seen enough; return the way you came.

A more scenic but less interesting option is to take the park road back toward the park entrance to the Hickory Hollow Trail, and dip into the hollow for a spell. You might consider going as far as the junction with the Stoney Brook Trail, which brings you to the park's most attractive section.

Trip notes: See map on p. 119. The park is open daily. There is no entrance fee. For more information contact the Park Manager, Little Bennett Regional Park, 23701 Frederick Rd., Clarksburg, MD 20871; 301-972-6581.

Directions: From the Capital Beltway (I-495) take I-270 north about 20 miles to the Md. 121/Clarksburg Rd. exit. Go north, and at the first stoplight—Frederick Rd. (Md. 355)—take a left. Proceed to the park entrance on the right. The nature center is located about a mile up the park road.

From Baltimore, take I-70 west, then go south on Md. 75. When the road ends at Md. 355, turn left toward Hyattstown; the park entrance will be on the left.

54. Harpers Ferry National Historical Park

In Harpers Ferry, West Virginia

Shenandoah Street and Appalachian Trail

1.6-mile loop/2 hours

Snuggled between the steep crags of the Blue Ridge mountains, at the point where the Shenandoah River meets the Potomac, Harpers Ferry is a quiet mountain village of stone-and-brick buildings and narrow streets. Its history, though, is anything but quiet, for it was here in 1859 that fiery abolitionist John Brown launched his ill-fated raid on the U.S. armory and arsenal. Though he ended up being hanged for the act a couple of months later, his actions helped precipitate the Civil War. Today, the heart of the city has been made part of the National Park System, and old buildings have been converted into interesting museums on Harpers Ferry's history.

Be sure to examine the exhibits and displays—they're extremely informative. But don't miss out on the town's extraordinary surroundings. This hike combines the region's colorful history with its idyllic setting. Begin at John Brown's Fort, at the corner of Potomac and Shenandoah Streets. This is the (reconstructed) building—really a fire engine station and guardhouse—in which John Brown and his followers barricaded themselves in a last-ditch attempt to ward off troops during that fateful raid. Peer inside at the old walls, read the plaque on the wall, then head down **Shenandoah Street,** past restored 19th-century buildings, to High Street, where you turn right. Almost immediately, on your left, you'll see some hand-carved stone stairsteps—cut in the rock at the turn of the 19th century to access the upper levels of town. Take them up the hill. You're not only immersed in history, you're also huffing and puffing your way up the **Appalachian National Scenic Trail,** the 2,000-odd-mile trail that ambles atop the Appalachians between Maine and Georgia. (Notice the white blazes that mark it.)

Soon on your left you'll see St. Peter's Catholic Church (now private), a beautiful stone edifice built in the 1830s with a tall graceful steeple. A little farther are the crumbling remains of St. John's Episcopal Church, which was rebuilt twice: once after a crippling fire in the 1800s and again after the Civil War. Just ahead perches Jefferson Rock—several hunks of Harpers shale piled atop each other—and its fabulous view of the steep Blue Ridge plunging dramatically into the valley. In the 1700s, Thomas Jefferson stood on this very spot and was inspired to write: "This scene is worth a voyage across the Atlantic." Indeed, it is.

The trail weaves along the mountainside for a while, offering occasional glimpses of the shimmering Shenandoah far below. You can't help but keep peering off to the left, to the ever impressive view of the river valley. When you come to the fork for Storer College, follow the Appalachian Trail to the left, downhill. At the next fork, take the high road, to the right. This will bring you down to the junction of US 340 and Shenandoah Street. Go left, virtually making a U-turn, onto Shenandoah Street. A little way down the road, you'll see a small trail just on the other side of a low fence. This trail follows the roadside back into Harpers Ferry. To the right lie the wilds of Virginius Island and the picturesque remains of the Shenandoah Canal. If you want to leave the road all together, you can follow one of the island's trails back into Harpers Ferry (see Virginius Island Trail below).

More hiking: You can link this hike to the **Loudoun Heights Trail** (see pp. 127-129).

Trip notes: See map on pp. 124-125. The national historical park is open daily. There is a $5 entrance fee payable at the Harpers Ferry National Historical Park Visitor Center. The visitor center has all kinds of information, including free park maps, books for sale, and rangers on tap to answer questions. For more information, contact the NPS, P.O. Box 65, Harpers Ferry, WV 25425; 304-535-6298. www.nps.gov/hafe.

Directions: From Frederick take I-70 west for just half a mile, then follow US 340 west for about 20 miles toward Harpers Ferry. After crossing the bridge over the Shenandoah River, turn right immediately on Shenandoah St., into Harpers Ferry National Historical Park. There is usually parking in the railroad station parking lot on Potomac St. Or, instead of turning right on Shenandoah St., proceed up the hill on US 340, turning left into the park at the traffic light; from here you'll have to take the shuttle into Lower Town (dogs not allowed on shuttle). The trailhead is at the corner of Shenandoah and Potomac Sts.

55. Harpers Ferry National Historical Park

In Harpers Ferry, West Virginia

Virginius Island Trail
0.75-mile loop/45 minutes

People flock to Harpers Ferry for its history—namely abolitionist John Brown's daring raid on the federal arsenal here in 1859—yet often ignore its early beginnings. It all started sometime before 1785, when Robert Harper erected his sawmill on Virginius Island, at the powerful confluence of the Shenandoah and Potomac Rivers. The result: an industrial boom that soon had the area—a thriving community of 200 people—banging, clanging, and steaming with productivity. George Washington took note of the locale's tremendous waterpower, and in 1799 put in motion the construction of a federal armory at Harpers Ferry. All this background is, of course, significant, since some of the region's major products were armaments and highly desirable to abolitionist rebels. Hence the John Brown raid.

Over time, most of the brick-and-stone buildings on Virginius Island have been swallowed by floods, and only ruins survive. Regardless, the National Park Service has erected a variety of plaques along a meandering path that pinpoint the vine-choked remains of important buildings and flesh out historical details. Strolling along, you can almost hear the sounds and see the smoke of industrial days.

Those industrialists couldn't have chosen a prettier place. And what's nice about the **Virginius Island Trail** is that nature has just about reclaimed it all. You meander right beside the fabled Shenandoah River, its riffles glistening in the sunlight. Mulberry trees abound. Bottomland hardwoods such as sycamore, white ash, and silver maple create a shady sanctuary on hot summer days. Northern cardinals and red-winged blackbirds dart from tree to tree, and great blue herons pause quietly on the riverbank.

The trail begins at the end of the Hamilton Street footpath, at the railroad trestle just outside Lower Town Harpers Ferry. Walking alongside the Shenandoah, you pass by the old cotton factory and blacksmith shop, then by the water tunnels that used to help supply water to the cotton factory. Near this point lies an intersection of trails; keep to the left. Continue past another old cotton mill and a machine shop. To see the remains of Herr's Dam, first completed in 1848, walk through the intake arches that stand just ahead.

Back on the main trail, you pass under the tracks for the Winchester & Potomac Railroad, which once connected Harpers Ferry to Winchester, Virginia. During the Civil War, Confederates used it to haul machinery to Richmond and other points south. Onward, cross the maintenance road, and follow the trail to the left. You come to the old Shenandoah Pulp Company—the site of Robert Harper's sawmill—and continue alongside a stone retaining wall. Just ahead is Lake Quigley—an old millpond—and a turbine pit that once was located beneath the machine shop of a rifle factory. Hall's Rifle Works, the first of two rifle factories built on the spot, churned out some 20,000 of John Hall's newfangled

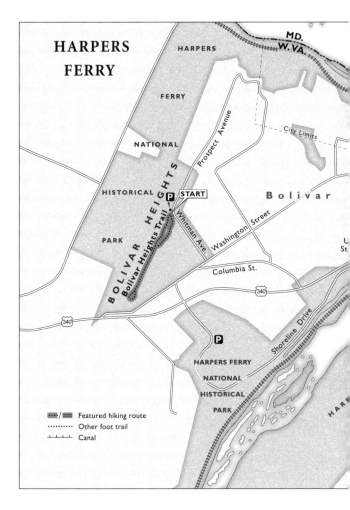

breech-loading rifles, which took one-third less time to load than the conventional muzzle-loader.

From here, the trail loops back through the sawmill ruins; at the trail junction continue straight ahead, beside the old Shenandoah Canal. Beyond the Herr and Snapp Foundry, the trail intersects with a park maintenance road. Go left, and when you reach the Randolph Bridge, take the trail that goes right, past the Child's House. At the next trail intersection, go left, past the Wernag's House and Wernag's Saw Mill, And then, turn left at the next trail intersection, and you're back to where you started.

More hiking: You can link this hike to the **Loudoun Heights Trail** (see pp. 127-129).

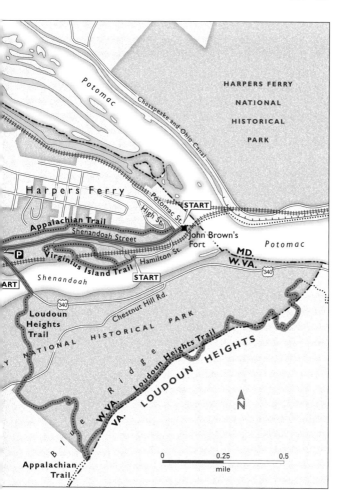

Trip notes: The national historical park is open daily. There is a $5 vehicle fee payable at the Harpers Ferry National Historical Park Visitor Center. The visitor center has all kinds of information, including free park maps, books for sale, and rangers on tap to answer questions. For more information, contact the NPS, P.O. Box 65, Harpers Ferry, WV 25425; 304-535-6298. The web site is www.nps.gov/hafe.

Directions: From Frederick take I-70 west for just half a mile, then follow US 340 west for about 20 miles toward Harpers Ferry. After crossing the bridge over the Shenandoah River, turn right immediately on Shenandoah St., into Harpers Ferry National Historical Park. There is usually parking in the railroad station parking lot on Potomac St.

Or, instead of turning right on Shenandoah St., proceed up the hill on US 340, turning left into the park at the traffic light; from here you'll have to take the shuttle into Lower Town (dogs not allowed on shuttle). The trail begins at the end of the Hamilton St. footpath, at the railroad trestle, just south of Lower Town Harpers Ferry.

56. Harpers Ferry National Historical Park

In Harpers Ferry, West Virginia

Bolivar Heights Trail
0.7-mile round-trip/30 minutes

It's hard to believe that the peaceful, leafy landscape of Bolivar Heights, located just west of Harpers Ferry's historic heart, has seen the bitter days of civil war. Yet Bolivar Heights hosted not one but two battles. The first was really a minor skirmish between 500 Virginia militiamen and 600 Union regulars, with no decisive victory for either side. But the second, which took place in September 1862, saw Southern hero Stonewall Jackson leading his troops in the capture of 12,500 Union troops—the largest single capture in the Civil War.

Along the **Bolivar Heights Trail,** with old black cannon and interpretive plaques to fuel your imagination, you can almost picture the soldiers camping out in pitched tents, stirring pots of beans over smoky fires, waiting for orders; you can almost see them relentlessly practicing military maneuvers; and you can relive the days of battle through the very words of soldiers, etched onto signboards. Wrote one Federal soldier: "The hissing and screeching of shot and shell discharged at us 'twas a strange medley for a Sabbath day's worship." And you can feel the soldiers' sorrow as they lowered fallen comrades into the ground.

Or, you can just choose to ignore the war history and appreciate the beauty of this spot: It's the perfect viewpoint from which to admire the precipitous gap between tree-covered Loudoun and Maryland Heights. The Shenandoah River sparkles in the distance, and with trees and grassy fields in the foreground, you couldn't find a nicer place to stroll.

The trail begins to the left of the parking lot. It's easy to follow (just to be sure, a big map at the trailhead shows you the way). A word of explanation: The Bolivar Heights Trail is actually two trails, the Loop Trail and the Redoubt Trail. Neither is very long. The Redoubt Trail, breaking away about midway along the Loop Trail, is a short, straight shot to an old artillery redoubt; backtrack to the Loop Trail, and complete the loop back to the parking lot.

Trip notes: See map on pp. 124-125. The national historical park is open daily. There is a $5 vehicle fee payable at the Harpers Ferry National Historical Park Visitor Center. The visitor center has all kinds of information, including free park maps, books for sale, and rangers on tap to answer questions. For more information, contact the National Park Service, P.O. Box 65, Harpers Ferry, WV 25425; 304-535-6298. The web site is www.nps.gov/hafe.

Directions: From Frederick, take I-70 west for just half a mile, then follow US 340 west for about 20 miles toward Harpers Ferry. After crossing the bridge over the Shenandoah River, proceed to the stoplight, and turn right. After rounding a right curve, turn left to Bolivar Heights. Park at the small parking area.

57. Harpers Ferry National Historical Park
In Harpers Ferry, West Virginia

Appalachian and Loudoun Heights Trails
4.4-mile round-trip/3 hours

A little hard to find, this trail leads into a little known world of Civil War ruins, a cool forest, trickling streams, and a stunning faraway vista of a toylike Harpers Ferry, nestled in the fabled Blue Ridge mountains.

From the dirt parking lot, walk up to US 340 and turn left onto the Shenandoah River bridge, whose narrow walkway brings you fairly close to fast-moving traffic—be careful. Below you, the Shenandoah swirls and churns around ledges of Harper shale. On the other side, carefully cross the road and climb over the guardrail. The white-blazed **Appalachian National Scenic Trail** (A.T.)—your trail—stairsteps up to the right, above the river, away from the noise and traffic.

The first mile tackles a fairly steep, rocky incline of Loudoun Heights. Up, up you go, through a forest of hardy oaks, hickories, and maples and across cool, clear-running streams. The soft white blossoms of sassafras and dogwood brighten the understory in May, intermingled with the vivid magenta of eastern redbud. In autumn, the scene is altered dramatically, with the dogwoods and maples and oaks now wearing showy hues of scarlet red, orange, and molten gold.

Partway up, you'll cross paved Chestnut Hill Road. As you huff and puff up the next part of the hill, look to the left for the old road that parallels the trail. This dirt route was probably built by the government sometime after 1827 to get at the trees up on the ridgeline. Back then, charcoal was needed to fuel the furnaces and forges at the Harpers Ferry armory, so colliers camped out on the mountainside beside slow-burning fires that converted the local timber into charcoal. If you look really carefully, you may spy some of the pits and ditches left over from their fires. By the 1850s, all this beautiful wilderness had been stripped bare. In the next decade, during the Civil War, Confederate soldiers trampled along that same dirt road, dragging supplies to the mountain summit.

Near the crest of the mountain, beware of the false trail that wanders off to the left. Your trail can't be missed: an obvious T-intersection with the blue-blazed Loudoun Heights Trail. The A.T. goes off to the right. Unless you want to go to Georgia (the A.T.'s terminus), bear left, onto the **Loudoun Heights Trail.** This trail is more or less flat, as it gerrymanders atop the ridgeline along the West Virginia/Virginia border. Walking along, you can occasionally gaze down on plush farmland to the right, and the Harpers Ferry valley to the left.

In 0.7 mile, some crumbling stone infantry fortifications, remaining from the Civil War, create an odd juxtaposition against the trees. About a half mile farther, you come to a clearing off to the left created by some power lines. You can either walk out to the bird's-eye view of Harpers Ferry offered here, or continue just a little bit farther down the trail for an even better view. In 0.3 mile, you pass by another clearing created by power lines. And then, half a mile beyond that, you come to Split Rocks. From here, the tiny brick buildings of Harpers Ferry snuggle far below in their mountain perch.

Turn around and head back the way you came.

Trip notes: See map on pp. 124–125. The national historical park is open daily. There is a $5 vehicle fee payable at the

Harpers Ferry National Historical Park Visitor Center. The visitor center has all kinds of information, including free park maps, books for sale, and rangers on tap to answer questions. For more information, contact the National Park Service, P.O. Box 65, Harpers Ferry, WV 25425; 304-535-6298. The web site is www.nps.gov/hafe.

Directions: From Frederick, take I-70 west for half a mile, then follow US 340 west for about 20 miles toward Harpers Ferry. After crossing the bridge over the Shenandoah River, turn right immediately on Shenandoah St. Park in the dirt parking area on your right. Or, to reach the park's visitor center, after crossing the bridge over the Shenandoah, continue up the hill on US 340 and turn left at the light into the park. You'll have to shuttle back to town. The trailhead is back up Shenandoah St., across the Shenandoah River bridge.

58. Antietam National Battlefield

Off I-70 near Sharpsburg, Maryland

Snavely's Ford Trail
2.5-mile loop/90 minutes

While Antietam is forever linked to its somber legacy as the bloodiest single day of battle in the Civil War, one that greatly altered the course of the Civil War, the battlefield today is a serene, beautiful place of wooded hilltops and murmuring streams. The perfect place to explore the battlefield's natural side is the trail that winds away from the historic Burnside Bridge, into a splendidly natural realm of trilling birds.

Begin at the Burnside Bridge parking circle, on the trail that zigzags down to the bridge. Graceful and serene, this bridge played a starring role in the Battle of Antietam. For it was here on that fateful September day in 1862 that an army of Union soldiers led by Gen. George B. McClellan attempted to push across, against an ongoing shower of Confederate fire. They finally made it, but too late; Southern reinforcements had just arrived. In the end, more than 23,000 men lay dead or dying. Although neither side gained a decisive victory, Confederate general Robert E. Lee's failure to carry the war effort into the North caused Great Britain to postpone recognition of the Confederate government. Abraham Lincoln took this opportunity to issue the Emancipation Proclamation, freeing all slaves and thereby making the abolition of slavery a central feature of the war.

As you turn right at the bridge and follow the river downstream on the **Snavely's Ford Trail,** you'll enter a tranquil province of oak, yellow poplar, sycamore, and American beech. The white blooms of dogwoods sprinkle the forest in early spring like snowflakes, and deer, raccoons, opossums, and squirrels forage for food. The creek riffles over boulders, snaking through the woods. Trout swim in the fast, cool currents, and bass, catfish, and sunfish are denizens, too.

After about a mile, a trailside marker indicates this was the chosen spot for Snavely's ford, where Union troops crossed over the river, without a bridge, in an attempt to surprise the Confederate right.

Onward, the trail wends uphill, away from the creek. You'll notice the vegetation around you begins to change. Different layers and zones of vegetation—small plants, shrubs, evergreens, and some hardwoods—mark a forest experiencing different stages of ecological succession. Over time, the hardwoods—beech, hickory, and maple—will win out, creating a lovely, mature deciduous forest. In the meantime, the young forest is a little bit wayward.

After climbing for a while, the trail comes upon rolling fields, and soon you see the gleaming white McKinley Monument towering ahead. Just beyond lies the Burnham Bridge parking area, the end of the hike.

Make it easier: About half a mile into the hike, take the wide fire trail back to the beginning.

Trip notes: The park is open daily. There is a $2 entry fee per person, $4 per family, payable at the visitor center. For information contact the Superintendent, P.O. Box 158, Sharpsburg, MD 21782; 301-432-5124. www.nps.gov/anti.

Directions: From Frederick, take I-70 west. Exit at US 40A and go through Middletown to Boonsboro. Turn left on Potomac St. (Md. 34W). In Sharpsburg, turn right on Md. 65 (Sharpsburg Pike) and follow signs to the Antietam National Battlefield Visitor Center. Pick up a battlefield map here and take advantage of the interesting Civil War displays. The film is a bit laborious to watch, but provides some good background.

To reach the trailhead from the visitor center, continue

on Md. 65, following the designated auto tour through the battlefield to stop #9 (Lower Bridge). Park in the parking area and follow the path to the bridge and trailhead.

59. South Mountain Recreation Area and Washington Monument State Park

Off I-70 west of Frederick, Maryland

Appalachian Trail
5.6-mile round-trip/ 3 hours

Connecting Georgia to Maine, the **Appalachian National Scenic Trail** (A.T.) rides the crest of the Appalachians for more than 2,000 miles, giving access to some of the East Coast's most magnificent mountain scenery. A hundred or more people walk the trail's entire length each year, camping out night after night beneath the starry sky. For those who don't have three or more months to spare, there are snippets in both Maryland and Virginia that make ideal day hikes. While the most popular portion winds through Shenandoah National Park, there's a quiet, remote leg in central Maryland that beckons the more adventurous. Beginning incongruously off I-70, it weaves along the long, skinny summit of South Mountain, the site of several Civil War skirmishes, and the spot where the first major battle on Maryland soil was fought in the war. At trail's end lies a state park that boasts the nation's first monument to the nation's first President. The hike is pretty anytime of year, but autumn brings the annual hawk migration—truly a spectacular sight from a special perch at the state park.

Starting out from the little parking area off US 40, walk past the bulletin board, down the old road about 50 yards. Here, pick up the blue-blazed spur trail, off to the left, into the woods. This will soon bring you to a footbridge over I-70, and the junction with the official white-blazed A.T. The trail rolls quietly along. Enjoy the classic Appalachian setting, with its great oaks and hickories, rhododendron and mountain laurel. Squirrels scurry in the underbrush, and if you're lucky you may spot a white-tailed deer or two.

After 2.8 miles, the trail brings you to the base of Monument Knob. Climb steeply uphill for 250 feet to Washington

Monument State Park, then turn right onto the paved road to the squat, jug-shaped, granite Washington Monument— built by the patriotic residents of nearby Boonsboro. On July 4, 1827, nearly every citizen marched from town 2 miles away and helped lay the stones. A narrow interior staircase winds up to a little observation tower, offering fabulous views of the farm-dotted piedmont far below.

This unassuming perch is one of Maryland's greatest spots to watch the annual hawk migration. When the air turns cool and the leaves commence their color change, hawks by the hundreds of thousands begin their journey south for the winter to sunny Mexico, Peru, and Argentina. Riding the updrafts created when winds from the piedmont crash into the steep Appalachians, hawks barely have to flap a wing as they follow the ancient flyway south along the long, narrow mountain range. Perhaps you'll be witness to a kettle—rising warm air that hawks ride like an elevator.

Two main kinds of hawks fly by here: broad-winged hawks, which generally float by in mid-September; and the sharp-shinned hawks, which wait until the first week of October to make their move.

When you're ready, turn back the way you came.

Insider's tip: At the point where the Appalachian Trail meets the state park road, turn left and head a quarter mile down the mountain to the core of Washington Monument State Park. There you'll find picnic tables, a recreation area, a little museum, and a soda machine, as well as the rest rooms.

Make it easier: You could cheat by parking at Washington Monument State Park and strolling about a quarter mile up the mountain to the tower. On the way back down walk a mile or so along the A.T., just to sample its beauty.

Trip notes: The trail is open daily. There is no entrance fee. For more information, contact the Appalachian National Scenic Trail, National Park Service, Appalachian Trail Conference, P.O. Box 807, Harpers Ferry, WV 25425-0807, 304-535-6331; or the South Mountain Recreation Area, 21843 National Pike, Boonsboro, MD 21713, 301-791-4767.

Directions: From Frederick, take I-70 west to the Md. 17 exit. Go north, turn left on US 40, and park at the Appalachian Trail parking area on the left, just before you reach the bridge over I-70.

60. Catoctin Mountain Park

Off US 15 north of Frederick, Maryland

Hog Rock Nature Trail
1.5-mile loop/45 minutes

S omewhere amid the dense, dark forest of Catoctin Mountain Park hides Camp David, the President's retreat since the 1940s, when Franklin D. Roosevelt chose Catoctin Mountain as the site of his Shangri-La. Many historic events have occurred here, including the planning of the Normandy invasion, the Eisenhower-Khrushchev meetings, the Camp David Accords with Menachem Begin of Israel and Anwar Sadat of Egypt, discussions of the Bay of Pigs and the Vietnam War, and many other meetings with foreign dignitaries and guests. You won't find the camp on the map, but the park boasts a nature trail that affords the ordinary citizen the same kind of leafy beauty enjoyed by the President—a stunning red maple forest that shimmers in autumn. As you walk along, you can thank Roosevelt for his vision through the New Deal's Works Progress Administration to preserve this beautiful eastern hardwood forest.

The well-marked **Hog Rock Nature Trail** begins at the Hog Rock parking area, about 1.3 miles north of the visitor center via Park Central Road. At the trailhead you'll find interpretive brochures, keyed to numbered posts along the way to help identify the various trees. Right off you're introduced to the stately sugar maple, unmistakably the most dominant tree here. In autumn, when frost turns the maple leaves crimson red, the typically sedate, green woodlands ignite like a forest fire, luring leaf peepers from far and wide. Other trees that complement the canopy include the tupelo, with their bulbous, wrinkly trunks; basswood, whose leaves are heart-shaped; shagbark hickories, which in fall produce nuts adored by squirrels and chipmunks; black gums; chestnuts; and oaks.

Jumbles of green-hued boulders grace the woodland floor—they're Catoctin greenstone, a metamorphic rock that originated from a lava flow some 600 million years ago. Little by little, the boulders are breaking down into soil, creating the setting's greenish cast.

After a quarter mile from the trailhead, go left at the fork. A half mile farther at the T-intersection, go left again. The sign here indicates you're headed to Hog Rock. And, indeed, just yards from this point you come to the trail's name-sake—the highest point in the park. Way back when, farmers used to bring hogs to the base of the rock to feed on chestnuts and acorns that dropped from above—hence the rock's strange name. The rock itself juts into empty space above the valley below, creating a perfect balcony perch overlooking green and golden fields. It's a nice spot for a picnic lunch, watching for the presidential helicopter to hover by.

The trail backtracks a couple of yards to the Hog Rock sign and continues through pretty woods, looping back onto itself. After half a mile you'll complete the loop at a T-intersection—go left a quarter mile, back to your car.

More hiking: From Hog Rock you can continue to Cunningham Falls; take the trail that drops down the hillside. When you get to Md. 77, cross it and take the 0.3-mile **Cunningham Falls Access Trail** (see p. 135) to the falls, located in adjacent Cunningham Falls State Park. To get back to your car, you'll have to climb back up the mountain and continue along the Hog Rock Nature Trail as described above.

Trip notes: The park is open daily, though Park Central Rd. is closed in winter. There is no entrance fee. The Catoctin Mountain Park Visitor Center has a small nature museum, plus all kinds of books and maps, plus rangers to answer questions. For more information, contact the Superintendent, Catoctin Mountain Park, National Park Service, Thurmont, MD 21788; 301-663-9330. The web site is www.nps.gov/cato.

Directions: From Frederick, go north on US 15 about 15 miles to the town of Thurmont. Here, follow Md. 77 west. In about 2.5 miles, at the junction with Park Central Rd., you'll reach the Catoctin Mountain Park Visitor Center. To reach the trailhead, turn right on Park Central Rd. and proceed 1.3 miles to the designated parking area on the right side of the road. Cross the street to the beginning of the trail.

61. Catoctin Mountain Park and Cunningham Falls State Park

Off US 15 north of Frederick, Maryland

Cunningham Falls Nature Trail and Cunningham Falls Access Trail
2.8-mile round-trip/2 hours

The tallest waterfall in Maryland, Cunningham Falls splashes 78 feet through a hemlock-choked gorge, creating one of the region's prettiest scenes. The most popular hike to the falls, considered one of Maryland's most beautiful trails, is the easy, 1.5-mile "lower trail," from Cunningham Falls State Park. To avoid the crowds you'll have to take this lovely wander in the early morning or the off-season.

On the other hand, try an alternate trail that winds through similar Appalachian woodlands, minus the people (and minus the state park fee), to the same splendid waterfall. The **Cunningham Falls Nature Trail** begins at neighboring Catoctin Mountain Park, from the parking area just to the left of the visitor center. (Cunningham Falls State Park and Catoctin Mountain Park are located adjacent to each other, and trails wind back and forth over the park boundaries.)

Striking off into the woods, you cross a little clear-running stream on a wooden bridge, then climb a fairly steep but short hill. As the trail more or less levels out, you can't help but notice the beauty surrounding you. Lovely white oaks dominate the peaceful woodlands, and lichen-covered rocks dot the forest floor. Birds sing, squirrels scurry, chipmunks dart across the trail. This is the domain of the pileated woodpecker, wild turkey, and elusive timber rattlesnake. And the best part: You'll feel like you have the whole forest to yourself.

After about a mile you come to a T-intersection, where a sign indicates that Hog Rock is off to the right and Cunningham Falls is to the left. Go left, cross Md. 77, and take the **Cunningham Falls Access Trail.** The trail wanders on a series of boardwalks beside boulder-strewn Hunting Creek, bringing you to the foot of Cunningham Falls. The forest's peaceful silence will probably be broken by the swarms of people here, but the falls, crashing into a pool below, aren't so quiet themselves. Chances are, you'll want to linger, perhaps even climb up the huge boulders for a closer look at the falls.

To return to the visitor center, retrace your footsteps.

Make it easier: Leave your car at the parking area on Md. 77 and take the 0.3-mile, wheelchair-accessible **Cunningham Falls Access Trail.**

More hiking: After viewing the falls, you can make a detour up to Hog Rock for a fabulous view. When you come back to the trail junction just after crossing Md. 77, instead of turning right back toward the visitor center, follow the trail up the mountainside. (This is a bit of a climb.) To return to the visitor center, you'll have to retrace your steps back to the trail junction and continue on the main hike.

Trip notes: The park is open daily, though Park Central Rd. is closed in winter. There is no entrance fee. For more information contact the Superintendent, Catoctin Mountain Park, National Park Service, Thurmont, MD 21788, 301-663-9330; or the Park Manager, Cunningham Falls State Park, Thurmont, MD 21788, 301-271-7574. The web site is www.nps.gov/cato.

Directions: From Frederick, drive north on US 15 about 15 miles to the town of Thurmont. Here, follow Md. 77 west. In about 2.5 miles, at the junction with Park Central Rd., you'll reach the Catoctin Mountain Park Visitor Center. The trailhead leaves from the far side of the parking lot located across from the visitor center.

62. Catoctin Mountain Park

Off US 15 north of Frederick, Maryland

Chimney Rock Trail
2.2-mile round-trip/2 hours

Catoctin Mountain Park is an unknown entity to many Washingtonians, though they reside less than an hour away. And what a difference an hour can make: In the same time it takes to fight commuter traffic from the suburbs into D.C., you can be luxuriating in the green mountain wilderness, surrounded by stately oaks, hickories, and black birches. One of the park's most popular hikes, the **Chimney Rock Trail** climbs to a jumble of overhanging rocks that protrudes over a breathtaking panorama of tree-carpeted ridges and blue sky.

The trail requires a bit of exertion, a small fact that doesn't deter the wide variety of people—including families with young kids—who easily make the trek. The hike begins at the parking lot located on Md. 77, about a mile or so east of the visitor center near the park administration building. To the left of a bulletin board, a small, unmarked trail wanders off into the woods, alongside the road. Take it. In about 10 yards, you come to the trailhead, a rocky path that climbs steadily through pretty oaks and maples. About 150 yards along the way you'll come to a trail crossing; just keep going straight ahead.

After 0.6 mile, the terrain flattens out, and the trail winds through more rocky woods, where chipmunks scamper about and pileated woodpeckers tap on fallen trees. You get the sense that you're high up on a mountain, which you are; that there should be views surrounding you, which there aren't—yet. Finally, looping around to a ridgeline, you come to a T-intersection. Chimney Rock is a few short strides to the left. The rock (actually a cluster of rocks projecting out into space) provides an idyllic place to take in the wonderfully remote scene around you. You can either sit complacently on the nearest rocks for good views, or jump and scramble farther out for breathtaking views.

Return down the mountain the way you came.

More hiking: You can continue on the trail to Wolf Rock, which also offers an inspiring view. Consult the park map for logistics.

The parking area at the park administration center is also the trailhead for the **Cat Rock-Bob's Hill Trail,** a fairly strenuous 7.5-mile (one way) climb between Md. 77 and the Manor Area of Cunningham Falls State Park. Along the way you're treated to a breathtaking 360-degree view (in winter) of the surrounding countryscape. Again, consult the park map for details.

Trip notes: The park is open daily, though Park Central Rd. is closed in winter. There is no entrance fee. The Catoctin Mountain Park Visitor Center has a small nature museum, all kinds of books and maps, plus rangers to answer questions. For more information, contact the

Superintendent, Catoctin Mountain Park, National Park Service, Thurmont, MD 21788; 301-663-9330. The web site is www.nps.gov/cato.

Directions: From Frederick, drive north on US 15 about 15 miles to the town of Thurmont. Here, follow Md. 77 west. In about 1.5 miles you'll see the park administration center on the right. Park in the parking area.

Western Panhandle

Squeezed between Pennsylvania and West Virginia high atop the Allegheny Plateau, this remote, unpopulated realm harbors dense forests, pure mountain streams, and a good dose of frontier history.

63. Chesapeake & Ohio Canal National Historical Park

Off Md. 51 near Paw Paw, West Virginia

Towpath Trail
1.2-mile round-trip/45 minutes

Dank, dark, mysterious, Paw Paw Tunnel penetrates a solid-rock mountain deep in the Appalachian Mountains. Built between 1836 and 1850 as part of the Chesapeake & Ohio Canal, the 3,118-foot, brick-lined engineering feat enabled canalboats to avoid a long, loopy, 6-mile stretch of the Potomac River called the Potomac bends. The towpath where muleboys once trod, illuminating the darkness with kerosene lamps, remains a narrow pathway above the dark canal waters. Technically speaking, the path is the same towpath that runs alongside the C&O Canal from Georgetown to Cumberland, Maryland, for 184.5 miles, popular with hikers and bikers alike. But this unusual leg is truly an entity unto itself.

The **Towpath Trail** begins on the left side of the parking area. Following the sign pointing in the direction of the tunnel, go uphill a little way and turn right onto the towpath. Another sign informs you that the tunnel lies 0.6 mile ahead. The sunny, leafy path beside the canal gives no indication of what lies beyond. Picnic benches dot the trailside, and off to the right, through the trees, shimmers the Potomac. If it's midsummer, you'll be hot and tired. But just wait….

The pathway zips up to the tunnel's yawning black hole, then plunges inside. It's instantly cooler, almost clammy, and exceedingly dark. Soon the only sounds you hear are your muffled footsteps, and the dripping of icy water from above. Thankfully, there's a railing between you and the canal's black waters to save you from taking an unnecessary plunge.

In the hushed, tomblike silence, it's hard to believe that in the canal's heyday more than a hundred years ago, this tunnel was a loud, boisterous place. Canalboat after canalboat bottlenecked just outside, waiting for a turn to pass through. There was no room for passing or turning around; a downstream boat supposedly had the right of way over an upstream boat, but stubborn captains made for colorful exchanges. One standoff lasted several days, until a company official threw green corn stalks onto a roaring fire at the upwind end of the tunnel, and forced the offenders out with smoke.

After 15 minutes or so, sunlight filters the darkness. The railing reappears in the light, and you can see the canal waters shimmering down on your left. And suddenly, you're outside, squinting in the sun. Walk out a bit on the wooden boardwalk, noting the impressive gorge that winds away from the tunnel—an engineering masterpiece in itself, it required just as much quarrying as the tunnel did. Turn around for a great prospect of the tunnel. Then head back the way you came.

Trip notes: The park is open daily. There is no entrance fee. For more information contact the C&O Canal National Historical Park, P.O. Box 4, Sharpsburg, MD 21782; 301-739-4200. The web site is www.nps.gov/choh.

Directions: From Frederick, take I-70 west to Hancock, where US 522 will take you south. At Berkeley Springs, continue west on W. Va. 9, a windy and scenic drive through the mountains. At the junction with W. Va. 29, go right. Continue beyond the town of Paw Paw just a mile or so on Md. 51. The turnoff for the tunnel, which comes up quickly, is located just beyond a railroad trestle, on the right side of the road.

64. Rocky Gap State Park
Off I-68 near Flintstone, Maryland

Evitts and Lakeside Loop Trails
2.1-mile loop/1 hour

In the heart of the Alleghenies, where snowdrifts are high and people few, Rocky Gap State Park provides the perfect foray into the wild country of Maryland's panhandle. The imposing mountains that buckle the landscape explain why settlers took so long in finding a passageway through. Indeed, even now that a major interstate threads through the mountains, making access to the park easier, the region remains beautifully isolated—even in summer.

Of course, there's often an exception, and in this case it's the state park's centerpiece. Measuring 243 acres, manmade Lake Habeeb sits like an indigo-colored jewel between two wooded peaks, luring plenty of families in summertime. But a deeply wooded wilderness surrounds the lake and gives cover to white-tailed deer, squirrels, even black bears. A perfect, easy trail winds through this remote corner, but

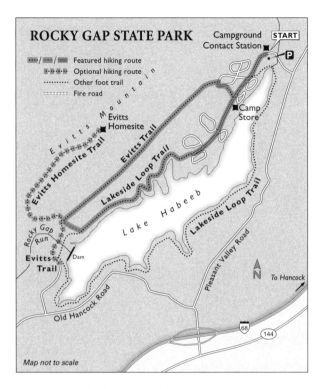

still many people don't venture far inside.

To explore this wilderness, park at the campground contact station and walk in through the gate (unless you're camping here). Walk about ten minutes to the camp store-beach area, and rather than turning left toward the beach, take the wooden staircase on the right. Soon you'll come to camping area D. Go left, uphill, to campsite no. 92, where a small sign marks the trailhead for the **Evitts Trail.**

At first this trail follows an old fire road, which climbs up Evitts Mountain. You probably won't even notice it, but the fire road veers off to the left after a couple hundred yards, but you should keep climbing on the narrower (unmarked) Evitts Trail. Farther along, this trail turns southwesterly, so you're cutting across the side of the mountain. You've entered the domain of the black bear—which is rarely spotted. More likely, you'll encounter gray squirrels and white-tailed deer. Chestnut oaks create much of the canopy, a fair indication that the rocky soil lacks nutrients; mountain laurel frill the trail in June, and blueberry bushes tangle the underbrush.

After about a mile, the trail bears right, uphill. Soon you'll be surrounded by pines—white, scrub, and pitch. And then you come to a crossroads. From here, the easiest hike entails

turning left on the fire road, which will bring you to the
Lakeside Loop Trail. Turn left on this trail and follow the
lake's sinuous curves back to the camp store-beach area.

More hiking: At the crossroads of the Evitts Trail and the fire
road, rather than turning left for the Lakeside Loop Trail, go
right on the **Evitts Homesite Trail** and proceed up the hill.
This 500-foot climb rewards you with fabulous views across
the valley. At the end of the trail lies an old homesite, said to
have belonged to a jilted pioneer who chose to live the rest of
his life in seclusion. The round-trip from the campground to
the cabin and back is 4.4 miles.

Another option at the Evitts Trail-fire road crossroads is to
turn right about 10 yards on the Evitts Mountain Trail, then
detour left, onto the **Canyon Trail** (also called the Evitts Trail).
This rocky, narrow path drops into an enchanting gorge of
Rocky Gap Run filled with dark hemlocks and rhododendrons
and serenaded by the dancing creek splashing over smooth
stones. The trail allegedly proceeds beyond the run, but it
becomes a bit confusing. It's safer to turn around and return
to the camp store-beach area via the Lakeside Loop Trail.

Trip notes: The park is open daily. There is no fee. For more
information contact Rocky Gap State Park, 12500 Pleasant
Valley, Flintstone, MD 21530; 301-777-2139.

Directions: From Frederick, follow I-70 west. At Hancock,
continue west on I-68. In about 30 miles, you'll come to the
well-marked exit for Rocky Gap State Park. To reach the
campground contact station, turn right on Pleasant Valley Rd.
(before the main parking area) for about 1.5 miles, and turn
left at the campground sign.

65. Swallow Falls State Park

Off US 219 near Deep Creek Lake, Maryland

Canyon Trail
1-mile loop/45 minutes

I t's one of Maryland's smallest state parks, yet 257-acre
Swallow Falls boasts not one but three waterfalls. This hike
makes a loop past the trio, through an ancient hemlock
forest and along the wild Youghiogheny River (the "Yock").
Mind you, all these scenic wonders are not in evidence when

you first pull up to the parking lot, near the contact station. It looks like any other state park—busier, if anything. But the scene changes as soon as you delve into the woods by the bulletin board. You'll notice how dark and cool it is beneath the canopy of hemlocks. Some of these ancient giants, having never been logged, date back more than 300 years. (Some were here before the first Pilgrim stepped ashore.) They create a sacred grove that almost demands a hushed, reverent silence.

When you come to a fork, go left, following the arrow toward Muddy Creek Falls (Swallow Falls is in the other direction—you'll return that way). Walk a little way on a wide gravel road; when you see a smaller trail on the right, take it into the woods. Soon you come to Muddy Creek Falls—you can't miss it. At 52 feet, the tremendous torrent of water is Maryland's largest waterfall. People like to walk out to the ledge above the falls and see how close they can get to the edge. (Parents should keep kids back.)

Take the wooden staircase down the cliff face, with fabulous waterfall views all the way down. You'll walk beside Muddy Creek until it converges with the Yock, and continue alongside the river. Winding among moss-covered rock ledges beneath towering trees, the trail, unmarked but called the **Canyon Trail,** wanders beside the river in one of the prettiest settings around.

Soon you hear water thunder, indicating Lower Swallow Falls must be off to the left. A wide band of water perhaps

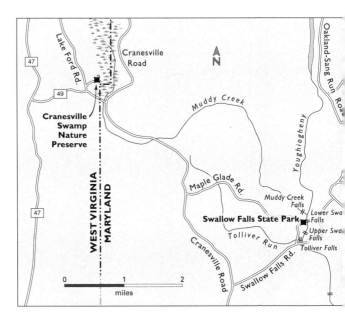

5 feet high, the falls attracts swarms of sunlovers in summer, who splash and scream and swim in its shallow depths. For a closer look, take the stairs that branch off from the main trail. From this vantage you'll also get your first glimpse of Swallow Falls.

Back on the main trail, the hike now visits a boulder-jumbled forest away from the water. At the split in the trail, the path to the right climbs back to the parking area. You don't want that. Upper Swallow Falls is off to the left. At 25 feet, the falls is one of the most famous landmarks in Maryland. Sunbathers lie on flat rocks or in the shallow waters above and below the falls, soaking up the sun's warm rays. That's lots of fun, but don't pass up a visit in autumn, when the people thin out and the bright red maples contrast nicely with the distant green hemlocks, or in winter, when snow blankets the landscape and the mighty falls freezes into a glistening ice sculpture. Downstream from the upper falls, the large sandstone outcrop, or plinth, with its steep sides, is called Swallow Rock. It's said that back in colonial times, swallows nested here, hence Swallow Falls.

Leaving the falls, take the trail up the stairs, following the sign that points the way back to the parking area (not campsites). Reenter the hemlock forest, and—ignoring the trails on the right that lead back down to the river—complete the loop, turning left at the Y-intersection. In a minute or two you'll be back to the parking lot's hullabaloo.

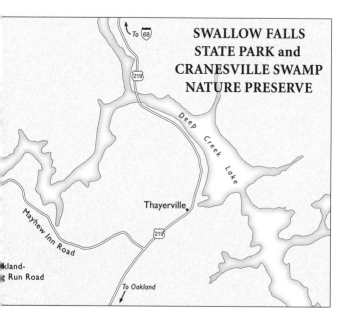

Make it easier: Just go as far as Muddy Creek Falls and turn around and come back. (This is a good option in winter, when icy paths make much of the trail slippery.)

More hiking: Instead of turning back to the parking lot at the end of the hike, continue along the trail by the stream and soon you'll come to Tolliver Falls, intimate in a dark, secluded glen.

Trip notes: Swallow Falls is open daily. There is a $2 vehicle fee on summer weekdays and a $2 per-person fee on summer weekends and holidays. Dogs allowed Labor Day to Mem. Day only. For more information contact the park, 222 Herrington Lane, Oakland, MD 21550; 301-387-6938 (summer) or 301-334-9180 (fall to spring).

Directions: See map on pp. 144-145. From Frederick, Maryland, drive west on I-70 and I-68 beyond Cumberland to the US 219 exit. Follow this south about 20 miles to just beyond Deep Creek Lake. Here, take the first major road on the right—Mayhew Inn Rd. Turn right, drive about 4 miles, and at the stop sign go left on Oakland-Sang Run Rd. Drive about a quarter of a mile and turn right on Swallow Falls Rd. The park entrance is about a mile down the road.

66. Cranesville Swamp Nature Preserve
Off US 219 near Deep Creek Lake, Maryland

Blue Trail
1-mile loop/30 minutes

Deciduous woods carpet western Maryland's remote Allegheny Plateau, exactly the kind of scene you'd expect in the mid-Atlantic. But here and there, tiny spots of subarctic swampland dot the landscape. In what is called a "frost pocket," cold air is trapped in montane valleys, creating the ideal environment for dozens of species of northern plants—including tamarack, bog goldenrod, and the tiny, insectivorous sundew. The result: a setting that seems much more typical of Maine or Canada. Certainly not of the mid-Atlantic.

On the Maryland/West Virginia border, the Nature

Conservancy preserves one of these biologically rich swamps and has built a loop boardwalk straight into its heart. Along the way, interpretive plaques describe the plants, animals, and communities.

Begin at the small Cranesville Swamp parking area; find the trailhead to the **Blue Trail** and head off through an upland forest full of ferns, club moss, and rhododendron. The trail soon comes to the edge of the wetland, then the boardwalk itself—and the swamp.

You may be caught off guard by how pretty this rustic, out-of-the-way setting is, with its gilded dabs of bog golden-rod and white puffs of cotton grass waving gently in the rust-colored meadow of sedge and ferns. It's especially pretty in October, when the fruit of the omnipresent cranberry matures, lending a burgundy aura to the scene.

Step out onto the boardwalk. To be technical, the first part of the boardwalk doesn't traverse swampland; it's all peat bog—an acidic wetland where few trees can grow. A swamp, as you'll see a little farther ahead, is also a wetland, but with trees. Almost immediately on your right, you'll spot a square-shaped, tannin-stained pool of water, mirroring the billowing clouds above. Way back when, someone discovered the peat underlying the rich carpet of sphagnum moss—layer upon layer of decomposed plant remains—and mined it here, probably for fuel.

A little farther ahead you'll come to a small open pond surrounded by broad-leaf cattails. And then, you leave the bog and enter the swamp. Here's where all kinds of wetland tree species grow: red spruce, hemlock, and the rare tamarack, to name a few. Of these, the tamarack is probably the most intriguing; a deciduous conifer, it drops its needles come fall. You can spot a few from the boardwalk; they're easiest to pick out in October, when the needles turn yellow. Nesting birds, too, are an attraction. Look for sora, northern saw-whet owl, alder and willow flycatchers, a variety of different warblers, eastern towhee, and Savannah sparrow.

The boardwalk takes you deeper into the swamp, where the sense of isolation is overpowering, almost as if you have, indeed, traveled to another place. It seems natural, in this northerly setting, that a giant moose might lumber out of the woods...but, of course, there are no moose in Maryland. There were once elk and bison in this region, but the remaining large mammal—sometimes found at the swamp—is the black bear.

The trail loops back to the upland forest, where the **orange** or **white trail** will bring you to a dirt access road. Follow this back to the parking area.

Trip notes: The preserve is open daily. There is no entrance fee. For more information contact either the Maryland/D.C. chapter of the Nature Conservancy, 2 Wisconsin Circle, Suite 600, Chevy Chase, MD 20815, 301-656-8673; or the West Virginia chapter, 723 Kanawha Blvd. east, Suite 500, Charleston, WV 25301, 304-345-4350.

Directions: See map on pp. 144-145. The preserve not too difficult to find, but pay attention. From Frederick, Maryland, drive west on I-70 and I-68 beyond Cumberland to the US 219 exit. Follow this south about 20 miles to just beyond Deep Creek Lake. Here, take the first major road on the right—Mayhew Inn Rd. Turn right, drive about 4 miles, and at the stop sign go left on Oakland-Sang Run Rd. Go a quarter mile and turn right on Swallow Falls Rd., proceeding 2.5 miles beyond the entrance of Swallow Falls State Park. At Cranesville Rd., turn right for a little over 4 miles. At Lake Ford Rd. (and the Cranesville Swamp Preserve sign) turn left. You'll come to two forks; at each one bear right. And soon you'll reach the parking area for Cranesville Swamp.

Baltimore and Beyond

Stream-laced woods and bird-filled marshes surround this busy harbor city on the Chesapeake.

67. Cylburn Arboretum

Off I-83 in north Baltimore, Maryland

Circle Trail
1-mile loop/20 minutes

As you follow the entrance road into Cylburn Arboretum, the Victorian stone mansion once belonging to the Tysons of Baltimore appears above a lush green landscape. Jesse Tyson built his country estate in the years following the Civil War, and for decades the cream of Baltimore society wandered across the expansive lawns and through formal gardens lit midsummer with Japanese lanterns. In the late 1950s, the grounds became a city arboretum—176 wooded acres laced with wide paths and specialty gardens. Among several different paths, the **Circle Trail** provides an excellent overview, making a wide loop through pretty deciduous woodlands with detours here and there to see wildflowers, a mature stand of trees, and other natural surprises.

From the front of the house, which now houses the Baltimore City Horticultural Division and volunteer staff offices, take the paved road downhill into the forest. Soon you'll see the sign for the Circle Trail; follow it right. The broad path meanders along a blufftop, overlooking Jones Falls Valley and taking you around three sides of the house. Along the way, native trees—oaks, hickories, tulip trees, and dogwoods—provide good shade on a hot summer day. Beautiful and serene, the trail is also educational: Small plaques identify many of the trees. Sassafras, dogwood, and mountain laurel make the arboretum a prime spring bloom destination.

Soon you're back to the house, where you can enjoy specialty gardens showcasing daylilies and roses.

Trip notes: The arboretum is open daily. There is no entrance fee. For more information, contact the Horticultural Division office, Cylburn Arboretum, 4915 Greenspring Avenue, Baltimore, MD 21209; 410-396-0180.

Directions: From Baltimore, take I-83 to the Northern Pkwy. exit and head west for 0.3 mile. Turn left onto Cylburn Ave., and proceed half a mile to Greenspring Ave. Turn left, then turn immediately left again into the arboretum.

68. Robert E. Lee Park

Off I-83 in north Baltimore, Maryland

Lake Roland Trail
4-mile round-trip/2.5 hours

T he placid blue waters of Lake Roland and its wild, tree-fringed shoreline might make you think you're far from civilization, when in reality you're smack in the middle of Baltimore's suburbs. The only clue is the inordinate number of dogs that share the trail—the park is a highly popular dog-walking place, with as many as 300 dogs visiting each weekend.

From Lakeside Drive, cross the footbridge below the old stone dam. Backing up Jones Falls—a pretty little stream, not a waterfall—the dam creates a magnificent green oasis for wildlife. Dawn or dusk, black-crowned night-herons pose as statues on the rocks below the dam, with the melodies of swifts and swallows often filling the air.

On the dam's other side, follow the asphalt road up the hill and to the right, where you'll spot a picnic area atop a hill, shaded by venerable white oaks and a popular spot to see migrating northern orioles. Take the trail to the right of this area, beside the lake. The trail loops around the picnic area and, about a quarter mile from the beginning, a smaller, unmarked dirt trail branches off to the right, downhill. Take it. (If you find yourself looping back toward your car, you've gone too far.)

Cross the light rail line and enter a quiet woods beside a secluded arm of the lake. From now on, keep the water's edge to your right and the old railbed to your left (formerly belonging to the Greenspring Valley Branch of the Northern Central Railroad). A mosaic of different habitats makes this a prime area for bird-watching. Ducks and geese skim the open water in winter, warblers sing from the trees of the river bottom forest, woodpeckers tap for insects in the upland forest, while great blue herons and kingfishers stalk the marshland reeds.

After hiking about half a mile beyond the light rail, you have a choice. You can either follow the embankment on the right, which explores the point where Jones Falls feeds into the reservoir. Or you can take the trail on the left and enter the woods. It doesn't matter, because just ahead the two trails merge, and you proceed alongside Jones Falls to a foot-bridge. This hike stops here and turns around.

Retracing your steps, watch on the right about a quarter mile from the footbridge for the wide, unmarked path that branches off to the right. As you climb the hill, stomping and slipping on loose, sharp, tan-gray stones, you'll think you're walking up a streambed. These stones belong to a pine barren, known locally as Bare Hills. Keep walking until you're suddenly enveloped in a curtain of green. Close your eyes to smell the fresh scent of pine. These are hardy Virginia pines, one of the few plants that can grow in the barrens' meager soil. This is a good place to watch for kinglets, nuthatches, and warblers. Continue to the top of the hill if you wish, then head back down the way you came.

Back at the main trail, turn right and backtrack beside the lake, across the light rail, to the picnic area, where you turn right and return across the dam to your car.

Trip notes: The park is open daily. There is no entrance fee. For more information contact the Baltimore City Parks Department at 410-396-7931. Or call 410-396-6106.

Directions: From the Baltimore Beltway (I-695), go north on I-83 to Northern Parkway East. Go north (left) on Falls Rd. for about a mile. Make a right onto Lakeside Dr. (if you go over a bridge, you've gone too far). Take a right at the sign that says "Robert E. Lee Park" (if you go to the light rail station, you've gone too far). In about half a mile, park on the side of the road. There's also an official parking lot for 50 cars upstream from the dam.

69. North Point State Park

Off I-695 near Edgemere, Maryland

Black Marsh Wildlands Trail
4.2-mile round-trip/1.5 hours

The smoke-belching chimneys just outside North Point State Park don't bode well for a wilderness hike, nor does the unremarkable landscape of trees and picnic tables surrounding the park's main parking area. And it's true that the first half-mile of this hike is nothing special, since it follows the forested park road you drive in on. But with a bit of patience, you'll be rewarded with one of the best hikes in the Baltimore area, complete with long-sweeping views of the fabled Chesapeake; a dark, sweet-smelling forest; and a marsh that's aflutter with shorebirds.

From the main parking area, backtrack along the same entrance road you drove in on. The fields that edge the road are some of the oldest farmed in Maryland, dating back some 350 years. After half a mile, you reach the trailhead (a gated road on the right) for the Black Marsh Wildlands; here you enter another world.

First the roadlike dirt trail delves into a shadowy, dark forest filled with towering tulip poplars, walnuts, sweet gums, willow oaks, blackjack oaks, and American hollies. The silhouettes of wild grape vines loop from tree to tree, creating an interesting geometric design. About 150 yards down the trail, you'll note a side trail wandering off to the right. It leads to Chesapeake Bay and a concrete pier, leftover from the days when an auto and passenger ferry ran between here and the Eastern Shore. You can't walk on the pier, but this is a fine spot to watch for shorebirds.

Back in the forest, the trail soon offers glimpses of the Chesapeake through the trees, and then you're right beside the shimmery water. On foggy days, the sky's pewter-gray clouds blend with the water's wide, gray surface like a Chinese watercolor painting. Just ahead, squeezed amid the underbrush, you'll see an old concrete building left over from early this century, when this tract of land belonged to the now defunct Bay Shore Amusement park, built in 1906. This old power house generated electricity for the trolleys that ran frolickers between Baltimore and the park.

In contrast, just beyond this point lies a wide-sweeping stretch of narrow-leaf cattails and three-square. Buffered by 435 acres of lovely trees, Black Marsh is a 232-acre tidal fresh-water marsh, alive with great blue herons and egrets, and even a nesting pair of bald eagles. It has been designated a State Wildland and Natural Heritage Area and is considered one of the finest examples of a tidal marsh on the upper Chesapeake. Walk slowly along the elevated trail, keeping an eye out for resident marsh birds such as American bitterns (a secretive, streaked brown heron), sparrow-size black rails, and in winter canvasback, goldeneye, and ruddy ducks. You may also spy great horned owls, northern harriers, and red-tailed hawks.

Just ahead, the marsh seems to dry up a bit as the trail bears right, into a thicket of white oaks. Unlike most white oaks, which can tower 100 feet or more, these are stunted by the nutrient-poor soil; bloated by salt, their girths are exceptionally wide. Not much else can grow in the area, just a few maples and hollies.

And finally, about a mile from the trailhead, you'll reach an observation platform overlooking the wide, open marshland. Cattails sway in the breeze, dark pools reflect big puffy clouds, and, if you're patient, you'll spot all kinds of birdlife.

Turn back the way you came.

Advisory: Bring insect repellent in summer.

Trip notes: The park is open daily. There is no entrance fee. For more information, contact Gunpowder Falls State Park, 2813 Jerusalem Rd., P.O. Box 480, Kingsville, MD 21087; 410-592-2897.

Directions: From I-695 east of Baltimore, take the Md. 20 (North Point Rd.) exit. Follow Md. 20 toward Fort Howard; the park entrance is half a mile beyond Miller Island Rd., on the left.

70. Patapsco Valley State Park (Avalon Area)

Off I-95 south of Baltimore, Maryland

Ridge and Valley View Trails
1.3-mile loop/30 minutes

A long, skinny wilderness weaving 32 miles through suburbia, Patapsco Valley State Park seems remote, faraway, wild—not as if subdivisions and shopping centers were just a stone's throw away. Indeed, this pristine, green river and its tree-clad valley look much as they did in 1608, when Capt. John Smith first discovered the river's mouth. That's why it's surprising to note that at the turn of the century lumbermen completely denuded the area, and that in the '70s a severe bout with pollution turned the river into a living cesspool. Trees have grown back beautifully, and clean water legislation has helped put an end to the dumping of sewage and industrial waste. Now bass swim its cool depths, and foxes, white-tailed deer, and beavers prowl the wooded shores—a perfect picture of river conservation.

Running from the river's source near Woodbine to the vicinity of Baltimore Harbor, the linear park contains five different recreational entities. Among them, the Avalon-Glen

Artney-Orange Grove area, located just off I-95 south of Baltimore, features several good hiking trails. This particular hike winds amid quiet wooded hillsides, offering pretty vistas (especially in winter, when the leaves are off the trees) of the venerable Patapsco.

Begin from the parking area in the Avalon portion of the park, walking downstream along the asphalt park road (River Road). In about 100 yards you'll see a gravel road on the left—the beginning of the **Ridge Trail.** Take this uphill, following the dark-orange blazes. The forest embraces you, taking you seemingly far into the wilderness. There's absolutely no sign of the 20th century, no sign of human life—one of the greatest ironies of this suburban park.

You'll climb a fairly steep incline; when you reach a fork, take the trail that veers sharply right, ever marked by dark-orange blazes. Climb another steep incline, and finally you reach the promised ridge of the Ridge Trail.

Now the trail rolls through the woods; all about you, tall, skinny trees—oaks, maples, and dogwoods—reach toward the sky. In April, while most of the forest still slumbers, trout lilies, spring beauties, marsh marigolds, bluebells, and trilliums carpet the forest floor, ephemeral harbingers of spring. Watch for white-tailed deer, raccoons, and striped skunks.

After about half a mile, look carefully for the white-blazed **Valley View Trail** on the right. But wait—before embarking on this narrow, undulating course, you may wish to proceed a couple hundred yards farther along the Ridge Trail, to the next white-blazed trail (also called the Valley View Trail). Dipping down the hill, you're treated to a wonderful overlook of the river, coursing placidly through the valley far below.

Back on the hike, the Valley View Trail dips and climbs across a leafy ridge, undulating through cool woods, eventually descending back down to River Road and civilization.

More hiking: If you still have some energy, instead of turning right on River Road back to your car, turn left and walk a ways beside the river. A mile or so down you'll reach the Orange Grove area, where, beside the rest rooms, you'll see the blue-blazed **Cascade Trail.** This short, steep hike wends through the woods to a pretty waterfall, shaded by hemlocks and birch.

Trip notes: The park is open daily. There is a $2 per-person fee on weekends April-Oct. For more information contact the park, 8020 Baltimore National Pike, Ellicott City, MD 21043-3499; 410-461-5005.

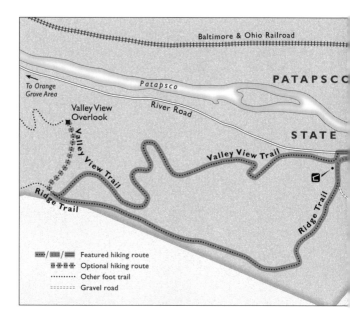

Directions: From I-95 south of Baltimore, take the I-195 exit east, toward BWI Airport. At the first exit, go south on US 1; proceed about 50 yards to South St., where you turn right. Almost immediately River Rd., the entrance to the park, will be on your left. (You'll pass beneath the Thomas Viaduct, the first multiple stone arch bridge built in the United States. It still carries a major railroad line to Washington, D.C.)

71. Patapsco Valley State Park (McKeldin Area)

Off I-70 west of Baltimore, Maryland

Switchback Trail
2.8-mile loop/1 hour

A mosaic of wooded uplands and verdant riverbanks, the McKeldin area of Patapsco Valley State Park perches at the confluence of the north and south branches of the Patapsco River. The best way to explore this leafy wonderland is along the **Switchback Trail**—which sounds more ominous than it is. Wide and

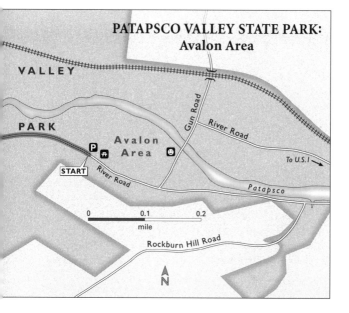

PATAPSCO VALLEY STATE PARK:
Avalon Area

VALLEY

PARK

Gun Road

River Road

Avalon
Area

To U.S.1

START

River Road

Patapsco

0   0.1   0.2
mile

Rockburn Hill Road

N

well marked, the path winds through a dense forest of
maple and river birch, sycamore and tulip poplar, offering
plenty of opportunities to survey the lovely green river.
The only downside are the mountain bikers who enjoy this
trail, too, and have a tendency to whiz down the hills.
So stay alert.

Begin the hike by parking in the lot just beyond the park
contact station. Then backtrack past the contact station,
down the park entrance road, about 50 yards to the trailhead. You can't miss the sign—SWITCHBACK TRAIL. At first the
trail seems terribly misnamed, as it shoots straight through a
forest dominated by chestnut oaks, adorned in May with the
frilly blooms of mountain laurel.

But in about a third of a mile, the trail zigzags down the
hillside, dropping sharply to the river floodplain. This area
can be wet and muddy, especially after a rainstorm. At the
bottom of the hill, the trail—resembling a road more than a
trail at this point—bears left, rolling through woods of
locust and sycamore. Nearing the Patapsco, bear left and
walk downstream, with the lazy river on your right and sil-
very maples all around. Watch for great blue herons and
kingfishers stalking the watery depths. Beavers and otters are
common, too.

Staying close to the river, ignore all secondary trails
along the way. Soon the hike climbs uphill to a paved park
road (and rest room, closed in winter). Here you have two

choices. The official trail proceeds straight ahead, across the road and down into the woods.

But try going right, along the road for a little way until it ends at an observation platform. Here you get a splendid view of McKeldin Falls as it drops 10 feet over a series of shady ledges into a cool green pool. After admiring the verdant pocket, you'll have to trailblaze a little. From the platform go left, downstream, scrambling down some large boulders to a gravel beach. A trail parallels the river here, which you follow as the river makes a wide bend, and then another.

At this point comes a trail intersection. You can choose to continue straight ahead, ever following the river, or go left to return to the Switchback Trail and turn right. Either way, you'll end up at the same place farther downstream, where the hike proceeds on the Switchback Trail. Before long, you reach the confluence of the south and north branches of the Patapsco River, merrily merging into the greater Patapsco.

The Switchback Trail follows the north branch of the river, a greener, more intimate stretch of water. The floodplain here is wide and moist, nurturing all kinds of spring wildflowers—bloodroot and violets, spring beauties and jack-in-the-pulpits—and the air smells of earth and roots. Don't be surprised if you meet a white-tailed deer, wood duck, or even striped skunk.

Wander along for 0.7 mile from the river confluence, until you reach a trail intersection. Sorry, but you have to take this uphill route—really a dirt road—which brings you back into the park's core area. Continue on the dirt road as its passes a copse of white pines to the paved park road; stay on the right at the fork and soon you'll be back to your car.

Trip notes: Patapsco Valley State Park is open daily. There is a $2 fee per person on weekends April-Oct. For more information contact the park at 8020 Baltimore National Pike, Ellicott City, MD 21043-3499; 410-461-5005.

Directions: From the Baltimore Beltway (I-695), take I-70 west from Baltimore for 8 miles. At Marriottsville Rd., turn right (north). The park entrance will be 4 miles on your right.

72. Soldiers Delight Natural Environment Area

Off I-795 north of Baltimore, Maryland

White Trail
3-mile loop/1 hour

While not classically beautiful, Soldiers Delight and its serpentine barren is lovely in a raw, elemental sense. Surely, with all the prairie grass and wide-sweeping vistas of sun-blasted rocks, you could very well be stomping through a midwestern prairie, complete with sweet-sounding song birds and birds of prey.

The **White Trail** begins at the visitor center located off Deer Park Road. View the exhibits on the serpentine habitat management and history, then pick up a trail map and head to the rear of the building for the Green and White Trails. Follow them to Red Dog Lodge, an old hunting cabin dating from the early 1900s. Here, continue ahead, crossing beneath the power lines and remaining on the White Trail.

The White Trail runs alongside and through areas that are being managed for serpentine habitat restoration. Immediately you sense the change of terrain; clumps of true prairie grasses (little bluestem, purplish three-awn, and Indian grass) dot the otherwise naked rock—quite a different scene from the surrounding fertile piedmont, where cherry, dogwood, and ash flourish. Take note of a piece of the metamorphosed igneous rock, which is full of different minerals. Inside it's greenish-black, indicating serpentine, while there are also magnesium, chromium, and nickel. No wonder plants have a hard time growing around here; only the hardiest—stunted blackjack and post oaks, Virginia pine (an invasive species), plus prairie grasses and wildflowers, can persevere. Of them, 39 species are rare, endangered, or threatened.

The White Trail bears right, heads downhill, and crosses Locust Run, a tributary of Chimney Branch. It then arcs around to more power lines. Crossing them, you eventually come to Deer Park Road and the Overlook Area. You can follow the trail back to the visitor center, or, using your map, access several other trails joining at this junction.

Insider's tip: The name "Soldiers Delight" dates back to the French and Indian War, when some local militia were stationed here, where the open nature of the place provided

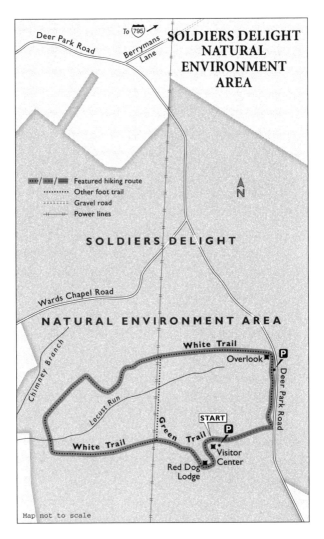

safety from ambush. It's said that local farms provided these soldiers with plenty of food, thus giving much "delight." During the Civil War, Soldiers Delight was the scene of skirmishes between Maryland volunteers of the Confederate Army and the regular troops of the North.

Trip notes: The environment area is open daily; the visitor center is open Wed. to Sun. There is no entrance fee. For more information contact the visitor center at 5100 Deer Park Rd., Owings Mills, MD 21117, 410-922-3044; or Patapsco Valley State Park, 8020 Baltimore National Pike, Ellicott City, MD 21043, 410-461-5005.

Directions: From the Baltimore Beltway (I-695), take I-795. Exit west on Franklin Blvd.; turn right on Church Rd. and, at the end, turn left on Berrymans Ln. Go half a mile, then turn left on Deer Park Rd. In 1.5 miles you'll come to the park entrance road.

73. Oregon Ridge Park
Off I-83 north of Baltimore near Shawan, Maryland

Logger's, Short Cut, Virginia Pine, and Lake Trails
1.6-mile loop/1.5 hours

At first glance, Oregon Ridge is a busy place, full of people who come for its popular summer concerts (Baltimore Symphony Orchestra), kid-filled swimming lake, and pancake breakfasts. But if you penetrate just a little deeper into the park, you'll discover woods filled with singing creeks and noisy songbirds.

Before heading out on the trail, take a peek in the Oregon Ridge Nature Center and pick up a trail map. Then head across the bridge to the left of the nature center. The man-made ravine you're walking across is actually a huge pit dug in the early 1800s, when iron ore was extracted for nearby Oregon Furnace. In those days, Oregon Ridge hosted several iron ore mines, a blast furnace, and an entire mining town.

On the other side of the bridge, several different trail options greet you. For this hike you go right, along the red-blazed **Logger's Trail**—appropriately named for the lumbermen who toppled the forest around the turn-of-the-century. Many of the park's trails are old logging roads, created by oxen dragging heavy logs down the hillside.

Soon a tributary of Oregon Branch parallels the trail, and you begin climbing Oregon Ridge, whose forested hillsides shadow the eastern end of Worthington Valley. The north-facing slopes are rather bare, save for scattered chestnut oaks. Compare these to the opposite slopes, tangled with mountain laurel and huckleberry that, even in late winter, add splashes of waxy-green color to the otherwise pallid understory. Don't be surprised if you startle white-tailed deer, wild turkey, or—if you're really lucky—a red fox.

Midway up the hill, a small dirt trail bears right, leading to a pretty little cove of tulip poplars. Explore the clear-running Tulip Tree Spring, fringed in late winter with bright green skunk cabbage and Christmas ferns. The moist banks harbor a plethora of spring wildflowers: In early May look for trilliums, columbine, rue anemone, bluets, and violets. Shaded by a huge tree, a split-log bench dedicated to an ardent trail guide sits before the creek's source issuing from beneath a big rock.

Back on the Logger's Trail, continue up through the trees—mostly white, black, scarlet, red, and chestnut oaks. When you come to a T-intersection, go right. Soon you'll come to a pipeline right-of-way. The light created by this man-made intrusion on nature nurtures the ideal environment for the bird's-foot violet, a spring blossom with bright purple flowers.

Turn right, following the clearing along the forest fringe. Soon the trail reenters the woods—watch carefully for the entrance on the left. Go a short way, past the white-blazed Short Cut Trail and the Laurel Trail, proceeding to the green-blazed **Virginia Pine Trail;** turn left on this. In about half a mile, cross the gasline right-of-way and reenter the woods on the orange-blazed **Lake Trail.** This little path winds above Oregon Lake, actually a huge mining pit now filled in summer with splashing kids. At one point you cross a tiny, somewhat deep ravine on a thin but sturdy fallen tree. (The park has fashioned a handrail to help you across.)

In no time, the trail drops you back to the parking area.

More hiking: Take a bigger loop to see the prettiest part of the park. After crossing the pipeline right-of-way for the first time on the **Logger's Trail,** go right on the **Short Cut Trail.** Take this to the yellow-blazed **Ivy Hill Trail** and go right. Now you're strolling along a gently rolling ridge top dotted with pines and yellow poplars and red maples. During spring, flocks of migrating warblers and scarlet tanagers wing through the treetops.

You'll notice a distinct change of scenery as the trail drops down to the crystal-clear Baisman Run. This green pocket nurtures a bounty of azaleas in mid-May, and throughout spring the ribbits and twangs of mating frogs fill the air. To the left, a miniature waterfall spills over rocks, and if you walk a few yards farther left you'll come to lovely Ivy Hill Pond, bordered by hemlocks, laurel, and oaks. Large, flat boulders edging the mirror-smooth pond make for a perfect picnic perch, from which you can scan the scene for spotted salamanders, red-spotted newts, painted turtles, and green herons.

Continue down the hill and ford Baisman Run on strategically placed rocks. Just ahead (before the hill) look for a small path—the **S. James Campbell Trail**—that shoots off to the left, through the underbrush to the water. This pretty section of the hike zigzags across the dancing stream, which harbors brook trout, black nose dace, creek chubs, and crayfish.

After about half a mile, you leave the run, climbing steeply up Oregon Ridge. At the top of the ridge, cross the gasline right-of-way and reenter the woods. You soon come to an intersection of trails: Go left on the Logger's Trail, then right on the green-blazed **Virginia Pine Trail.** Proceed back to the parking area as described in the main hike. The total length of this loop is 3.6 miles.

Trip notes: The park is open daily. There is no entrance fee. Pick up a trail map at the nature center. For more information contact Oregon Ridge Park at 410-887-1818.

Directions: From the Baltimore Beltway take I-83 north to the Shawan Rd. exit. Go west 1 mile, turn left at the first stoplight, then bear right immediately between the Oregon Grill and a red shed. This road leads half a mile to the nature center.

74. Gunpowder Falls State Park

Off I-83 north of Baltimore near Hereford, Maryland

Gunpowder Falls South and Panther Branch Trails
4-mile loop/2 hours

Gunpowder Falls State Park is one of Maryland's great natural treasures. Featuring several different recreational areas along the Gunpowder Falls Valley, the park offers more than 100 miles of trails. But no falls. Early colonists called the swift-moving water above the tidewater Gunpowder River, the "falls" of the river. This particular hike takes in a wild and winding stretch of the waterway, then follows the smaller but just as picturesque Panther Branch.

The hike begins downstream (east) from York Road. Walk across the grassy meadow and, about 40 yards up from the river, follow the path that begins from an opening in the brush. The narrow trail crosses a little stream, then comes to a trail sign indicating that the white-blazed **Gunpowder Falls South Trail** goes left, and the blue-blazed Panther Branch Trail goes right. Go left (you'll be returning on the Panther Branch Trail). The trail cozies up beside the river, a rock-strewn ribbon of water flowing swiftly beneath a verdant veil of oaks and maples. This is one of Maryland's premier trout streams, and fly-fishermen—seemingly mesmerized as they throw their lines in long, loopy figure-eights—dot the stream.

Soon you come to a trail junction with an unmarked trail. Staying on the white-blazed trail, go right, winding up and up through the woods, away from the river. And soon, through the trees, you can see the sparkling "falls" far below. Rolling along through pretty woods adorned with ferns and serenaded by chattering birds, the trail eventually brings you back down to the river's edge. Here you find another fork in the trail, with an unmarked trail heading down to the water and the white-blazed trail bearing right. Go right, staying on the Gunpowder Falls South Trail.

The trail meanders along the river for a while, then the river disappears. Pass by the pink-blazed Sandy Lane Trail on the right and continue onward.

After crossing over a little stream, and then another one soon after, be alert to the fact that in a quarter mile you'll need to keep a keen eye out for the blue-blazed **Panther Branch Trail.** The blue blazes are hard to spot, as is the trail itself. A double white blaze on a tree is your clue. If you reach a good-size stream, Panther Branch, you've missed the turn by 20 or 30 yards. The Panther Branch Trail—which you'll stay on for the rest of the hike—wraps off to the right. Go uphill, over a ridge, and soon you're walking beside Panther Branch, a pretty woodland stream tumbling over smooth mossy rocks. Its namesake is thought to be a panther that once resided in a cave along the branch.

Keep going with Panther Branch on your left. After 0.6 mile, the trail climbs beside a pleasant brook, then enters a whole new world. You cross a meadow dotted with goldenrod and purple thistles, a seemingly endless wave of yellow and gold and purple. Then the trail enters a pine forest; turn right on the wide, roadlike dirt path, lined with towering trees.

The road jogs left, then right, plunging through deciduous woods. About 50 yards beyond the point where the path goes downhill, you leave the dirt road. Turn right on the still-blue-blazed trail, on a narrower path through the woods. It emerges in a clearing, enters another pine plantation, and crosses another grassy clearing. At the corner of another pine plantation, turn right at the trail intersection. And soon you come to a three-way junction. The pink-blazed Sandy Lane Trail heads downhill back to Gunpowder Falls. You don't want that. And you don't want the wide fire lane, which looks like it might be heading in the direction you want to go. Instead, still following the blue blazes, wrap sharply back to the left, making a U-turn.

Soon after, you come to two more trail junctions. At the first one, go right. At the next one, go left. You curl beside a narrow stream and, just beyond, the roar of autos mixes with the songs of birds, indicating the end of the trail is near. Sure enough, you'll soon recognize the trail sign that you passed a couple of hours ago…at this junction, go left and return to your car.

Make it easier: For a 2.2-mile walk, take the **Gunpowder Falls South Trail** as far as the **Sandy Lane Trail,** where you go right. At the top of the hill, loop back to the beginning of the hike via the blue-blazed **Panther Branch Trail** (as directed above).

Trip notes: The park is open daily. There is no entrance fee. For more information contact Gunpowder Falls State Park, P.O. Box 5032, Glen Arm, Maryland 21057; 410-592-2897.

Directions: See map on pp. 166-167. From the Baltimore Beltway (I-695), take I-83 north about 13 miles to the Md. 137 exit; follow Md. 137 east to Hereford and a T-intersection at York Road (Md. 45) and go left. The trail will be 1.7 miles north, just before the road crosses the bridge over Gunpowder Falls. Park in one of the small lots on either side of the road.

75. Gunpowder Falls State Park
Off I-83 north of Baltimore near Hereford, Maryland

Gunpowder Falls South Trail
3-mile round-trip/2 hours

In the age of the Romantics, artists lugged their easels to nature's most inspiring places—fast-moving rivers, jagged mountains, rocky seashores pounded by iridescent waves—where they created masterpieces drenched in golden light. This hiking spot near Baltimore possesses the kind of raw beauty that would have appealed to the best of the Romantic landscapists. Don't be surprised if you round a bend and come across a latter-day Albert Bierstadt.

Here, the clear, green Big Gunpowder River tumbles

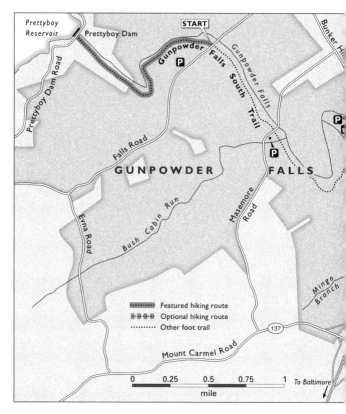

through a narrow, verdant valley, pouring over steep drops, splashing over boulder-strewn rapids, filling deep cool ponds. Shafts of gilded sunlight beam through the valley's luscious canopy, bursting into millions of sequins as they hit the river surface. White-tailed deer roam the banks, and—most critical—the place is enough off the beaten path that you probably won't meet another hiker; maybe just an artist or two.

Oh—and then there are the fly-fishermen. For as much as the Gunpowder appeals to artists, it's even more popular with trout fishermen. The nearby Prettyboy Dam creates a constant, freezing-cold source of running water so that trout thrive here throughout the year. Fishermen come from far and wide to methodically cast their lines, on a catch-and-release basis.

All this spectacular, wild beauty is accessible to the hiker via the narrow, somewhat rocky **Gunpowder Falls South Trail,** which hugs the streambank. This is a hike to savor. Bring a picnic and perch atop one of the large, flat boulders that speckle the river. Or bring your bathing suit and—if

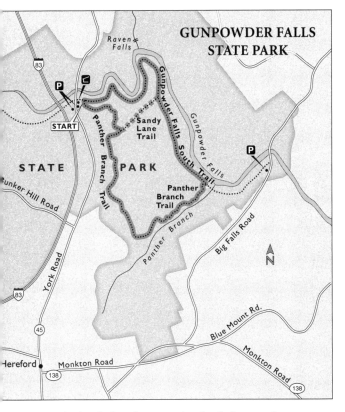

you don't mind cool water—the river's deep pools are enchanting places to take a dip, especially during summer's sweltering days.

Before embarking on this great trail, walk part way across the bridge for a wonderful introductory view of the river. Even if you didn't bring your easel and paints, you'll be glad you brought your camera.

The hike itself is easy to follow; from the trailhead, just keep the water on your right. When you reach the dam, turn around and return the way you came.

Trip notes: The park is open daily. There is no entrance fee. For more information contact Gunpowder Falls State Park, P.O. Box 5032, Glen Arm, Maryland 21057; 410-592-2897.

Directions: From the Baltimore Beltway, go north on I-83 to the Mount Carmel Rd. (Md. 137) exit. Turn left and proceed on Md. 137 to Evna Rd. Bear right, and in several miles turn right at the fork onto Falls Rd. Follow Falls Rd. to the small parking area on the left, about 100 yards before the bridge over Gunpowder Falls. Walk down Falls Rd. to just before the bridge; the trailhead is marked on your left.

76. Prettyboy Reservoir

Off I-83 north of Baltimore near Rayville, Maryland

Frog Hollow Creek trail
4-mile round-trip/2 hours

Exploring woods sprinkled with flowering dogwood, azalea, and mountain laurel and teeming with white-tailed deer, this trail leads to forest-fringed Prettyboy Reservoir.

The **Frog Hollow Creek trail** (actually a combination of fire roads) begins along the fire road off Parsonage Road, marked by a chain-link fence. Almost immediately you cross the fern-clad, crystal-clear Frog Hollow Creek; in spring the swampy area resonates with the twangs, ribbits, and bellows of thousands of frogs that reside here.

First climbing, then undulating, then flattening out, the trail delves deep into an oak-and-hickory forest, carpeted in spring with dainty spring beauty, rue anemone, columbine, and trillium. After crossing Salamander Creek (the second creek you come to after Frog Hollow Creek), keep straight ahead on the fire road. (A not-so-obvious trail leads to the right. Ignore it.). After awhile, you come to a T-intersection; turn left. At paved Spooks Hill Road, turn left again and walk along the road's shoulder about 100 feet. Reenter the woods on the fire road to the right. Almost immediately the road forks. Go left. You'll walk a ways, then see the lake's sparkle through the trees on the right. The fire road becomes a narrow trail, which continues winding through the woods until you reach a pretty little point overlooking the reservoir. Cooled by a refreshing breeze, this remote hideaway is especially alluring on stifling summer days. Beauty entwined with function: The reservoir holds more than 20 billion gallons of water from the Gunpowder Falls river, providing Baltimore with much of its water supply.

You can return the way you came, or take a slightly different route. To do this, backtrack to Spooks Hill Road and, instead of turning left, back the way you came, go right. Walk down the paved road about 50 yards to another fire road, on the left. This road will eventually bring you to a little creek; cross over it, turn right—and you'll recognize this as the trail you first headed out on. A few more ups and downs, and you're back to your car.

Make it easier: Rather than beginning the hike on Parsonage Rd., drive farther down the road for about half a mile to Spooks Hill Rd. and turn right. Drive just over a mile, and on your left you'll see a fire road—the latter part of the hike. Park along the shoulder of the road and follow the fire road as indicated in the directions above, and soon you'll come to the pretty setting on Prettyboy Reservoir.

Trip notes: The trail is open daily. There is no entrance fee. For more information contact Prettyboy Reservoir, Dept. of Public Works, 410-795-6151.

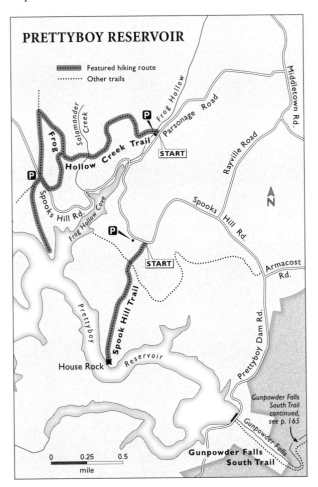

PRETTYBOY RESERVOIR

Featured hiking route
Other trails

Frog Hollow

Salamander Creek

Frog Hollow Creek Trail

Parsonage Road

Middletown Rd.

Rayville Road

START

Spooks Hill Rd.

Frog Hollow Cove

N

Spooks Hill Rd.

Armacost Rd.

START

Spook Hill Trail

Prettyboy

Reservoir

House Rock

Prettyboy Dam Rd.

Gunpowder Falls
South Trail
continued,
see p. 165

Gunpowder Falls

**Gunpowder Falls
South Trail**

0   0.25   0.5
mile

Directions: See map on p. 169. From the Baltimore Beltway (I-695), go north on I-83 to the Middletown Rd. exit. Turn left and travel about 2.5 miles to Parsonage Rd. Turn left and go 1 mile. At this point, you'll see a field on your left; on the right is a bright-orange chain marking a fire road. Park along the shoulder and head out on this fire road.

77. Prettyboy Reservoir
Off I-83 north of Baltimore, Maryland

Spook Hill trail
2-mile round-trip/ 45 minutes

T he name of this hike conjures up visions of bats and spiders and broom-wielding witches. Indeed, its centerpiece—Spook Hill—is a woodsy area renowned for its ghostly tree groves and eerie bellowings. But what you'll mostly find is an average-looking forest crisscrossed with old lumber roads. Stick with it and you won't be disappointed, because at trail's end awaits a wonderful rocky point jutting into the tree-fringed Prettyboy Reservoir—the perfect picnic perch.

From the chain-link entrance to the fire road, the **Spook Hill trail** cuts through the woods; ignore several old lumber roads that carve across the trail. If you always proceed straight ahead, you'll do just fine. After passing through an area of big pine trees, you come to a clearing where a fire road intersects with your trail. Again, just keep walking straight (though the trail itself bears slightly to the right).

After awhile, the fire road ends; continue straight ahead on a narrow trail that winds beneath trees, and soon you come to the rocky point on Prettyboy Reservoir, with fabulous views of water and trees and sky. Certainly you'll agree that the somewhat banal hike was worth all this beauty. By the way, the scary sounds fill the air only in springtime, when the frogs of nearby Frog Hollow commence their annual mating chorus.

Points to ponder while picnicking: The rock you're sitting on, called House Rock, provided shelter for Native Americans. It was submerged in 1936 with the creation of the reservoir, to provide the City of Baltimore with water. A small creek nearby, named for a poor mare that in the 19th century got stuck in the mud and drowned, gives the Prettyboy Reservoir its curious appellation.

Trip notes: The trail is open daily. There is no entrance fee. For more information contact Prettyboy Reservoir, Department of Public Works, 410-795-6151.

Directions: See map on p. 169. Take I-83 north of Baltimore to Middletown Rd. Turn left to Rayville Rd., where you turn left again. After 0.9 mile, turn right on Spooks Hill Rd. for 0.7 mile to an obvious bend in the road, where several houses cluster. Park your car just beyond the bend on the side of the road (mind the no parking signs). Walk to the houses, where you'll see a gravel road cutting between them. Follow this gravel road to the bright orange chain marking the beginning of a fire road. This is your trail.

If you're coming from the Frog Hollow Creek trail on Parsonage Rd. (see pp. 168-170), continue on Parsonage Rd. for about half a mile to Spooks Hill Rd. Turn left on Spooks Hill Rd. and drive for 0.6 mile to the sharp bend. Park on the side of the road and proceed as stated above.

78. Shure's Landing Wildflower and Natural Area

Off I-95 north of Baltimore near Havre de Grace, Maryland

Wildflower trail
2-mile round-trip/40 minutes

Rare and endangered blooms and birds highlight this easy stroll beside the Susquehanna River. The trail is part of a grand effort to convert an old rail corridor and natural areas along the Susquehanna into a greenscape of interlocking trails, one that would also feature cultural, historic, and recreational facilities. Called the Lower Susquehanna Heritage Greenway, this trail system will one day connect the town of Havre de Grace with Conowingo Dam.

The **wildflower trail** begins at Fisherman's Park, near Conowingo Dam. You don't even have to step on the trail to enjoy this prime bird-watching spot. Birders congregate in the parking lot overlooking the river in quest of bald eagles, lured here especially in winter by ice-free water below the dam. The area's forested slopes and shorelines are also breeding habitat for many kinds of warblers (including the northern parula, cerulean, hooded, veery, and prothontory), gulls, herons, and magnificent ospreys.

A sign at the parking lot's southern end indicates the trailhead. Wide and flat, the gravel pathway ambles through peaceful woods of tulip poplar and sycamore, with the pretty Susquehanna rippling on the left, rocky slopes rising on the right. In mid- to late April, a multitude of wildflowers trans-forms the hillside into a veritable garden. Star of the show is the trillium, representing the largest stand of its kind in Maryland. Though white, these trillium are actually a rare form of red trillium—their colorless petals are caused by a rare pigment production mutation. Joining them are Dutch-man's-breeches, dogtooth violets, spring beauties, and wild ginger, with showy aster and goldenrods following in sum-mer and fall. Shure's Landing Wildflower and Natural Area is also known for its several colonies of ferns and an endan-gered daisy species.

Just a couple of hundreds yards down the trail stands an observation platform overlooking the river, shaded by giant maples and sycamores. The path becomes progressively nar-rower and, after about a mile, you leave the natural area. At this point, this hike backtracks to the parking area. You can, however, proceed another 4 miles along the river, to a trestle crossing Deer Creek. And about half a mile beyond that awaits the Rock Run Historic Area in the heart of Susque-hanna State Park, a picturesque clutch of 19th-century buildings, including an old stone mill.

Trip notes: The trail is open daily. There is no fee. For more information, contact the Executive Director, Maryland Greenways Commission, 580 Taylor Avenue, Annapolis, MD 21401; 410-974-3589.

Directions: From I-95 north of Baltimore, take the Lapidum Rd. exit north; Lapidum runs into Stafford Rd. within Susquehanna State Park. Follow Stafford to Md. 161 (Dar-lington Rd.), turn right, and take the first right, on Shuresville. Bear right on Shures Landing Rd. and proceed to the end.

79. Elk Neck State Park

Off I-95 north of Baltimore, Maryland

Turkey Point Trail
2-mile round-trip/45 minutes

A long, timbered peninsula jutting out into Chesapeake Bay, Elk Neck is a haven for wildlife: Wild turkeys, white-tail deer, woodpeckers, even bald eagles abound. But the main draw to this state park lies at its tip—Turkey Point. Here, a century-old lighthouse overlooks the blue Chesapeake, and steep bluffs provide prospects of sailboats dashing with the wind. It's a breathtaking sight, one that makes you want to sit and linger and keep the world at bay.

The wide, dirt **Turkey Point Trail** begins from the parking lot at the very end of Md. 272. Before starting off, be sure to peek over the cliffs on the right, which plunge steeply to the Northeast River. Gazing into the scene, you may glimpse a bald eagle soaring out over the water. Now head down the trail beneath a thick canopy of scarlet, chestnut, and white oaks, sprinkled with pitch and Virginia pines. You soon enter a small field, perhaps dotted with bales of hay, definitely aflutter with sparrows.

And then you come to a larger field, and the junction of two trails. A small sign here indicates that the lighthouse is to the left, the direction you want to go (you'll make a loop, returning on the other trail). In no time, you reach the tall, whitewashed lighthouse (now closed), perched atop a grassy rise. Benches beckon to sit and relax, though just as tempting is the edge of land that lies just beyond, dropping dramatically down to the bay. A rock wall permits you to sit and study this spectacular vista of water and land.

In autumn, this point features some of the best hawk-watching around. The hawks' long journey south to their wintering grounds (some go as far as Ecuador) brings them right past the lighthouse…on a crisp, cool day you can spot 20 or more hawks an hour winging by. In late September and early October, watch for sharp-shinned hawks and kestrals, while mid-October brings red-tailed and red-shouldered hawks. Ospreys can be seen throughout September and October, as well as bald eagles. And the very patient may be rewarded with the sighting of a rare peregrine falcon or, perhaps, a golden eagle.

When it's time to leave, head down the grassy slope. Be sure to look over your shoulder now and again at the impressive view of the lighthouse-crowned knoll. Farther ahead, on the other edge of the grassy field, you'll see a narrow trail darting into the woods. Take this, descending to the water's edge. Before you know it, you're eye-level with the Chesapeake, with a cool breeze riffling through your hair. A large stone dike prevents erosion by keeping the waters from lapping against the shoreline; its large, flat surface provides a perfect place to sit, picnic, and enjoy the view.

Continue walking along the dike, with the water to your left. In 10 or 20 yards you'll come to a dirt and gravel trail entering the woods. This will lead you away from the water, uphill, and back to the big meadow. At the close of the loop (at the lighthouse sign), bear left, and head back to the parking lot the way you came.

Trip notes: The park is open daily. There is no entrance fee. For more information, contact Elk Neck State Park, 4395 Turkey Point Rd., North East, MD 21901; 410-287-5333.

Directions: North of Baltimore on I-95, take the Md. 272 south exit. The park is located 10 miles beyond the town of North East at the end of the road.

Maryland Tidewater

South of the colonial city of Annapolis,
the fabled Chesapeake's waters lap
upon a lesser known land
of gold-and-green fields, pocket
forests, and ancient cliffs.

80. City of Annapolis
1.25-mile loop/1 hour

B oasting one of the nation's greatest concentrations of 18th-century buildings, a historic harborfront, and the famous U.S. Naval Academy, Annapolis offers a scenic stroll back into history and tradition. Serenely perched at the confluence of the Severn River and Chesapeake Bay, the city dates from 1649, when a group of Puritans from Virginia settled on the Severn's north bank; 35 years later, Anne Arundel Town (later renamed Annapolis) was laid out on the opposite bank. In 1694 this flourishing port town became the colonial capital—and one of colonial America's most cosmopolitan cities. Between November 1783 and August 1784, the Continental Congress met at the Annapolis State Capitol, ratifying the Treaty of Paris to end the Revolutionary War. During this time, George Washington came before Congress here to resign his commission as Commander in Chief of the Continental Army.

This walk begins in the heart of the old town, at the **State House** *(State Cir. 410-974-3400)*. The legislature first met here in 1780, making it the nation's oldest state capitol in continuous use. It was used as the national capitol from 1783 to 1784. Inside hangs a Charles Willson Peale portrait of George Washington at the Battle of Yorktown. Nearby, the Victorian Gothic **St. Anne's Episcopal Church** *(149 Duke of Gloucester St. 410-263-2396)* is a beautiful brick structure rebuilt in 1858—the third church on the site since the parish was founded in 1692. The silver communion service inside was presented by King William III in 1695.

Drop down to College Avenue and turn right, past **St. John's College,** which dates back to King William's School, founded in 1696. The Sons of Liberty met in front of the 400-year-old tulip tree that still stands in front of McDowell Hall.

To sample colonial life, turn right on King George Street, then right again on pretty Maryland Avenue to the **Chase-Lloyd House** *(22 Maryland Ave. 410-263-2723. March-Dec. Mon.-Sat., closed Jan.-Feb.; adm. fee)*. This Georgian town house, noted for its fine interior detail, was once the home of Samuel Chase, a signer of the Declaration of Independence who became a Supreme Court justice. Another interesting residence awaits just across the street. The old **Hammond-Harwood House** *(19 Maryland Ave. 410-269-1714. Adm. fee)* was the 1774 Georgian home of legislator and planter Matthias Hammond. It is considered architect William Buckland's last outstanding American Colonial building. Elegant colonial furnishings offer a glimpse into the life of the privileged during the Revolutionary War.

Surely the grandest house in town is around the corner on Prince George Street. The elegant **William Paca House and Garden** (*186 Prince George St. 410-263-5553. Limited hours Jan.-Feb.; adm. fee*) was built in 1765 in the Georgian style by signer of the Declaration of Independence and state governor William Paca. Two acres of backyard gardens contain formal parterres and terraces, complete with a fish-shape pond, a Chinese Chippendale bridge, and a wilderness garden. If you tour only one house in town, make it this one.

Continue down Prince George Street, turn left on East Street, and take a quick right on King George Street and enter through the main gate of the **U.S. Naval Academy** (*52 King George St. 410-263-6933*), the undergraduate college of the U.S. Navy. Established in 1845, the academy's 300 acres bustle with square-jawed midshipmen. Stained-glass windows designed by Tiffany cast colored medallions of light upon the stark interior of the domed chapel. Marines guard the marble crypt of Revolutionary War naval hero John Paul Jones, sur-

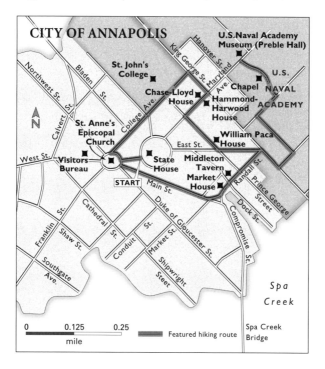

CITY OF ANNAPOLIS

U.S. Naval Academy Museum (Preble Hall)

Hanover St.

King George St.

Maryland Ave.

Northwest St.

Bladen St.

St. John's College

Chase-Lloyd House

Chapel

U.S. NAVAL ACADEMY

Hammond-Harwood House

Calvert St.

College Ave.

St. Anne's Episcopal Church

William Paca House

East St.

West St.

Visitors Bureau

State House

Middleton Tavern

Randall St.

Prince George Street

START

Main St.

Market House

Cathedral St.

Franklin St.

Shaw St.

Conduit St.

Market St.

Duke of Gloucester St.

Dock St.

Compromise St.

Southgate Ave.

Shipwright Street

Spa Creek

0   0.125   0.25
mile

Featured hiking route

Spa Creek Bridge

rounded by ceremonial flags. Also here, Preble Hall houses a museum of arms, ship models, uniforms, and maritime art.

In case you've forgotten that Annapolis is the sailing hub of the Chesapeake, backtrack from the main gate on King George Street to Randall Street and turn left. In a couple of blocks you'll come to the **City Dock** area—the old colonial port, once surrounded by warehouses and ship carpenter's lots. Dating from those times, the **Middleton Tavern** *(Market Space and Randall St. 410-263-3323)* operated as a tavern and ferry landing between 1745 and 1790, and American Patriots lodged here; now it serves up decent seafood specialties. The watery area in front of **Market House**—built in 1858 and still bustling with food shops—has been dubbed "Ego Alley," where yachtsmen show off their pride-and-joys. At the head of City Dock stands a newly erected statue of Alex Haley. It was here in 1767 that Haley's ancestor, Kunta Kinte, immortalized in his Pulitzer prize-winning family history, arrived with other Gambian Africans to be sold into slavery.

End the stroll along the waterfront, away from the city clamor. Sit by the water's edge with your feet dangling over the pier, watching motoring boats, wheeling gulls, lapping waves. Then, if you're hungry or feel like poking in some shops, head up Main Street, which brings you back to St. Anne's Church.

Trip notes: The sites have individual openings and fees as listed in the text. For more information, contact the Annapolis and Anne Arundel County Conference and Visitors Bureau, 26 West St., Annapolis, MD 21401; 410-280-0445.

Directions: Begin at the Annapolis Court House, in the heart of old Annapolis. Parking available on surrounding streets.

81. Patuxent River Park
Off Md. 4 south of Upper Marlboro, Maryland

Black Walnut Creek boardwalk trail
1-mile loop/30 minutes

A 2,000-acre natural area, Patuxent River Park protects a beautiful stretch of the Patuxent River at Jug Bay beloved by birds and birders alike. This short hike explores both woodlands and marshlands along the river, with chances of spotting more than 200 different species of birds, including swans, Canada geese, greater yellowlegs, and cormorants fanning out their wings to dry like ancient goddesses. This is an important site for waterfowl during the non-breeding season, with up to 22 different species present in winter. This is also an important migratory stopover for the Sora rail.

From the park office, find the flagpole and descend the stairs to a pier overreaching the glassy river. With binoculars you can pick out birds both floating in the open waters of Jug Bay and perched along the water's edge—especially in winter, don't forget to scan the tree branches for bald eagles. Then walk up the road a bit to a wooden gate on the left and enter the Black Walnut Creek Nature Study Area. Right away you're on a boardwalk above a marshy area alive with wildlife. At the T-intersection go left, past a stand of bald cypress—among the northernmost locations that they grow. Along the river grows wild rice, a favorite among birds migrating along the waterway and food for as many as 25,000 waterfowl during the winter months.

Proceed into the deciduous forest predominantly comprised of oaks (white, chestnut, northern red, and scarlet), sweet gum, and beech, abundant with springtime warblers. Farther ahead, an observation tower overlooks the open waters, offering more prime birding.

Then backtrack along the trail; but at the trail intersection, rather than returning on the right, the way you came, proceed straight into the woodlands—the domain of woodpeckers, white-tailed deer, and gray squirrels. You pass by another observation tower, this one for woodland creatures, and soon cross over wee Black Walnut Creek. Follow the trail up the stairs to a flat area and the W.H. Duvall Tool Museum. From here, finish the hike by walking up the gravel road, back to the park office.

More hiking: Adjacent to Patuxent River Park is the **Merkle Wildlife Sanctuary.** This refuge is devoted to the birds, with plenty of promised sightings of Canada geese, ospreys, and more. Four different trails wind through the sanctuary. Stop by the visitor center for a trail map. For more information, contact the Maryland Dept. of Natural Resources, State Forest and Park Service, 11704 Fenno Rd., Upper Marlboro, MD 20772; 800-784-5380.

Trip notes: The park is open daily. Special-use permits, required for all activities, are available for a fee at the park office; $5 per car for Prince George's and Montgomery County residents, $7 for nonresidents. For more information, contact

Patuxent River Park, 16000 Croom Airport Rd., Upper Marlboro, MD 20772; 301-627-6074.

Directions: From the Capital Beltway (I-95), take Md. 4 east to US 301 south. In 1.5 miles turn left on Croom Station Rd. In 2.5 miles, turn left on Md. 382 for 1.5 miles to Croom Airport Rd. Go left for 2 miles to the park entrance, where you take another left. The park office is 1.5 miles down the road.

82. Battle Creek Cypress Swamp Sanctuary

Off Md. 4 south of Prince Frederick, Maryland

Boardwalk loop
0.25-mile loop/30 minutes

Walking the boardwalk at Battle Creek Cypress Swamp is like walking back 100,000 years in history, to a time when saber-toothed cats and mammoths roamed the earth. Surely the majestic cypress trees—their knobby knees poking through murky waters—don't belong to modern-day Maryland! Indeed, this parcel of land is a tiny remnant of the vast coastal swampland that once covered the southern part of the state.

Before embarking on the trail, peruse the exhibits at the visitor center. Among the many interesting things found here are some live specimens of the more obscure swamp residents that you probably won't see out on the trail—including a copperhead or two.

The **boardwalk loop** starts out the back door of the visitor center, down the stairs. The boardwalk itself is quite short: You could do the whole loop in 15 minutes. But take your time. This dark, brooding, primeval world, where bright green ferns carpet the ground and honey-colored light diffuses through the cypresses' dark foliage, is a great place to marvel at the diversity of nature and watch for swampland denizens. Of course, the primeval beasts are long extinct, but if you're quiet, you may glimpse spotted and painted turtles basking in the sun; black rat snakes wrapped around tree trunks, waiting for prey; a green frog warily watching from beneath a green leaf. Since many of the residents are nocturnal, look for the footprints that raccoons, muskrats, deer, skunks, foxes, and otters have left behind during nighttime forages. And along the banks of Battle Creek, admire the crayfish chimneys—stacks of mud pellets that mark the entrances to submerged burrows.

The star of the show is, of course, the bald cypress itself. Towering 100 to 150 feet above the water, they dominate the swamp. You can't miss them, with their bulbous base and knobby knees (an extension of their root system—though some say they breathe through these). An interesting note: It takes very select seasonal conditions for the bald cypress to propagate. Sometimes years pass between generations. You can actually note the different generations throughout the swamp.

The boardwalk will bring you round, back to the visitor center.

Trip notes: The park is closed Mondays. There is no entrance fee. For more information, contact the Battle Creek Cypress Swamp Sanctuary, Calvert County Natural Resources Division, Calvert County Courthouse, Prince Frederick, MD 20678; 410-535-5327.

Directions: From the Capital Beltway (I-95), take Md. 4 south to Calvert County. Just south of Prince Frederick, turn right on Sixes Rd. In about 2 miles look for a sign and turn left on Gray's Rd. The sanctuary is located on the right in about 1 mile.

83. Flag Ponds Nature Area
Off Md. 4 south of Prince Frederick, Maryland

Duncan's Pond and North Ridge Trails
1.4-mile loop/45 minutes

Salamanders, frogs, and other herpetofauna may not be aware of it, but they have a friend in Flag Ponds Nature Area—a peaceful sanctuary where they don't have to worry about crossing busy roads to reach their breeding grounds. Meantime, their presence takes on a more poignant note when you understand that amphibians are the first animals to succumb to soil toxicity—that their role in nature is similar to that of the proverbial canary in a mine shaft. For this reason, the Department of Natural Resources has undertaken a large-scale herp consensus at various sites through Maryland—including Flag Ponds—to see exactly where they (and we) stand.

On the lighter side, Flag Ponds—named for the abundant blue flag iris—is an attractive park just a few miles north of its more famous cousin, Calvert Cliffs. Most people flock to Flag Ponds in summertime to sunbathe on the beach, without realizing that nearby lies a beautiful hike through the coastal plain forest filled with amphibians.

This hike begins from parking lot no. 1 near the visitor center. Walk down the dirt-gravel road toward the beach. You pass through a gate and, farther along, the trailhead to the North Ridge Trail. You don't want that. Turn left at the next trailhead, onto the **Duncan's Pond Trail.** You plunge into thick, cool woods—a mix of maple, sweet gum, tulip poplar, American beech, and white oak. Soon you'll come to an observation platform overlooking duckweed-choked Duncan's Pond. It may not be much to look at, but dragonflies abound, and this is a great place to bird-watch: Red-winged blackbirds visit in late spring and summer, while ducks come in late fall. If you wish to watch for wildlife in complete obscurity, proceed ahead to a side trail (marked by a sign) leading off to the right to an observation blind.

Back on the hike, the trail slithers through the forest, soon becoming a boardwalk over a silent swamp speckled with green ash and red maple. The openness makes the swamp a perfect place to watch for birds and other animals: pileated woodpeckers, wood ducks floating by on the ebony water, sweet-singing warblers, owls, and plenty of frogs.

After a hundred yards or so you leave the boardwalk, coming to a trail junction with the **North Ridge Trail.** Go right, along the edge of the swamp. In a little way, the trail wraps sharply around to the left, away from the swamp. Now brace for a fairly steep climb, made a little easier by some stairs. What you're essentially doing is leaving the floodplain, climbing into the wooded upland. The soil becomes drier, the vegetation less lush. Be on the lookout for woodchucks, rabbits, and raccoons, along with bluebirds.

At the top of the stairs, you have a choice. You can go right on the North Loop Trail for a 0.6-mile extension of the hike. Or you can continue left on the North Ridge Trail, directly back to parking lot no. 3. (If you watch carefully for a side trail near the end of the North Ridge Trail, it will bring you to parking lot no. 2). Walk down the park entrance road to find your car in parking lot no. 1.

More hiking: Take the **North Loop Trail** for a 0.6-mile extension of the hike.

Trip notes: The park is closed Mon. to Fri. Labor Day to Mem. Day. There is a $6 entrance fee ($4 for Calvert County residents). For more information, contact the Calvert County Natural Resources Division, Calvert County Courthouse, Prince Frederick, MD 20678; 410-535-5327.

Directions: From the Capital Beltway (I-95), follow Md. 4 south into Calvert County. Just 10 miles south of Prince Frederick, look for the sign and turn left into the nature park.

84. Calvert Cliffs State Park

Off Md. 4 south of Prince Frederick, Maryland

Red trail
4-mile round-trip/2 hours

Overlooking the blue Chesapeake, Calvert Cliffs provide more than a scenic backdrop to this hike. For these mighty bluffs contain one of the world's richest fossil deposits, embedded 12 to 17 million years ago when a warm, shallow sea covered the area. Little by little, wind and rain have eroded the soft sandstone, exposing more and more fossils; one by one, they crumble onto the beach or into the surf, and some are washed ashore. A short stroll along the beach becomes a treasure hunt—you can find the remains of all kinds of ancient marine creatures, including shellfish, angelfish, crocodiles, sharks, whales, porpoises, and dolphins. The best part: You get to keep what you find.

While these fossil-filled cliffs are a huge draw, the trail that leads to them through striking coastal plain forest is reason enough to visit Calvert Cliffs State Park. The trail begins from the parking area; follow the red-blazed path across the wooden bridge, which overlooks a picturesque pond full of noisy frogs. You enter the woods, and after about a quarter mile, the **red trail** bears right—you're on your way. You wind through a beautiful, stream-laced coastal plain forest filled with maple, sweet gum, tulip poplar, American beech, and white oak. In June, the white, puffy blooms of mountain laurel festoon the trailside, and tiger swallowtail butterflies flutter by.

Take note of the stream, because in three-quarters of a mile from the parking area, it orchestrates a dramatic change in scenery. Backed up by an earthen berm, it creates a nontidal wetland full of wildlife. Do try to visit in spring, when an amphibian symphony features the spring peeper and its rendition of a twanging rubber band, and the deep-throated bullfrog. The only tree that survives here is the green ash, which may look dead—but its straggly, unfoliated condition is merely a coping mechanism to survive the harsh, water-logged conditions of this marshy area. Scan the spindly branches for herons and kingfishers.

At one point, a boardwalk knifes out over the marshland, bringing you into its heart. Stand just a couple of minutes here and you'll surely spy a melee of turtles—some nearly a foot in diameter—and bulging-eyed frogs hiding beneath lily pads. Blackbirds dart playfully, and off to the right stands a 4-foot-long beaver dam.

Just beyond the boardwalk, you come to a gravel service road. Bear right, and in no time the refreshing bay breeze riffles through your hair. The Chesapeake's waters lap gently upon a narrow beach, where families picnic and sunbathe. Calvert Cliffs—which tower along 30 miles of bayshore, from Chesapeake Beach to Drum Point—stand at either end of the beach. The erosion from waves, landslides, storms, and frost is so bad that trees hang precariously from the cliff top, and down below fallen ones scatter like matchsticks. Because of the danger, you won't be allowed to get too near the cliffs, so concentrate your fossil hunt on the beach. The shark's tooth is especially abundant, with your best chances along the water's edge. Look carefully—there are plenty of broken shells to fool you. Then return to your car the way you came.

Trip notes: The park is open daily. There is a $3 vehicle fee. For more information, contact Maryland State Forest and Park Service, c/o Point Lookout State Park, P.O. Box 48, Scotland, MD 20687; 301-872-5688.

Directions: From the Capital Beltway (I-95) take Md. 4 south. The state park is located 14 miles south of Prince Frederick. Look for the park entrance on the left, just beyond the entrance to the Calvert Cliffs Nuclear Power Station.

Eastern Shore

Across the Chesapeake Bay Bridge east of Annapolis, a quiet farmscape remains closely tied to the ebbs and flows of the Chesapeake, beloved by birds and birders alike.

85. Eastern Neck National Wildlife Refuge

Off Md. 20 southwest of Chestertown, Maryland

Tubby Cove Boardwalk, Duck Inn Trail
Tubby Cove Boardwalk: 400 yards round-trip/15 minutes
Duck Inn: 1-mile round-trip/20 minutes

A good reason to visit Eastern Neck National Wildlife Refuge in the waterlogged winter months is to see the exquisite tundra swans. Every October or November, they migrate from the Arctic to overwinter on this 2,285-acre island at the mouth of the Chester River. You don't even have to step a foot on a trail to see them—chances are, driving across the low-lying wooden bridge that connects the island to the mainland, you'll spot a cluster of them bobbing on the choppy gray water; snowy white and regal, they seem out of place, surreal, in this wild, lonely setting.

Established in 1962, Eastern Neck protects more than just swans—it's a major feeding and nesting site for thousands of migratory and wintering waterfowl, the most common being Canada geese (20,000+) and canvasbacks (15,000+). Year-round you'll see great blue and green herons and egrets standing sentry along the marshes and tidal mud flats, along with mallards, black ducks, and dandylike wood ducks. Mute swans, a nonnative species of swan often mistaken for the tundra swan, also reside here (they have orange bills while tundra swans have black). Eastern Neck provides refuge to three endangered or threatened species as well: the bald eagle, which has nested and successfully fledged eaglets every year since 1986; the Delmarva Peninsula fox squirrel, which once roamed as far north as Pennsylvania and New Jersey; and the peregrine falcon, which occasionally stops by on its annual fall migrations.

Eastern Neck has several interesting, albeit short, trails, two of which are especially worthwhile. The first is the **Tubby Cove Boardwalk,** whose trailhead you'll see on your right soon after entering the island. It hovers above a marsh, leading to a tiny woodsy island where an observation platform looks out over the Chesapeake Bay's open waters. You could do this hike—really, more of a stroll—in 10 minutes; but go slowly, read the interpretive plaques, and watch for wildlife. This is a good place to spot resident mute swans, red-breasted mergansers, and buffleheads.

Take a short drive farther down the island to pick up the **Duck Inn Trail,** a short traipse through pines, sweet gums, and dogwoods to a small beach on the Chester River. In all its secluded tranquility, it's hard to believe that in colonial days this area bustled with the activities of packet ships that made regular stops at nearby Bogles Wharf. Today there's scarcely any sign of modern life.

To the left of the beach, a sweet little inlet is surrounded by a marsh. To the right spreads a panorama of Bogles Cove—just one of the many indents of land that frill the Chester River. Return to your car the way you came.

If you haven't had enough of this fascinating place, stop by the refuge visitor center for information on other hikes. A new hike, on the 0.1-mile **Bayview/Butterfly Trail,** leaves from the parking lot, bringing you to the refuge's best view of the bay.

Trip notes: The refuge is open daily. There is no entrance fee. Deer hunting is allowed in fall (but not Sundays). For further information contact the Refuge Manager, Eastern Neck National Wildlife Refuge, 1730 Eastern Neck Rd., Rock Hall, MD 21661; 410-639-7056.

Directions: From Chestertown, drive southeast on Md. 20 for 13 miles to the town of Rock Hall. Here, turn left (south) on Md. 445 and drive 6 miles to the bridge across Eastern Neck Narrows. Continue straight ahead, onto the island. The Tubby Cove Trail will be on your right in about half a mile. For the Duck Inn Trail, drive another half mile down the park road, turn left on Bogles Wharf Rd., and in 0.1 mile park your car in the gravel lot on the right.

86. Horsehead Wetlands Center
Off US 50/US 301 just east of the Chesapeake Bay Bridge

Boardwalk and Marshy Creek Trails
1-mile loop/30 minutes

Just minutes east of the congested Chesapeake Bay Bridge, the Horsehead Wetlands Center harbors a plethora of birdlife. Birds seem to know they're safe from hunters here, promising sightings of all different kinds—from wood ducks to ospreys to green herons. The visitor center has minor exhibits and programs, and nearby there's a short trail past three ponds frequented by clipped birds typical of the nation's different flyways, including the Pacific (emperor geese, white-fronted geese), central and Mississippian (American widgeon, lesser and greater scaup), and the more familiar Atlantic (snow geese, wood ducks, redheads, and blue-winged teal). There's also a raptor mews of nonreleasable birds. (Without explicit interpretive plaques, though, this area is not really that interesting.)

But the main draw at the Horsehead Wetlands Center is the walk around Lake Knapp to the edge of Chesapeake Bay. On this serendipitous adventure into the wilds, you never know what you're going to come across. Perhaps a huge heron floating just above your head, or an osprey sitting quietly on its nest, or dozens of ducks skidding across the cattail-laced lake.

The hike is actually comprised of two trails—the Boardwalk Trail and the Marshy Creek Trail. Exiting the visitor center, walk to the right, to the first road you come to, on the left. This is the **Boardwalk Trail,** which takes you past wildflower-dotted meadows. Though you can't see it through the high grasses, Lake Knapp is off to your right.

Soon you come to the J.C. White Blind, which provides a perfect (albeit cobweb-strewn) perch to anonymously watch the birds of Lake Knapp. There's an osprey platform out in the middle. Bald eagles have been spotted gliding by overhead. Also watch for bufflehead; Canada geese (over half a million pass through Maryland annually, and many stay on the Eastern Shore all year); blue-winged teal (in early fall); tundra swans (half the world's population winters in the bay area); northern pintails; and many more. At the very least you'll glimpse the standard egret or heron.

The trail continues onward to the wetland boardwalk, bringing you out over the tidal salt marsh. This buffer between land and bay provides a perfect year-round home to waterfowl, which nibble its common reeds and plant shoots. An observation tower offers a marsh overview. Scan the grasses and water for tundra swans, buffleheads, loons, terns, and wading birds.

Two different (short) boardwalks branch from here. The one to the left brings you near the bay; the one to the right doesn't look like much, but at its end lies a salt pan. Because this natural, water-filled depression has a higher salt content than the surrounding area, its organisms are completely different from those found in the surrounding marsh: Mud snails, water snakes, and marsh wrens are commonly sighted.

Backtrack to the lodge, and continue clockwise around the lake. You'll enter a wooded area, and the trail becomes the

Marshy Creek Trail, a haven for northern cardinals, eastern towhees, warblers, and other songbirds. Keep walking straight, staying left at two trail junctions, and you'll reach the Marshy Creek Observation Tower, overlooking Marshy Creek. Watch for great horned owls, great blue herons, tundra swans, and Canada geese frollicking in the waters beyond.

Backtrack along the trail to the first turnoff you come to, and go left. When you reach a fork, a left turn will bring you back to the parking area. If you're not quite ready to leave this wildlife wonderland, then go right instead; soon you'll come to East Blind, providing one last look on Lake Knapp.

Trip notes: The center is open daily. There is a $3 entrance fee per person. For more information contact the Wildfowl Trust of North America, P.O. Box 519, Grasonville, MD 21638; 410-827-6694.

Directions: The wetlands are located 6 miles east of the Chesapeake Bay Bridge, near the village of Grasonville. After crossing the bridge, follow US 50/US 301 for 5 miles across the bridge at Kent Narrows. Take the third exit, for Chester River Beach Rd. At the top of the ramp, turn right toward Md. 18, then left at the T-intersection onto Md. 18 in Grasonville. Make the first right on Perry Corner Rd. The entrance is located about a quarter mile on the right and is clearly marked. Discovery Ln. is a dirt road that dead-ends at the parking lot. Go to the visitor center to pay the entrance fee and pick up a map.

87. Wye Island

Off US 50 near Wye Mills, Maryland

Ferry Point Trail
1.5-mile round-trip/30 minutes

When early English settlers first stepped ashore in the New World, many chose the fertile lands of Maryland's Eastern Shore for their new homes. With the wealth they accumulated from fields and fields of tobacco, they built large plantation houses on bluffs overlooking the green Chesapeake. The Eastern Shore of today, though still agricultural, scarcely resembles those early years; corn and soybeans have replaced tobacco, and few manors survive. There are, however, pockets where you can get a whiff of yesteryear, when tobacco was king, and the landed gentry sat on open verandas enjoying cool bay breezes.

One such place is Wye Island, a wonderfully undeveloped niche of fields and woods—and, if you're en route to the beaches, a perfect place to stretch your legs along the way. It's pleasant to simply wander across the quiet and serene farmlands any which way, or even stroll down the dirt lane that bisects the island. But there are three designated trails to take, one of which is especially enchanting. The **Ferry Point Trail** wends through a tunnel of beautiful osage orange trees—a popular garden decoration in colonial days—down to the Wye River, site of an old ferry landing.

The trail begins near the end of the island's main road; signs lead the way to the small parking area. From here, enter the trail through the middle of the fence and begin your journey beneath the osage trees. Long, graceful branches arch over the entire length of the pathway, evoking images of grand entrees to regal manors. Note the unusual crenallated red-colored bark, the perfectly shaped leaves, and the large osage oranges that still grow wild.

Don't rush, for this is a hike to savor. Stroll along, enjoying the chatter of songbirds, the clatter of insects. Soon the trail swings right, revealing a splash of blue at the end of the leafy burrow—the Wye River. After awhile, you reach the river at a tiny beach, a great place to picnic, or to simply sit and watch fishing boats and pleasure crafts float by. When you're ready, return the way you came, enjoying it all anew.

Trip notes: The trail is open daily. There is no entrance fee. For more information contact the Wye Island Natural Resources Management Area, 632 Wye Island Rd., Queenstown, MD 21658; 410-827-7577.

Directions: From the Chesapeake Bay Bridge, follow US 50 east. Proceed 3 miles beyond the US 50/US 301 split, on US 50 to Carmichael Rd., on the right. Turn right and follow the road for 5 miles to the bridge across Wye Narrows. Continue on the road to the end of the island, following signs to the parking area.

88. Blackwater National Wildlife Refuge

Off US 50 east of Salisbury, Maryland

Marsh Edge Trail, Woods Trail
Marsh Edge Trail: 0.75-mile loop/20 minutes
Woods Trail: 0.5-mile loop/15 minutes

Hundreds of miles of marshes and estuaries filigree the Chesapeake Bay shoreline, reaching a crescendo of natural beauty in southern Maryland. Here, the Blackwater River moseys through tidal flats past tree-clad islands before joining with the Chesapeake Bay. In the heart of this soggy landscape sprawls Blackwater NWR.

The refuge's extensive marshes make prime habitat for migratory birds—Canada geese, great cormorants, pied-bill grebes, yellowlegs, killdeer, least sandpipers, snow geese— which congregate here especially between mid-October and mid-March. You might also spot a bald eagle; about 15 pairs nest at Blackwater, the greatest number in the eastern U.S. after Florida. Look for them along the marsh edge, where they perch on snags protruding from the inky water, and atop tall trees, where they nest.

Blackwater is also a prime spot to catch sight of the rare Delmarva Peninsula fox squirrel—a grizzled critter twice the size of the normal gray squirrel, with foxlike ears. They prefer woodland floors to trees, with lots of open space to scurry across the earthen floor.

The refuge doesn't encourage walking on its lands, since human presence disturbs the wildlife. Cars are permitted along Wildlife Drive (the vehicle serves as a blind so animals aren't scared of them), as are biking and hiking. There are also two very short hiking trails that provide a more intimate glimpse at the refuge's intriguing marsh and woodland habitats.

First, the **Marsh Edge Trail** is an interpretive walk (pick up a brochure at the visitor center or at the entrance to the trail). From the parking area along Wildlife Drive, you immediately plunge into a forest of loblolly pine and hardwood. This area of the marsh is the transition zone, where forest meets marsh. Called an "edge," this environment supports a high diversity of plants—a sure sign that wildlife may be feeding nearby. Some that you may see: opossums, nutrias, gray squirrels, and raccoons.

Soon the trail reaches the marsh's edge—overlooking the ebony, glass-smooth Blackwater River. A wooden bench here provides a nice spot for quiet contemplation. Check out the osprey nesting platform sticking out of the water to see if anyone's home; ospreys winter in South America, but return to the Chesapeake area in mid-March to nest. Across the marsh you'll see Barbados Island, where a pair of bald eagles has nested since 1975.

Around the bend, Olney three-square (2-foot-long grass) carpets the marsh's open waters. Blooming from late June to September, this plant—which dominates the marsh at Blackwater—provides important nutrients for ducks, geese, muskrats, and nutrias. Just beyond, a boardwalk extends out over the water, providing a fine prospect of one of the world's richest ecosystems. Indeed, each marsh acre produces about ten tons of organic material, twice the amount of a typical hayfield. A profusion of unseen fish and shellfish breed in this nutritious gumbo, in turn luring birds and animals.

Farther along, the trail forks. Go right for a good view of open water. The dense marsh vegetation that used to cover the water has been lost—a fate troubling much of Blackwater. Since 1933, more than 7,000 acres have disappeared, thanks to a rising sea level, nutria, wind and wave erosion, high water salinity during droughts, and changes in the flow of the Blackwater River. What this essentially means is loss of natural habitat for the animals and birds.

Backtrack to the main trail and continue on. Before you know it, you return to the parking lot. Next, on to the Woods Trail. Hop in your car, turn right out of the parking lot, then left on Wildlife Drive. In 0.7 mile you'll reach the parking area for this trail.

As the name implies, the **Woods Trail** visits a mature upland forest of pine and mixed hardwoods—a favored spot among Delmarva Peninsula fox squirrels. The chance of spotting one of these rare creatures is the main reason for taking this figure-eight trail; regardless, it's a pretty stroll through the woods. Soon after leaving the parking area, you reach a trail intersection—the heart of the figure eight. If you go right, you can do a short second loop. Bear left to loop back to the parking lot.

But don't leave too quickly. Sit on one of the wooden benches and wait patiently, quietly…you never know when a Delmarva Peninsula fox squirrel may show up.

To return to the visitor center, hop back in your car and follow the rest of the Wildlife Drive. At the end of the drive, signs will point the way back to the visitor center.

Trip notes: The Wildlife Drive is open daily. There is a $3 vehicle fee. For further information, contact the Refuge Manager, Blackwater National Wildlife Refuge, 2145 Key Wallace Dr., Cambridge, MD 21613-9535; 410-228-2677.

Directions: Just beyond the town of Cambridge on US 50, turn right (west) on Md. 16 (Church Creek Rd.) and proceed for 6.5 miles. At the village of Church Creek, turn left on Md. 335. Now go about 4 miles to Key Wallace Dr. and turn left. The visitor center driveway is a mile ahead, on the right. Obtain a map and directions here for the Wildlife Drive.

89. Trap Pond State Park
Off Del. 24 east of Laurel, Delaware

Cypress Point Nature Trail
1.5-mile loop/45 minutes

O ne of the most fascinating places on the Eastern Shore has nothing to do with beaches or boats or quaint colonial architecture. Quiet and primordial, the bald cypress swamp at Trap Pond State Park—the country's northernmost stand of bald cypress trees—more resembles a southern bayou than mid-Atlantic woodlands. The remains of an ancient swampland that once covered much of the Atlantic coastal plain, these bulbous-trunked trees provide a fascinating glimpse into another world.

In the late 1700s, settlers realized the value of these beautiful trees: The rot-resistant wood made for sturdy boats, posts, and shingles. They dug Trap Pond to power their mills … and down toppled the ancient trees. As the tree canopy opened up, the sun dried the underlying peat bogs, making the whole area susceptible to fire. Indeed, one blaze in the 1930s raged for eight months.

Though the swamp isn't what it used to be, it's still an awe-inspiring, mysterious place. Plenty of trees still fringe the pond, providing a glimpse into yesteryear. In winter, the entire pond is quiet save for the steady blaring of Canada geese overwintering here, and ice locks the bald cypress trees in an enchanting fairy-tale scene. The place looks altogether different in spring, when the shaggy cypresses are green with needles, and snowy water lilies dapple the smooth, ebony waters.

The best way to see the cypresses is via the easy-to-follow

Cypress Point Nature Trail. This short trail leaves from the Cypress Point parking area and wanders along Trap Pond's shoreline, where bald cypresses congregate in all their splendor. At one point, a short boardwalk juts out over the black water, providing a perfect perch to examine these truly interesting trees. Deciduous conifers, they lose their needles each autumn, hence the term "bald" cypress. Knobby "knees," thought to be part of the trees' aerial root system, poke out of the water like periscopes. This is also a good spot to watch for wildlife: painted and spotted turtles sunbathing on logs, bullfrogs, and tree frogs. One rather interesting denizen that you probably won't see is the carpenter frog, also known as the bog frog for its affinity for cypress swamps. A wide variety of southern birds can be spotted here, including prothonotary, parula, and yellow-throated warblers, as well as the shy Swainson's warbler, rarely seen because it only lives in dense swamps.

After about half a mile, the trail loops back through woodlands containing at least 12 different kinds of oak, including blackjack, normally not found near swampland.

And before you know it, you're back at your car.

Trip notes: The park is open daily. An entrance fee of $5 for out-of-state and $2.50 for in-state residents is charged May-October. For more information, contact Trap Pond State Park, Rd. 2, Box 331, Laurel, DE 19956; 302-875-5153.

Directions: From Laurel, Delaware, take Del. 24 east for 5 miles. At Cty. Rd. 449 turn right for 1 mile, to the park entrance.

90. Chincoteague National Wildlife Refuge

On Assateague Island east of Chincoteague, Virginia

Wildlife Loop
3.2-mile loop/1.5 hours

Whole landscapes sleep in wintertime. Animals hibernate; trees and fields are brown and drab. Everywhere, it seems, but Chincoteague National Wildlife Refuge, where a veritable winter wildlife festival is in full swing. The refuge's whole raison d'être is to preserve the habitat of migrating waterfowl, and it seems to be working, because the place is alive with Canada geese, tundra swans, and snow geese that have migrated thousands of miles to spend the winter. And that's just for starters. Pick up a bird list at the visitor center to help identify the hundreds of other birds you may spot here.

The refuge is located at the southernmost tip of Assateague Island, a thin Atlantic barrier isle along the Atlantic flyway. In the 1940s, people became concerned for the future of migrating birds—especially the greater snow goose, whose habitats all along the East Coast were quickly being developed into condos and hotels. At that time, only several hundred snow geese were making their annual trek to Assateague; quite a difference from the thousands and thousands that used to come before. So in 1943, 14,000-acre Chincoteague National Wildlife Refuge was established, its natural marshland enhanced with freshwater impound-ments that provide plenty of food for birds. Today, more than 32,000 geese—Canada and snow—overwinter here, along with 14,000 ducks and 400 swans.

The best way to experience Chincoteague's wild beauty is along the **Wildlife Loop,** which encircles Snow Goose Pool. A paved road beginning from the parking area at the Chin-coteague Refuge Visitor Center, it is closed to cars every day until 3 p.m., leaving it for bikers and hikers in the morning and early afternoon. The trail takes off beneath a canopy of loblolly pines where, if you're patient, you may catch sight of a rare Delmarva Peninsula fox squirrel or a Sika deer. Right away comes a T-intersection. Go right along the one-way road, following the sign. You pass by some freshwater impoundments on the right—any birds?—and wooded shrubs on the left. And then you come alongside Snow Goose Pool. Try to be here during sunrise, when the dark, glassy pond reflects the purplish blue sky and the silhouettes of Canada geese, great blue herons, and hundreds of ducks ink the twilit scene.

In 0.3 mile, the trail passes the Black Duck Trail, a spur that leads to the main refuge road and the Woodland Trail; fringed with small trees and shrubs, it's a good place to spot swallows, wood ducks, and woodpeckers. Farther ahead, the Wildlife Loop leaves the water, delving into a ghostly forest of dead trees. Sadly, these trees were killed by saltwater that flooded the area during a series of storms in 1992 and an outbreak of the southern pine beetle in 1994. Just beyond, you'll see the trailhead for the 1.2-mile Swan Cove Trail, which wanders to the primary dunes. The primary dunes are the island's front line of defense against the onslaught of surf and angry winds. The freshwater ponds along the way harbor all kinds of wildlife—most notably any number of wading birds. The trail leads to Toms Cove, which provides access to the ocean beach, quite a different scene from the nearby marsh. In summer, it's body-to-body sunbathers, in winter a windy, lonesome stretch of pounding surf.

Continuing along the Wildlife Loop, you come to a boardwalk leading out over Snow Goose Pool. If you're here in winter, especially at twilight, you will be welcomed by the riotous prattle of hundreds and hundreds of snow geese— coming from Canada in October, they spend every winter here. Band by band they circle in the sky above, lower and lower, until they splash down in the dark waters, joining their comrades in a plush, white carpet of feathers.

Back on the trail, you soon leave the snag-filled forest and traverse a berm across the impoundment, providing more birding opportunities. Farther ahead, the road bears left, following the edge of the forest. Another boardwalk leads out to an observation platform. The trail continues between the woods and pool, soon entering the loblolly forest and bringing you back to the start. A couple of hundred yards before the exit, the short Marsh Trail wanders past small pools where birds congregate, and deer, red foxes, and squirrels come to forage, providing one last chance to scan for wildlife.

Trip notes: The Wildlife Loop is open to vehicles from 3 p.m. to dusk only; the gates are open only to walkers and bikers before then. The loop may be closed until noon during hunting season—phone ahead in fall. There is a $5 vehicle fee. For information, contact the Refuge Manager, U.S. Fish & Wildlife Service, Chincoteague NWR, 8231 Beach Rd., Assateague Island, Chincoteague, VA 23336-0062; 757-336-6122.

Directions: From Salisbury, take US 13 south. Soon after entering Virginia, bear left on Va. 175. Drive over a causeway to the town (and island) of Chincoteague. After crossing the drawbridge you'll come to a T-intersection at a stoplight. Turn left onto Main St. Proceed several blocks to Maddox Blvd. and turn right. You'll cross another bridge onto Assateague Island and Chincoteague National Wildlife Refuge. About a quarter mile beyond the contact station, turn left to the visitor center and park in the lot. The entrance to the Wildlife Loop is opposite the visitor center.

91. Assateague Island National Seashore

Off Md. 611 south of Ocean City, Maryland

Life of the Dunes Trail
0.75-mile loop/45 minutes

■■

Sculptured and serene, Assateague's dunes sit prettily in their oceanside setting. But if you're a plant or animal, you face one of the planet's harshest environments, where you must adapt ... or die. Here, the sandy surface reaches 140°F in summer; hurricane-force winds sweep through periodically. And then you have to deal with the extreme salinity and lack of soil moisture and nutrients— not the easiest place to live.

Assateague Island National Seashore has set up a short interpretive walk through this difficult environment: **Life of the Dunes Trail.** You learn all about how plants adapt—how fuzzy petals absorb water, how long root systems anchor fly-away sand, how gutsy plant life anchors millions of pieces of flyaway sand to form the dunes in the first place.

Animals somehow endure this seemingly forbidden place. You probably won't see much—most don't venture out until the cooling shroud of dusk. An interpretive plaque shows how to identify tracks of a hognose snake, ghost crab, red fox, doodlebug, and others. More readily seen are all different kinds of birds; Assateague is a major stop along the Atlantic flyway.

The loop trail is easy to follow. Begin from the designated parking area; the trail brings you straight into the dunes. In about a quarter mile, you come to a trail junction; go left (the other trail will be your return route). Proceeding along this stretch, sniff the air and you'll smell tar; and then you'll see a long, incongruous black slab. Continue a little farther to a signpost, which explains that you're following the remains of Baltimore Boulevard, a road built by developers in the 1950s. A nor'easter in 1962 destroyed the road, sweeping away any future hopes for development. Only the gulls use it now; from high in the sky they drop clams on its hard surface, then swoop down to claim their fresh meat.

At the far end of the trail stands a wooden platform, where you can sit quietly and watch what stirs. An interpretive plaque talks about Assateague's dune life, and its inner dune community, in which you're seated.

Next, walk down some stairs and begin the other side of the loop. You enter the thicket zone, where dunes meet the forest. All kinds of dune and forest plants mingle here—poison ivy, muscadine grape, and blackberry together with such stunted trees as wild black cherry, loblolly pine, and red maple. The trail soon comes back to the trail junction, where you turn left and return to the parking area.

Trip notes: The park is open daily. There is a $5 vehicle fee. An interpretive booklet, offering more detail than what is stated on the plaques along the way, is sold at the visitor center. For further information, contact the National Park Service, 7206 National Seashore Ln., Berlin, MD 21811; 410-641-1441. The web site is www.nps.gov/asis.

Directions: Just west of Ocean City, take Md. 611 south onto Assateague Island. Proceed past the park toll booth to the end of the road, where a sign marks the trailhead.

92. Assateague Island National Seashore
Off Md. 611 south of Ocean City, Maryland

Life of the Marsh Trail
0.5-mile loop/15 minutes

The short **Life of the Marsh Trail** delves into the wild heart of the marsh, where a cornucopia of animal and birdlife depends on the land, water—and each other—for survival. Begin from the parking lot along the boardwalk trail. Soon you emerge on a wide-open expanse of golden marshlands that, at first glance, appears empty and forlorn. But linger for a little while and the abundant wildlife will begin to show itself. Assateague's fabled wild horses like to graze here; you may see their glossy brown or white coats speckling the grasslands. Birdlife includes wading birds and shorebirds, gulls, songbirds, even hawks and owls. Snowy egrets stand statuesque along the shoreline, their unflickering eyes targeting fish. Greater yellowlegs, their compact bodies held aloft by stiltlike, bright yellow legs, poke long bills into the murky sediment. Northern harriers fly low over the water, patrolling the marsh for rodents.

The animal life, aside from the horses, isn't so obvious. Plenty of animal droppings and footprints in the mud, however, attest that red foxes, Sika deer, and white-tailed deer are about.

As far as plant life goes, the marsh is filled with salt marsh cordgrass and salt meadow hay, which thrive in high-saline environments. On the elevation rises, marsh elder, ground-sel, wax myrtle, and bayberry grow, with loblolly pine and wild black cherry filling in the upper elevations.

Interpretive plaques talk about local flora and fauna, as well as the effects of man, physical traits such as salt pans, and the role of marshes in the ecosystem. Midway, a short spur brings you to the bayshore, where you can compare life in the marsh and Chincoteague Bay.

It's soon back to the parking area, but take your time. Wander, and watch nature at its finest.

More hiking: The national seashore has another short trail nearby, the **Life of the Forest Nature Trail,** which winds for half a mile through maritime woods. The most common tree you'll see here is the loblolly pine, beneath which wild horses and deer take refuge during storms. Other common trees to watch out for are northern bay berry, wax myrtle, and wild black cherry—all of which are stunted by sea breeze and salt spray. This is an especially good place to see migrating songbirds. If the weather is warm, be sure to arm yourself with insect repellent.

Trip notes: The park is open daily. There is a $5 vehicle fee. An interpretive booklet is sold at the visitor center. For further information, contact the National Park Service, 7206 National Seashore Ln., Berlin, MD 21811; 410-641-1441. The web site is www.nps.gov/asis.

Directions: Just west of Ocean City, take Md. 611 south onto Assateague Island. Proceed past the park toll both to Bayside Dr.; turn right to the parking lot and trailhead.

93. Assateague Island National Seashore

Off Md. 611 south of Ocean City, Maryland

Wilder beach walk
Up to 12 miles round-trip

Just south of Ocean City's neon bustle lies a place as remote and wild as any desert island. Preserved by the National Park Service, the northern tip of Assateague Island is completely, totally undeveloped. The only way to penetrate this heavenly sanctuary is by foot …the perfect excuse for a beach walk.

Assateague is a barrier island, a thin, low-lying strip of sand eternally resculptured by ocean currents, hurricane-force winds, and crashing waves. From year to year—indeed, from day to day—its topography changes…stretching, shortening, stretching again. Over eons, the sand mass has crept landward, inch by inch. Sometime far in the future, it will probably meet the mainland.

But for now, this alluring place, called the wilder beach by park employees, is one to explore and enjoy. Walking silently along the empty sandscape to the rhythmic lapping of waves, you may think you're alone. But you're not. From little beach fleas to intriguing ghost crabs, from red foxes to fabled wild horses, the island is full of life. And then there are the birds. Assateague lies along the Atlantic flyway, so throughout the year you're guaranteed plenty of bird sightings. It's perhaps the state's best shorebird habitat. May is the peak of spring migration, when colorful clouds of warblers stop by. In late summer and fall, watch for herons, egrets, terns, sandpipers, loons, and peregrine falcons. Snow geese, black ducks, mallards, and pintails, among others, overwinter here.

You can visit here any time of year; the scenery is always breathtaking. But there's something enticing about winter, when pewter skies and a swollen, gray-blue surf lend a dash of wild excitement. In January and February, especially after a big storm, beachcombing is at its prime. While summer turns up the normal stuff—oyster and clam shells, crab carcasses, polished glass—the winter surf delivers such exotic treasures as sea horses and sea urchins, wrinkly whelk shells and sea stars, sand dollars and moonstones, perhaps even a piece of an old shipwreck (though shipwreck artifacts are protected by law; inform a ranger if you find one).

The **wilder beach walk** begins from the day-use parking area of Assateague State Park—an overpopulated strip of sand in summertime. Cross the dunes along the boardwalk and, at the ocean, turn left (north). In front of you lie 6 glorious miles of solitary beachscape. Soon, the sounds of sunbathing, surf-splashing vacationers are far behind and, before you know it, your mind is as fresh and clean as the golden sand and salty breeze. You can go as far as the narrow inlet separating the island from Ocean City before turning back the way you came.

Insider's tips: For a primer on barrier island life, stop at the Barrier Island Visitor Center, located just before the island entrance. Remember that beach walking is more strenuous than hiking on dirt trails. The easiest time to walk is at low tide, on the hard, packed sand. Also, summer heat and mosquitoes can be unbearable—bring a hat and insect repellent.

Trip notes: The beach is open year-round. You can park at the Assateague S.P. parking lot, where there is a per-person fee of $2 between Mem. Day and Labor Day; the state park is closed in winter. You can also park at the Barrier Island Visitor Center and walk across the bridge to the state park beach (0.75 mile). For further information contact Assateague Island National Seashore, 7206 National Seashore Lane, Berlin, MD 21811; 410-641-1441. The web site is www.nps.gov/asis.

Directions: Just west of Ocean City, take Md. 611 south onto Assateague Island. Park in the state park's day-use parking area straight ahead.

94. Cape Henlopen State Park

Off Del. 9 just east of Lewes, Delaware

Beach Loop
1.8-mile loop/2 hours

Windswept and battered by waves, lonely Cape Henlopen juts out into the sea, a place so isolated that it looks much as it did when Spaniards first spotted it about 1544. Though the Dutch in the next century founded a small fort here and used the place as a whaling colony, no permanent settlement ever took root. However, with the arrival of World War II in the 20th century, the strategic site supported a key military post, primarily to watch for enemy activity offshore. Little by little, the military has since returned the lands to the state, so now it exists as a wild, fairly remote state park, edged with pristine shoreline idyllic for beach walking.

Fringed by a wide, sandy beach and containing ranks of sand dunes and forests of holly, cedar, and loblolly pine, Cape Henlopen's diverse landscape supports a plethora of wildlife...you may not immediately spot the velvet ants, pine lizards, hairy wolf spiders, rabbits, snakes, or voles—they generally venture out beneath the cooling veil of evening. But you can make out their tracks etched in the sand.

One animal that deserves special mention is the helmet-shaped horseshoe crab. In spring, hundreds of these big, primitive creatures—a species unchanged for 300,000 years—sidle onto the bayshore, where they dig shallow holes and lay thousands of tiny, pea green eggs—as many as 80,000 each. At the same time that the crabs lay their eggs, half-starved, squawking birds, using some kind of internal time clock on their migration from South America, flock to the scene and jab the sand for the protein-rich eggs (approximately 9,000 a day for two weeks). With thousands of miles to go before arriving at their nesting and breeding grounds in the Arctic, these tiny red knots, ruddy turnstones, sanderlings, and semipalmated sandpipers double their weight in a mere two weeks.

Here, too, you'll hear about (but probably not see) the threatened piping plover, a small shorebird the color of sand. Whole portions of the dunes may be closed in summer to allow these birds to nest in peace. Beware of serious-looking rangers, who won't let you anywhere near the nesting sites.

A good way to take in all this wild beauty is along the **Beach Loop.** Though the park has given this hike an official name, there are no actual groomed trails or signposts. It follows the gentle waters along the bayshore side of the cape, rounds the cape's tip, and returns along the Atlantic's pounding surf.

Park your car in The Point parking lot. Take the pathway to the west of the lot, which leads down to Breakwater Harbor, an inlet of Delaware Bay. Sheltered and serene, this picturesque cove boasts a lighthouse perched on the tip of a jetty. The beach here is a shell collector's paradise, what with all the oyster, mussel, clam, and horseshoe crab shells cast ashore.

Walking toward the tip of the cape, note the long spits of

mud and sand that extend into the harbor, one of the many signs of erosion occurring on this ever transitional cape. Over time, these tongues will grow higher and longer, until they become dunes far removed from the shoreline. The existing dunes to the right are the protected domain of the piping plover, along with least and common terns.

You'll know you're reaching the tip of the cape when the breeze whips against your face; soon you reach the point where land and bay and ocean meet. A long open stretch of sand meets the deep blue waters here, and just offshore an automated lighthouse flashes its warning light to ships and boats offshore. You sense you're at the end of the world. And you very well could be, since shorebirds, perhaps a brown pelican or two, will probably be the only signs of life.

The hike now heads back along the cape's oceanside, a dynamic setting of pounding surf and gusting winds. Here you experience firsthand the ongoing assault of the elements on the cape's eastern shore. You begin to understand how, over time, the wind and waves tirelessly chip away at its profile, slowly, determinedly changing its shape. Indeed, the peninsula's eastern shore is creeping westward bit by bit, while the tip marches north about 50 feet a year.

You'll know you're nearing the parking area as more and more people—surf anglers, volleyball players, ball-playing kids, hand-holding couples—take over the beach. The hike ends at the first bridge you come to, which leads back to The Point parking area.

Advisory: Walking on sand is difficult. Though this hike is short, remember that it'll be a bit harder on your legs than walking along a dirt trail.

More hiking: The state park offers a couple of other trails that are worth taking. The 1.2-mile **Pinelands Nature Trail,** which begins across the road from the Seaside Nature Center, winds among sand dunes, unusual flora, pine woods, and old cranberry bogs. Edging the trail along the way are bunkers left over from World War II, when the U.S. Army established a military base here to take advantage of the strategic position overlooking the open Atlantic. Another trail, the 3.1-mile **Dune Overlook Trail,** begins across from the 24-hour beach access road and ambles down Dune Rd. past the campground. It boasts three different spurs—the first leading to a World War II observation tower, the second exploring the mysterious walking dunes, and the third ending at a spartina marsh.

Trip notes: The park is open daily. Walking around the bay side of the point is forbidden during piping plover breeding season, March 1 to October 1. An entrance fee of $5 for out-of-state and $2.50 for in-state residents is charged May through Oct. For more information, contact Cape Henlopen State Park, 42 Cape Henlopen Dr., Lewes, DE 19958; 302-645-8983. The web site is www.destateparks.com/chsp.

Directions: From Lewes go east on Del. 9 for 1 mile past the ferry terminal to the park entrance. Proceed straight, beyond Seaside Nature Center. At the fork, go left, then left again at the T-intersection. This will bring you to The Point parking lot.

95. Prime Hook National Wildlife Refuge

Off Del. 1 south of Dover, Delaware

Boardwalk Trail, Dike Trail
Boardwalk Trail 0.5 mile/15 minutes
Dike Trail 1 mile/30 minutes

Prime Hook National Wildlife Refuge offers a supreme stroll through a landscape so quiet, so remote, so pristine, that only the birds will know you're here. Tens of thousands of birds pass through this mosaic of marsh, woods, and upland fields every year—but relatively few people. The best time to visit is fall and spring, during the peak migration periods. In fall, you're guaranteed sightings of Canada geese, snow geese, black ducks, wood ducks, and mallards. You should also see herons and terns, and maybe even some songbirds. In May, shorebirds and warblers wing through.

The place, however, isn't just for the birds. Spring is a good time to scan the marsh for reptiles and amphibians. The most common sightings include frogs such as spring peeper, cricket, and bull; and turtles such as red-bellied and painted. Snakes—garter, black rat—are frequently spotted, as are redbacked salamanders and American toads. The headquarters near the trailhead has a complete list of birds and amphibians to watch for.

The hike begins on the north side of the parking lot, at the boardwalk sign. A brochure available here describes the refuge and interprets the trail you're about to walk on.

Strolling along the mowed, grassy **Boardwalk Trail** through upland forest, you'll probably spot a cottontail or two nibbling on the grass, darting shyly into hedgerows of multiflora as you pass. And even if you don't spot a wood-chuck, try to avoid stepping into one of their holes, which tunnel through the ground below. Just ahead lies the old Morris family cemetery, testimony to the fact that humans once eked a living out of this remote land. The family house stood nearby until 1968, though dates on the tombstones—mostly around the mid-1800s—indicate that the land was inhabited long before.

Farther ahead, leave terra firma as you step upon a board-walk and stroll out over dark, glassy Shell Beach Pond. The white-blooming water lilies, green, wide-eyed frogs, and sun-ning turtles create a quaint scene straight out of Beatrix Potter.

The boardwalk quickly drops you back on solid ground, and you enter a small forest sprinkled with holly trees, then a wooded swamp. This part of the hike isn't so interesting, but keep your eyes peeled for wildlife. There's a bench for resting and watching.

Soon you come to a trail junction. Go left onto the earthen dike that edges the swamp. Follow this trail as it zigs sharply right across a little trickle of water, and zags immedi-ately left onto a mowed trail. Walk straight ahead, and soon you meet the Headwaters Ditch straight on.

Now you have a choice. You'll note you're standing on a service road that borders the ditch. If you walk to the right, you'll soon return to your car. But if you go left along the service road, also called the **Dike Trail,** you have a whole other adventure awaiting you.

The service road enters another portion of the marsh, dot-ted by tree-covered hummocks once used as temporary camps by Native Americans, when they came here to fish and hunt. Because the hummocks are higher and drier than the rest of the marsh, they tend to harbor a variety of birds typically not found in such an environment. Be on the lookout for owls, flickers, mockingbirds, and warblers. In about half a mile you come to Petersfield Ditch, the end of the road. Turn around and take the service road back to the parking area.

More hiking: While in the area, drive over to Killens Pond State Park *(Rte. 384, S of Felton. 302-284-4526),* where the 3.2-mile **Pondside Trail** loops around a 66-acre mill pond.

Trip notes: The refuge is open daily. There is no entrance fee. For further information contact the Refuge Manager,

Prime Hook National Wildlife Refuge, Rte. 3, Box 195, Milton, DE 19968; 302-684-8419. The web site is www.fws.gov.

Directions: From Dover, go south on US 113 to Milford; take Del. 1 south to Del. 16 (Broadkill Beach Rd.). Turn left (east) and go 1 mile. Then turn left again, into the refuge, and proceed 1.6 miles to the parking lot.

96. Bombay Hook National Wildlife Refuge
Off Del. 9 north of Dover, Delaware

Boardwalk trail
0.25-mile loop/20 minutes

A British man visiting Bombay Hook one summer day was amused that he needn't even get out of his car at this wildlife refuge to spy big birds. "Back home," he said, "we have to walk miles and miles in order to see even the little ones." Here, a diketop road allows visitors to drive all around the refuge, providing a first-rate view of herons, egrets, kingfishers, shorebirds, waterfowl, and much, much more. If you wish to get more intimate with the marshlands, walking trails provide even more opportunities to spot birds … and probably see some bigger animals as well.

Perched at the point where the Delaware River broadens into Delaware Bay, this 15,978-acre wetlands is one of the most important stopping points along the Atlantic flyway for migrating and overwintering birds. Its name dates back to early Dutch settlers, who came here in the 1600s to trap muskrats and terrapins, hunt waterfowl, and ply the waters for crabs, fish, and oysters; they called the place Boompies Hoock, or "little-tree point," which more or less stuck.

Established in 1937, the sanctuary protects all kinds of birds, including ospreys, bald eagles, and peregrine falcons, which either nest here or stop by on their annual migrations. More than a hundred thousand waterfowl—including snow geese and Canada geese—arrive in autumn, either settling down for the long winter or resting up before heading farther south. Spring is the best time to look for shorebirds: plovers, greater or lesser yellowlegs, sandpipers, dunlins, dowitchers, and the list goes on. For a complete listing of birds, stop by the refuge headquarters/visitor center.

The refuge boasts several walking trails, all of them short. Of these, the **boardwalk trail** is especially popular for two reasons: It travels through a diversity of landscapes—brackish pond, freshwater pond, salt marsh, and woodland; and it offers a chance to spot all different kinds of wildlife, including fiddler crabs.

The trailhead is located along the refuge driving tour, between auto stops nos. 2 and 3. The trail is easy to follow, but it might help imagining a figure-eight shape; your start is at the bottom of the eight. Immediately you plunge into woods filled with persimmon (which produces a round, orange fruit quite popular among raccoons, opossums, and foxes); wild cherry; and sweet gum trees (distinguished by their star-shaped leaves). At a junction of trails, bear left and soon you'll come alongside a brackish pond edged with bulrushes. Be still, and perhaps you'll glimpse a wood duck skimming across the algae-covered water.

Farther along, the trail crosses over a little boardwalk— the center of the figure eight. In summer look into the depths of the water for minnows and killifish. Soon you come to another trail junction, where you veer left. The trail reenters the woodlands, and then, suddenly, the landscape changes. The trees give way to high marsh, a pretty, golden scene of wind-tousled salt meadow cordgrass. The trail becomes a boardwalk, leading out to Raymond Gut. (A gut is a little saltwater appendage to a tidal creek or river.) If the tide is out, look along the muddy banks for fiddler crabs, which dart crazily about. The males have one claw that is much larger than the other, hence the name "fiddler." Here, too, you may spot marsh and blue crabs, along with different kinds of shorebirds and waterbirds. The mud-and-vegetation mounds in the salt marsh are muskrat homes.

As you proceed along the boardwalk, the view opens up to sweeping marshland, stretching as far as the eye can see. Stroll along slowly, keeping your eyes open for birdlife. At the very least, you'll spot some ducks, which nest in the wetlands. Some of the more popular species include mallards, blue-winged teal, gadwalls, and shovelers.

Ahead, the boardwalk ends, dropping you back into the woods. Walking along, you might note the wooden deer hunting stand off to the left; deer hunting is permitted in the refuge to help keep the deer population down. (The trail is sometimes closed during hunting season.) You cross over the same little boardwalk you traversed before, and at the trail junction, bear left. Soon a freshwater pond peeks through the trees on the left, a popular gathering place for binocular-clad birders.

The trail brings you to one more junction, where you veer left back to your car.

Trip notes: The visitor center is closed on summer and winter weekends, but the refuge is usually open daily. Call ahead during hunting season, when the trail is sometimes closed. There is a $4 vehicle fee. For further information contact the Refuge Manager, Bombay Hook National Wildlife Refuge, 2591 Whitehall Neck Rd., Smyrna, DE 19977-9764; 302-653-9345 or 302-653-6872 (visitor center).

Directions: From Dover, go north on US 13 to Del. 42. Take Del. 42 east to Leipsic, then go north on Del. 9 until you see the refuge sign at Whitehall Neck Rd. Turn right and proceed to the refuge. The trailhead is located between stops nos. 2 and 3 along the auto tour.

Wilmington
Area

Plush green fields, pellucid streams, and colonial villages sprinkle the genteel countryside outside of industrial Wilmington.

97. Bellevue State Park

Off I-95 northeast of Wilmington, Delaware

Bicycle and bridle trails
2-mile loop/45 minutes

Age-old sycamores, stone-speckled streams, blackberry brambles, flowery meadows: This hike takes in the mannerly beauty of a former DuPont estate. Here, William DuPont, Jr., lived in the mid-1900s, fostering his love for tennis and horses by building wonderful tennis courts (the Wimbledon trials have been held here), an arena, equestrian stables, and racetrack. Since his property became a state park in 1975, people have flocked here to take advantage of the now public facilities. What most people don't seem to realize, however, is that much of the estate has been allowed to revert to its natural appearance, providing the perfect place for an easy stroll.

From the parking area, walk south toward the tennis courts and turn left (east), onto the paved bicycle trail. You'll walk around a green barn, over a little stream, and come to a four-way intersection of trails. Go straight, slightly uphill on the dirt trail. As lovely woods engulf you, slow your pace, take a deep breath, relax. The only sounds are chattering songbirds and the wind breezing through the trees.

When you come to another intersection, bear right, uphill. At the top of the hill, take a quick jog to the right and continue in that direction. The path soon becomes an elegant avenue shaded by sycamores and maples—probably the original estate entranceway.

At the end of the lane lies a big meadow. Go right, on a grassy path, with the meadow on the left, and enter the woods ahead. Magnificent trees embrace you—towering black and red oaks, tulip trees, and sweet gums. An ice-cold stream dances over smooth stones, and red-winged blackbirds dart from tree to tree. In spring, jack-in-the-pulpit, trout lily, mayapple, and wild geranium brighten the woodland floor.

The trail climbs a bit and soon comes to another meadow, where you'll see one trail leading straight ahead and another that goes left. Take the one to the left, fringing the woods. Slowly you approach a lone sycamore tree, with great, upswept arms. Mustardweed, monarch butterflies, and purple thistles dot the surrounding meadow in summertime, resembling the countryside paintings of Andrew Wyeth, who was born in nearby Chadds Ford, Pennsylvania.

Just beyond the sycamore tree, you'll see a trail meandering left. Take this, along the edge of the woods. The field is still to your right.

Soon you reach a T-intersection. This is the point where you entered the stream-crossed woods. Go right. In about 100 yards you'll reach the allée—where you go left. Retracing your steps through the woods, you'll soon be back at the parking lot.

Trip notes: The park is open daily. There is a $5 out-of-state and $2.50 in-state fee on weekends in May, September, and October; and daily Mem. Day to Labor Day. You can pick up a map at the entrance gate. For more information, contact Bellevue State Park, 800 Carr Rd., Wilmington DE 19809, 302-577-3390; or the Delaware Division of Parks and Recreation, 89 Kings Hwy., P.O. Box 1401, Dover, DE 19903, 302-739-4702.

Directions: From downtown Wilmington, go 4 miles north on I-95 to the Del. 3/Marsh Rd. exit. This will bring you to Carr Rd. Turn left and continue across Marsh Rd. A half mile ahead, turn right into the park entrance. Follow the park road 0.7 mile, past the bandstand on the right, to the last parking area.

98. Brandywine Creek State Park

Off I-95 north of Wilmington, Delaware

Marsh Trail, Walnut Lane, and Hidden Pond Trail
2.5-mile loop/1 hour

Fabled for its genteel beauty, the Brandywine Valley has long been cherished for its rolling meadows, wooded hills, and slow-moving Brandywine Creek. The Wyeth family has lived in the area for three generations, capturing its pastoral essence on canvases that now hang in the world's top museums. But this gentle landscape was settled long before, in the 1700s, by a family called DuPont. They began with gunpowder, providing ammunition for the Revolutionary War. With modernization they switched to chemicals and textiles, and the rest, as they say, is history.

Until 1965, the DuPonts owned the park's land, where they grazed dairy cattle on plush hillsides. The lovely stone walls embroidering the meadows in the southwestern section of the park were built by Italian masons in the late 1800s to border their pastures.

This hike takes in former Dupont lands, a mosaic of woods, meadows, marshes, and, of course, the Brandywine. Begin to the right of the nature center, following the paved path to the trailhead. Immediately you enter a stunning stand of old-growth tulip poplars—some as old as 190 years. Neither tulip nor poplar, these trees, often reaching heights of 100 feet or more, are named for their tulip-shaped flowers. Sprinkling the canopy are red oaks, white ashes, and several kinds of hickories, while flowering dogwoods burst into bright white and pink in early spring.

Pretty soon you come to a fork in the trail, offering various trail options. Follow the **Marsh Trail** (blue) to the right. You'll come to a couple more junctions; follow the blue trail each time. Soon you'll be walking beside a green meadow, edged with dark green forest. Dotted with picnic tables and bordered with picturesque stone walls, this place beckons for a picnic.

Farther ahead, you'll pass through a stone wall, leaving the green expanse and snaking down into the woods. The grassy trail becomes an old rocky road called **Walnut Lane,** dating back to DuPont days. After strolling a bit farther, follow the blue arrow left, down into the swamp area. (If you come to the white barn, you've gone too far.) Soon you'll arrive at another little road; turn left. Wetlands edge the trail to the right. You will pass an unmarked trail. At the next trail, turn right; this will lead you to the Brandywine River.

Beginning nearby as two streams—the east and west branches—the Brandywine dawdles through verdant hills dotted with fat cows, and across wildflower-dotted meadows before joining the majestic Delaware River just 20 miles away. Turn left and enjoy the pleasant walk along this lovely waterway, in the shade of sycamores sweetly scented with honeysuckle. You'll continue to the white-blazed **Hidden Pond Trail.** Turn left here, back toward the nature center. Follow the yellow trail and the red trail back through the tulip woods. When you reach a gap in a stone wall near the nature center, you'll see that you can walk across the grass, back to your car in the parking lot.

More hiking: Instead of turning left on the Hidden Pond Trail, continue straight, beside the river. The trail loops

around to the left; return to the nature center via the red and
white trails.

Trip notes: The park is open daily. There is a $5 out-of-state
and $2.50 in-state fee on weekends in May, September, and
October; and daily Mem. Day–Labor Day. The nature center
sells interpretive brochures for the Tulip Woods Trail and the
Marsh Trail. For more information, contact the Brandywine
Creek State Park Nature Center, P.O. Box 3782, Wilmington,
DE 19807; 302-655-5740 (nature center) or 302-577-3534.

Directions: From I-95 in Wilmington, go north on Del. 52
for nearly 3 miles. Turn right on Del. 100 and, in 2.5 miles,
you'll come to the intersection with Del. 92 and Adams Dam
Rd. The entrance is on Adams Dam Rd. Follow the park
road to the nature center, where you can park your car.

99. City of New Castle
2-mile loop/2 hours

P rim colonial houses, fragrant boxwood gardens,
shaded cobblestone lanes, and steepled churches fill
the charming old town of New Castle, leading walkers
into the serenity of a bygone era. Perched strategically on the
banks of the northern Delaware River, the little settlement
was founded as a Dutch fort in 1651 and subsequently ruled
by the Swedes, the Dutch again, the British, the Dutch again,
and the British again. Then in 1704, when Delaware established its own legislative assembly, New Castle—the colony's
largest city—became its colonial capital.

George Washington and Thomas Jefferson conducted
business here, and as more and more people whispered about
the prospect of democracy, New Castle's courthouse and taverns became hubs of conversation. When the Revolutionary
War broke out, New Castle was named the capital of the new
state of Delaware. But, alas, the state government had to flee
to Dover in 1777, when British warships threatened the town,
never to return. Though there was a period of growth in the
1800s, New Castle never regained its prominence and, after
being bypassed by the main railroad line, its backwater fate
was sealed. The town's loss then is our gain—it remains an
absolutely charming time capsule of colonial times.

This walk begins at the old **Court House** *(211 Delaware St. 302-323-4453. Closed Mon.),* built in 1732—making it one of the country's oldest courthouses. Delaware became a state here on June 15, 1776, and from its balcony on July 24 of that same year, the Declaration of Independence was first read to the citizens of Delaware. An interesting footnote: In the 1763-67 land surveys of Mason and Dixon, the cupola's spire was used as a center point of the 12-mile radius that forms Delaware's northern boundary with Pennsylvania. Guided tours of the bright, sunny courthouse shed good light on town history.

Stepping outside, turn left on Delaware Street, then cross Market Street. Before you stands the town hall, built in 1823. Originally the first floor and the arch were designed as a fire station. Walk through the arch and enter **Market Square,** used as a market as early as 1651, when the town was laid out. In 1682 William Penn, the Quaker founder of Pennsylvania, first stepped ashore in the New World at New Castle; a statue in the square commemorates his arrival.

Cross Second Street to the **Presbyterian Church,** founded in 1657 as Dutch Reformed and still in use. Crumbling, weathered, unmarked graves date back to the Dutch period.

The walk continues back across Second and Market Streets to the Market Plaine, or **Green.** Citizens used to graze their sheeps and cows here, before a prison and gallows were built. It's now a pleasant public park. Continue up (away from the courthouse) Market Street to the long, brick building bordering the Green. This is the old arsenal, built by the federal government in 1809 to hold ammunition for the War of 1812, and then used during the Mexican War; now it's a fine restaurant.

At the far end of the Green, you can't miss **Immanuel Episcopal Church** *(100 Harmony St. 302-328-2413).* Enter through the cemetery, a quiet place of forgotten gravestones recalling such early residents as George Read, a signer of the Declaration of Independence (The Signer, as proud locals refer to him). The church was founded in 1689 as the first Anglican church in Delaware. A fire completely gutted the historic structure in 1980, and the building was subsequently reconstructed using its original walls and foundation.

Exit the graveyard and continue up Market Street to Harmony Street, and turn left. Walk a block past the church's crumbling stone walls. At Third Street, turn left. This is perhaps New Castle's most picturesque street, with most of its buildings dating from the late 18th or early 19th centuries. First you pass the academy; dating from 1798, it was the first private school for privileged children. It became a public school in the mid-1800s and remained as such until the 1930s.

The next interesting building on the right is the octago-
nal 1892 **Old Library Museum,** the newest building on the
block. Keep walking down Third Street. You can't miss the
circa 1700 **Old Dutch House** *(32 E. 3rd St. 302-322-2794.
March-Dec. Tues.-Sun., Jan.-Feb. Sat.-Sun. only; adm. fee),*
with its slanting eaves, perhaps the town's oldest house. Fur-
nished with period antiques, including an ornate courting
bench and a Dutch oven that long-ago residents left behind,
it's a fascinating place to learn about the Dutch way of life
here long ago.

Continue to the end of Third Street, then turn right on
Delaware Street. Cross Fourth Street to the 1738 **Amstel
House** *(4th and Delaware Sts. 302-322-2794. Adm. fee),* one
of New Castle's most elegant houses. Governor Van Dyke
once lived here, and George Washington attended the wedding reception of the governor's daughter here in 1784.

Cross Delaware Street and turn left (east), strolling back
past the courthouse, all the way down to the Delaware River.
Take your time to peek into the antique shops, perhaps taking a bite to eat at one of the taverns or cafés. Nearly at the
river, you'll see a paved hiker-biker trail taking off to the
right through grassy **Battery Park.** This trail winds beside
the Delaware River for a couple of miles, providing picturesque vantages of boats bobbing in the water, driftwood-
strewn beaches, and a bird-filled marsh. In the early 1700s,
this part of town harbored cannon emplacements against
pirate attacks. At the end of the trail lie the earthwork terraces of early fortifications.

Back at the foot of Delaware, you are standing on the site
of the old town wharf. New Castle was once one of America's most important ports, abuzz with all types of activity.
Then head back up the other side of Delaware Street, to the
first street on the right. This is **The Strand,** long ago the
bustling waterfront street filled with taverns, brothels, and
inns. Elegant houses were built in the 18th century, a few of
which still stand today. About midway down the tree-shaded
street, you'll come to **Packet Alley,** once a busy passageway
for travelers on their way to Baltimore, Washington,
Philadelphia, Boston, and New York. A little farther down,
on the left, you'll come to the stately **George Read II House**
*(42 The Strand. 302-322-8411. March-Dec. Tues.-Sun., Jan.-
Feb. Sat.-Sun., and by appt.; adm. fee),* dating from 1801.
This federal mansion—22 rooms and 14,000 square feet of
living space—is famous for its Palladian windows and silver-
plated hardware on solid mahogany doors. It was lived in

until 1975, when its owner bequeathed it to the Historical Society of Delaware. The house has since been restored and is open for tours. Don't miss the lovely gardens, installed in 1847; they are the oldest surviving period gardens in the state.

Continue along The Strand to Harmony Street and turn left. You'll pass the diminutive **Rising Sun Tavern** *(private),* one of the city's many 18th-century inns and taverns. At Second Street, turn left, passing **Armstrong's Row,** a collection of row houses dating from the federal period, and **Aull's Row,** dating from the 1790s. Proceed down Second Street, and soon you'll return to Delaware Street and the courthouse.

Trip notes: Sites have various hours and fees as indicated in the text. For more information contact the Delaware Tourism Office, 99 Kings Hwy., Dover, DE 19901; 302-739-4271 or 800-441-8846.

Directions: The walk begins in front of the Court House, at 211 Delaware St., in the colonial heart of New Castle. Parking available on nearby streets.

100. Pea Patch Island

Via ferry from Delaware City, Delaware

Prison Camp Trail
0.75-mile loop/30 minutes

A ten-minute ferry ride brings you to the middle of the Delaware, where Pea Patch Island sits in a world all its own. Most people come here to visit Fort Delaware, a brick-and-granite bastion originally built to defend the sea approach upriver. Indeed, it's hard to miss the imposing, star-shaped edifice standing on the island's high ground and well worth a peek inside. During the Civil War, some 13,000 Southern sympathizers and Confederate prisoners suffered inside its damp, chilly walls.

Outdoor lovers will be more interested in the fact that the tiny island (288 acres) harbors the largest heronry north of Florida. Thousands of large wading birds, including nine different species of heron, egret, and ibis, congregate here, at the island's northern tip. No one is allowed inside, but a short hiking trail wanders through pretty woods to an observation tower that looks out on the birds' domain.

Because much of the island is marshy, the ferry docks at the end of a long pier. After debarking, you'll be greeted by a truck-pulled jitney, which takes you through a brackish marsh to the fort's entrance (or you can choose to walk along the short paved road instead). Once standing before the fort, walk to the left (north), across the grassy expanse, to the trailhead for the **Prison Camp Trail,** an ominous name for a perfectly lovely walk. Various long-gone points of military interest are keyed to an interpretive brochure sold at the fort's gift shop.

The trail plunges into the bottomland hardwood forest of red maple, sassafras, sumac, box elder, and wild cherry. Butterflies dart here and there and cottontails nibble on the grass. Soon you come to the observation platform, which looks across the marsh to a wooded stand of trees and shrubs. With binoculars, you can pick out large, floppy heron nests in the tall trees and among the reeds, and in spring you might spy a downy chick or two. Binoculars help in determining which bird is what—watch for great blue herons, little blue herons, tricolored herons, glossy ibis, great egrets, snowy egrets, and cattle egrets. The nesting season is between mid-March and mid-July.

Farther ahead, the trail edges a marshland then curves beside several sandy beaches. Across the river you can see the New Jersey shore, and with binoculars pick out Fort Mott, just to the north.

As you exit the woods, the fort emerges in front of you. Either walk back to the ferry landing by angling off to the right, across the open expanse of grass, or wait in front of the fort for the jitney to pull you back.

Trip notes: Ferries run weekends from the last weekend in April through the last weekend in September, between 10 a.m. and 6 p.m. They also run Wednesday, Thursday, and Friday from mid-June to Labor Day, between 10 a.m. and 6 p.m. There is a $6.50 fare for adults and $4 for children to ride the ferry. For more information, contact Fort Delaware State Park, P.O. Box 170, Delaware City, DE 19706; 302-834-7941 or 302-739-4702 (all Delaware state parks).

Directions: The ferry to Pea Patch Island runs from the Fort Delaware State Park Visitor Center in Delaware City, at the foot of Clinton Street. It also runs from Fort Mott, New Jersey.

Resources

WASHINGTON AREA HIKING CLUBS

American Hiking Society *(1422 Fenwick Ln., Silver Spring, MD 20910. 301-565-6704. www.americanhiking.org)* A recreation-based conservation organization dedicated to maintaining trails throughout America. Check the AHS calendar on the web for upcoming events.

Appalachian Mountain Club, Washington, D.C. chapter *(www.outdoors.org. www.amc-dc.org)* One of twelve chapters of the club founded in 1876 to promote outdoor activities and conservation in the Northeast. Volunteers lead hikes, bike rides, and trail clean-ups. Call the activities line for updated events, 202-298-1488.

Capital Hiking Club *(6519 Bannockburn Dr., Bethesda, MD 20817. 301-229-5816. www.teleport.com/~walking/chc.shtml)* Guided hikes throughout the Washington, D.C., region. Check the web site for events schedule.

Center Hiking Club *(c/o Marion Knight, 5367 Holmes Run Pkwy., Alexandria, VA 22304. 703-527-2349 or 703-751-3971. www.smart.net/%7Edmaidt/chc_home.html)* Established in 1939, this volunteer organization is devoted to enjoying the outdoors. Several activities every weekend of the year offered. Main interest is hiking, but also camping, canoeing, biking, and backpacking.

Maryland Outdoors Clubs, Inc. *(P.O. Box 4052, Gaithersburg, MD 20885. 301-601-5007. www.Maryland-outdoors-club.org)* An outdoors and social club focusing on a variety of activities for active individuals, including hiking, biking, camping, and skiing, mostly in Maryland.

Mountain Club of Maryland *(4106 Eierman Ave., Baltimore, MD 21206. 410-377-6266)* Founded in 1934, this organization leads hikes into the mountains near Baltimore. Trips vary in length and difficulty, including overnight and backpacking hikes.

Northern Virginia Hiking Club
(www.members.aol.com/nvhc) Offers an extensive hiking calendar with information, costs, and contact telephone numbers for upcoming hikes in the Washington area. For recording of upcoming activities call 703-440-1805.

Potomac Appalachian Trail Club *(118 Park Street, SE, Vienna, VA 22180. www.patc.net)* Headquartered in the Washington, D.C., area, this club maintains and improves 970 miles of hiking trails, 30 shelters, and 28 cabins in Virginia, West Virginia, Pennsylvania, and D.C. Monthly events include hikes, excursions, and work trips. For a recording of upcoming activities, call 703-242-0965.

Sierra Club *(Sierra Club New Columbia Chapter, Sierra Club National Legislative Office, 408 C St., NE, Washington, D.C. 20002. 202-488-0505. www.sierraclub.org or www.sierraclub.org/chapters/dc)* Founded in 1892, this nationwide, 500-member-strong environmental organization offers members the chance to participate in local outings and chapter activities, as well as volunteer to support local environmental issues. Maryland *(301-277-7111 or 410-813-2225. www.sierraclub.org/chapters/md)* and Virginia *(804-225-9113. www.sierraclubva.org)* both have chapters as well. For a recording of upcoming events call 202-547-2326.

Washington Women Outdoors *(19450 Caravan Dr. Germantown, MD 20874. 301-864-3070. patriot.net/~wwo)* Activities for women include hiking and backpacking, as well as watersports, rock climbing, biking, and cross-country skiing.

MAPS

The U.S. Geological Survey produces topographic maps showing prominent natural and cultural features that are extremely popular with hikers. The best for hiking are those at scales of 1:24,000 (1 inch = 2,000 feet). Also available for sale are topographical maps featuring national parks, national monuments, and other National Park System units. You can order them by contacting the USGS Information Services, Box 25286, Denver, CO 80225, 888-275-8747 or 303-202-4700. Or check out the web site at www. mapping.usgs.gov/mac/isb/ pubs/booklets/usgsmaps/usgsmaps.html. Recreational stores, such as REI and Eastern Mountain Sports, sell them as well.

PARK CONTACTS

National Park Service *(www.nps.gov)* Web site contains detailed information on all national parks, national monuments, and other National Park System units.

Chesapeake & Ohio Canal National Historical Park *(C&O Canal NHP Headquarters, Box 4, Sharpsburg, MD 21782 . 301-739-4200. www.nps.gov/choh)* This 184.5-mile towpath between Georgetown in Washington, D.C., and Cumberland, Maryland, offers endless hiking possibilities.

Virginia Department of Conservation & Recreation *(www.state.va.us/~dcr/parks/index.htm)* The web site has a useful index for state parks and natural areas.

Northern Virginia Regional Park Authority *(5400 Ox Rd., Fairfax Station, Virginia 22039. 703-352-5900. www.nvrpa.org)* More than 10,000 acres of woodlands, streams, and rolling Virginia countryside preserved within 19 regional parks, featuring golfing, swimming, and hiking.

Fairfax County (Virginia) Park Authority *(12055 Government Center Pkwy., Suite 927, Fairfax, VA 22035. 703-324-8702. www.co.fairfax.va.us/parks/outdoor.htm)* More than 350 parks on more than 18,300 acres, with recreational opportunities including hiking, picnicking, swimming, fishing, tennis, and golf.

Maryland Department of Natural Resources *(800-830-3974. www.dnr.state.md.us./publiclands)* Facilities include parks, forests, and wildlife management areas. For specific hiking information, a good web site is www.dnr.state.md.us./outdoors/hiking.html.

Maryland-National Capital Park and Planning Commission *(Community relations office 301-495-2503. www.clark.net/pub/mncppc/montgom/parks/facility.htm)* The web site offers a round-up of parks in Montgomery County, Maryland.

Delaware Division of Parks and Recreation *(89 Kings Hwy., Dover, DE 19901. 302-739-4702. www.destateparks.com)* Maintains 13 state parks and related preserves and greenways throughout Delaware, totaling more than 17,000 acres.

Delaware Tourism Office *(99 Kings Hwy., Dover DE 19901. 302-739-4271. www.state.de.us/tourism/office/main.htm)* Travel information, including state parks.

CYBER INFORMATION

www.emsonline.com Eastern Mountain Sports's web site offers good information including an adventure finder for vacation dreaming, clinics, and checklists for a variety of activities, including backpacking and bird-watching.

www.gorp.com Gorp Outdoor Recreation Pages provide a regional hiking guide—including information on hikes in

Shenandoah National Park, rambles in Delaware, and short stints along the Appalachian Trail. Plus detailed information on gear, books and media, tours, and more. Check out the special section on "Articles, guides, books, trips, and more of interest to walkers, hikers, and trekkers."

www.rei.com REI provides detailed information on equipment, as well as the chance to sign up for various clinics and guided hikes in spectacular places.

www.washingtonpost.com/wpsrv/sports/longterm/outdoors/hiking/front.htm The *Washington Post* web site provides a link to an outdoors and hiking page.

Barbara A. Noe is the associate travel editor at National Geographic Books and an avid hiker, bicyclist, and runner who has spent a great deal of time exploring the countryside around Washington, D.C. She lives in Arlington, Virginia.

National Geographic 100 Easy Hikes in Washington, D.C.,
Northern Virginia, Maryland, and Delaware
by Barbara A. Noe

Published by the National Geographic Society
John M. Fahey, Jr., *President and Chief Executive Officer*
Gilbert M. Grosvenor, *Chairman of the Board*
Nina D. Hoffman, *Senior Vice President*
William R. Gray, *Vice President and Director, Book Division*
Elizabeth L. Newhouse, *Director of Travel Publishing*
Barbara A. Noe, *Associate Editor*
Caroline Hickey, *Senior Researcher*
Alan Kahan, *Art Director*
Carl Mehler, *Director of Maps*
K.M. Kostyal, John Thompson, *Text Editors*
Keith R. Moore, Thomas L. Gray, *Map Research*
Gregory Ugainsky, *Map Production*
Lise Sajewski, *Editorial Consultant*
Richard S. Wain, *Production Project Manager*
DeShelle Downey, *Staff Assistant*

Library of Congress Cataloging-in-Publication Data
Noe, Barbara A.
   100 easy hikes : Washington, D.C., Northern Virginia, Maryland, Delaware / by
Barbara A Noe.
      p. cm.
   ISBN 0-7922-7588-8
   1. Hiking—Washington Region—Guidebooks. 2. Hiking—Delaware—Guidebooks. 3.
Washington Region—Guidebooks. 4. Delaware—Guidebooks I. Title: One hundred easy
hikes. II. Title.
GV199.42.W17 N64 2000
917.504'44—dc21   99-462358
                                                                CIP

Visit the Society's web site at www.nationalgeographic.com

Cover photo: Two hikers sit beside a Blue Ridge waterfall. By
Buddy Mays.